RESTAURANT HANDBOOK

TOOLS & RULES

4th Edition

Roderick A Clelland

FUNDAMENTALS OF RESTAURANT MANAGEMENT

Vector Time Tools Publishing
© 2013

VECTOR TIME TOOLS PUBLISHING

Selected material from
FUNDAMENTALS OF RESTAURANT MANAGEMENT
Roderick A. Clelland

4th Edition

Copyright © 2013 - 2011, 2009, 2007 by Vector Time Tools Publishing. All rights reserved. Except as permitted under the United States Copyright Act of 1976, no part of this publication may be reproduced or distributed in any form or by any means, or stored in any data base retrieval system, without prior written permission of the publisher.

ISBN–13: 978-1484806517

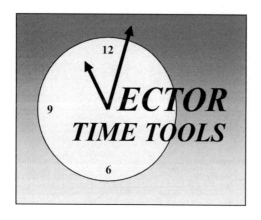

FORMAT – HOW TO USE THIS HANDBOOK

This book uses the format of the engineer's handbook. It is designed for quick look-up of fundamentals without wading through filler-verbiage. It is clear, cogent, and comprehensive.

You do not need to read from beginning to end. Rather, you can go directly to your subject of immediate interest for decision compelling information.

Six standalone textbook-like sections cover every topic of successful restaurant practices from initial concepts to comfortable steady cash-flows. You have check-lists, formulae, templates, forms, and examples for best-practices to guide best-outcomes, including rules-of-thumb.

Note: that for every rule-of-thumb you can find some restaurant that violates a rule and still does well. The *tools & rules*, here, force your attention – as with a pilot's checklist – to carefully consider the cost/benefit of violating a particular rule. After all, your concept should be unique to differentiate and fit a competitive market niche. Each item on a list will not always fit your own concept, but you will ignore it without a mistaken omission.

Some tools must evolve. The *tools & rules* that help provide customer value – systems, supply-chains, data-capture, and equipment – continue to evolve with technology. Rules for happy staff do not evolve. The values that customers seek do not evolve, since basic qualities of service, atmosphere, and excellent food are timeless in their endless and creative varieties.

Note: This book uses some textbook formatting, but is free of the constraints of the academic environment. Academe can be insulated from reality on-the-ground. We are free not to dress-up any subject in order to make it politically correct. Instead, we focus on real practices that will strongly influence successful outcomes.

Be creative with *tools & rules,* but always understand why the rules are there.

ACKNOWLEDGEMENTS

My first restaurant was only possible with the help of the brilliant and talented Joseph Michael Tierney, Jr. MBA, who lost his life in a white-water accident at age 28. Creative partners: Glen Wilt, Jr. PHD, Peter Nikas Esq., Pete McClennan, George Errecalde, and George McGowan guided superior outcomes measured in profits and popularity.

TABLE OF CONTENTS - Section One

START–PLAN–FINANCE–LOCATE–DESIGN

THE BUSINESS
- STATE OF THE INDUSTRY   1- 1

THE CUSTOMER
- CUSTOMER SATISFACTION SURVEYS   1- 2
- SUSTAINED COMPETITIVE ADVANTAGE   1- 3

PLANNING AND ORGANIZATION
- CONCEPT   1- 4
- START UP   1- 6
  - ORGANIZATION STRUCTURE   1- 6
- PROJECT MANAGEMENT   1- 7
- BUSINESS PLAN   1- 8
  - PLAN FUNDAMENTALS   1- 11

FINANCE
- SOURCES   1- 12
- NEGOTIATING WITH INVESTORS   1- 13
- FRANCHISE   1- 13

PHYSICAL PLANT
- LOCATION   1- 14
  - SELECTION OF GEOGRAPHIC AREA   1- 14
  - SITE SELECTION   1- 16
    - SOURCES OF DATA FOR DECISIONS   1- 16
  - SITE NEGOTIATIONS   1- 17

DESIGN
- KITCHEN DESIGN   1- 18
  - WORK FLOW IN THE KITCHEN   1- 19
  - KITCHEN SIZE   1- 20
  - WORK STATION DESIGN   1- 21
  - THE KITCHEN DESIGN PROCESS   1- 22
  - FLEXIBILITY AND MODULARITY   1- 23
  - KITCHEN RENOVATION   1- 25
    - BUDGET   1- 25
- CUSTOMER AREA DESIGN   1- 26

OPENING   1- 27
SUMMARY   1- 28

Appendix – Section One
Break-even Analysis

TABLE OF CONTENTS - Section Two

QUALITY – MENU SCIENCE

VALUE - QUALITY
  QUALITY OF PRODUCT   2- 2
MENU
  MENU DESIGN – PHYSICAL   2- 4
  MENU CONTENT   2- 5
  MENU MANAGEMENT – SCIENCE   2- 6
  MENU PROFITABILITY ANALYSIS   2- 6
  MENU ITEM - RECIPE COSTS   2- 7
  DIRECT FOOD COSTS   2- 8
  MENU STRATEGIES   2- 8
    PORTION SIZES   2- 9
    MENU BREADTH AND VARIETY   2- 10
    MENU HEALTH AND NUTRITION   2-11
  CHANGING THE MENU   2- 11
    PRICING STRATEGY   2- 12
    YOUR TARGET MARKET   2- 12
    CUSTOMER PERCEPTIONS   2- 13
    PRICING AND VOLUME   2-13
    PRICING DECISION CONSIDERATIONS   2- 14
    COMMON SIMPLE PRICING METHODS   2- 14
    PRICE INCREASES   2- 15
    PSYCHOLOGICAL PRICE BARRIERS   2- 16
  WINE MENU   2- 16
QUALITY OF SERVICE
  DELAY OF SERVICE AND THE CUSTOMER   2- 18
    THE IMPATIENCE CURVE   2- 18
    THE POINT-OF-NO-RETURN   2- 19
  REGISTER CONTROLS   2- 20
  CUSTOMER COMPLAINTS   2- 21
  COMPLAINT CORRECTION   2- 22
    NO EXCUSES   2- 23
  COMMON COMPLAINTS   2-23
  TEAMS
  TEAM STRUCTURE   2- 25
QUALITY OF ATMOSPHERE
  SOCIAL   2- 27
  PHYSICAL   2- 27
TOTAL QUALITY MANAGEMENT
SUMMARY

TABLE OF CONTENTS - Section Three

HUMAN RELATIONS – TEAM EXCELLENCE

MANAGEMENT
- MANAGER PERSONAL CHARACTERISTICS AND SKILLS   3- 2
- MANAGER JOB REQUIREMENTS   3- 2
- TIME MANAGEMENT RULES   3- 4
- FLOOR MANAGER   3- 5
- PRAISING STAFF   3- 7
- CORRECTING STAFF   3- 7
- STAFF MEETINGS   3- 8

HIRING STAFF
- FINDING STAFF   3- 10
- SELECTING   3- 11
- APPLICANTS   3- 12
- INTERVIEW TECHNIQUES   3- 13
- WAITSTAFF PERSONALITY CHARACTERISTICS   3- 13
- HIRING YOUNG PERSONS   3- 14
  - ORIENTATION CHECKLIST   3- 15
- HIRING FOR THE HOST/HOSTESS FUNCTION   3- 16
- EMPLOYEE TERMINATION   3-16

MOTIVATE
- ATTITUDE AND EXCELLENCE   3- 17
- CULTURE   3- 18

BUILDING MORALE
- ASSESSING MORALE   3- 20
- MANAGEMENT ROLE   3- 21

MOTIVATORS
- COMPENSATION / PAY   3- 22
- ACCEPTANCE BY PEERS   3- 22
- STATUS – GROWTH & ACHIEVMENT   3- 23
- INVOLVING STAFF   3- 24

STRATEGIC GOAL SETTING
- MEASURING PERFORMANCE   3- 24
- INCENTIVES FOR MEETING GOALS   3- 25
- PERFORMANCE REVIEWS   3- 26
- DELEGATING   3- 26
- RESOLVING STAFF CONFLICT   3-27
- CORRECTING STAFF WITH PEER REVIEW   3- 27

POLICY
- MISSION - GOALS - POLICIES – PROCEDURES   3- 27
- MOTIVATION FOUNDATIONS   3- 31
- TEAM DYNAMICS   3- 35

SUMMARY – MOTIVATION

TABLE OF CONTENTS – Section Four

TRAINING

    RETURN ON INVESTMENT 4- 3

WHO - FACILITATOR
    PRIMARY vs. SECONDARY TRAINERS 4- 4
    FACE-TO-FACE SKILLS 4- 4

WHO – LEARNER 4- 5

HOW - PLANNING & PREPARATION 4- 6
    CUSTOMIZE 4- 8
    ENVIRONMENT 4- 9
    BASICS 4- 9
    CLARITY 4- 10
    MOTIVATE 4- 10
    DELIVERY 4- 11
    FOLLOW-UP 4- 11
    METRICS 4- 12
    MENTORING vs. TRAINING 4- 13

HOW – BACK-OF-HOUSE 4- 14
    HOW TO TRAIN – PROCESSES 4- 14

HOW – FRONT-OF-HOUSE 4- 15

HOW - NOT 4- 15

WHAT - WHY OF EACH JOB FUNCTION 4- 16
    BIG PICTURE 4- 17
    SUPPLY CHAIN
        INTERNAL CUSTOMER 4- 17
    SPEED OF SERVICE 4- 17

WHAT – FRONT-OF-HOUSE
    SENSE OF PEOPLE SKILLS 4- 18
    SALES TRAINING 4- 19
    CONCEPTS TO COVER AS FUNDAMENTAL 4-20
    CROSS-TRAINING 4- 24
    SAFETY – HEALTH 4- 26

WHERE

WHEN - CONTINUOUS IMPROVEMENT 4- 26

TOOLS
  JOB DESCRIPTIONS 4- 27
  PERSONNEL MANUAL 4- 28
  CHECKLISTS 4- 30

JOB FUNCTIONS – FRONT
  MANAGERS 4- 30
  FRONT DESK 4- 31
  WAITSTAFF 4- 32

SUMMARY

TABLE OF CONTENTS – Section Five

CONTROL – OPERATIONS

    ACCOUNTING FOR DAILY OPERATIONS 5- 2
    POINT OF SALE CONTROLS 5- 3

PRIME COSTS
    COST OF GOODS SOLD 5- 6
      PURCHASING 5- 6
        NEGOTIATING WITH SUPPLIERS 5- 6
      INVENTORY CONTROL – SUPPLY CHAIN 5- 7
        INVENTORY LEVEL MAINTENANCE 5- 8
      THEFT CONTROL 5- 9
      BAR CONTROL 5- 12
      LABOR COST CONTROL – PRODUCTIVITY 5- 13
        LABOR COST PERCENTAGE 5- 13
    COST ANALYSIS 5- 18
    BREAKEVEN 5- 18

OVERHEAD CONTROL
    FACILITIES COST 5- 19
    DEALING WITH GOVERNMENT REGULATORS 5- 21

OPERATIONS
    OPERATIONS MANAGEMENT 5- 22
      FOOD HANDLING 5- 24
        WALK-IN MANAGEMENT 5- 25
      RED MEAT 5- 25
      DAIRY 5- 26
      BEVERAGES 5- 26

FACILITY MANAGEMENT
    EQUIPMENT 5- 29
      MAINTENANCE 5- 30
      INDIVIDUAL EQUIPMENT 5- 31
        KNIVES 5- 30

HEALTH / SANITATION / CLEANLINESS
    FOOD ILLNESS 5- 33
    PEST CONTROL 5- 35
    FIRE SAFETY 5- 36
    FIRST AID – CUTS – BURNS – SLIPS 5- 35
    DISH WASH / CHINA POLICY 5- 37
    JANITORIAL 5- 37
    CHECKLISTS 5- 37

RESERVATIONS 5- 39

SUMMARY
    Glossary Section 5
    Appendix Section 5

TABLE OF CONTENTS – Section Six

VALUATION FOR BUY/SELL

    REASONS TO KNOW THE VALUE 6- 1
FAIR MARKET VALUE 6- 1
SELL 6- 2
BUY 6- 4
INCOME CAPITALIZATION
  CASH FLOWS DISCOUNTED 6- 5
  CAPITALIZATION RATE OR MULTIPLE 6- 6
COST OR REPLACEMENT
  ASSET VALUATION 6- 9
    LAND 6- 9
      HIGHEST AND BEST USE 6- 10
     BUILDING 6- 11
     OTHER ASSETS 6- 11
AREA SALES COMPARISON 6- 13
NEGOTIATE
  THE DEAL 6- 14
  PLAN 6- 15
  ATTITUDE 6- 16
  STRATEGY 6- 17
    STRATEGIES FOR SELLERS 6- 20
    TECHNIQUES & TACTICS 6- 21
LEASE 6- 23
FINANCE 6- 25
SUMMARY

CHECKLISTS – TEMPLATES - FORMS
  VALUATION BY CAPITALIZATION CHECKLIST
  BUYING CHECKLIST
  OPERATION
  FINANCIAL INFORMATION
  BUILDING AND LAND
  COMPETITOR ANALYSIS
  LEASE
  PURCHASE AGREEMENT

PREFACE – Success & Error

Evidence shows that near 45% of restaurants fail in the first year. This dismal statistic must cease. It represents a tragic misapplication of peoples' energy, fortunes and lives. This failure rate is a hard and tragic drain on the whole economy. Hindsight will show that the failures were a result of poor decisions and poor execution. Poor execution can come from inadequate resources, time, talent, dollars, and knowledge. But we would never even get to poor execution if we had not already made poor decisions. Both decisions and execution must be based on knowledge. This handbook supplies all the tools for sound decisions and execution. The problem is: that it takes time and energy to gain this knowledge. Time is our most perishable resource. This book will detail why restaurant operations-management requires a broader range of skills and knowledge than most any other kind if management. Time is always in short supply.

Time is best saved when we follow time-proven *tools & rules* that evolved through the long experience of successful others. We all gain wisdom by experiencing error, but we can avoid fatal error by using tested guidelines and common sense.

Common sense however requires this caveat. Restaurant failure can be likened to pilot error; poor decisions and execution. Old pilots know that outside visual cues can be impaired such as; clouds, fog, haze, flight over water or at night and a deadly combination thereof. Tragedy comes from trusting the seat-of-the-pants senses. Pilots learn to keep their eyes scanning across trusted instruments. Several attitude and navigation aids always pinpoint the pilot's position relative to a safe destination. Checklists force the use of all this input to assure smooth cruising.

Restaurant operators must use similar diligence and techniques to safe destinations.

AUTHOR – PROFILE/PERSPECTIVE

Before building my first restaurant, I did much secondary research. (1) I looked at every restaurant-management book in print, starting with the university library. (2) My consulting business partners, in our travels to major cities, sought out perennials. We found the most popular restaurants, as identified by published lists of top-grossers year-after-year, and by local acclaim. We analyzed each with two perspectives. (A) We looked for what set them apart from lesser operations, and (B) What did they share in common with other perennials.

We were able to create our first restaurant as a highly popular success, without misstep. We used objective proven science and we borrowed examples of artful creative genius. The MBA approach to the business proved efficient, but we quickly learned that creating a restaurant was not a quick and easy part-time task. Primary research requires doing.

Knowledge, skills and wisdom must come from daily exposure to real events with the opportunity to learn from mistakes. Twenty years of rewarding design, building, staffing, operating and selling of restaurants gives insight to best practices and lifetime rewards.

AUTHOR - BONA FIDES

To plan, design, finance and build a restaurant (Section 1) was easiest for me, because I had extensive study of architecture and engineering before switching to a finance business major, and I had worked in construction all through the school years. Still, to jump into a project in your early 20's without direct experience in the specific business requires following proven *tools & rules* developed over time.

We all know what we like to eat, and basics of deliciousness remain constant. To create a profitable menu, however, requires use of menu- science. (Section 2)

The primary key to success is exceptional people (Section 3). How you select, mentor, train and motivate will be the deciding factor in sustained profitability.

Training (section 4) relies on proven practices from human-relations science. Teamwork is a dynamic complex process, but a large body of proven tools will maximize learning and guide a healthy and fun culture.

Operations/Control (Section 5) will require the greatest focus of attention and time. We are lucky that basic business rules are again an excellent guide to safe efficient control.

The designed plan for each one of my restaurants was to sell after one or two years of operations. Each one sold for above a five times earnings price because of popularity. Meanwhile we sold licensing with consulting contracts for markets in other cities. As a licensed real-estate agent – to save fees for self-buy – it made sense to use the body of RE business aids to properly determine values for real-estate in order to buy/sell (Section 6).

RESTAURANT HANDBOOK

TOOLS & RULES

Roderick A. Clelland

FUNDAMENTALS OF RESTAURANT MANAGEMENT

PRINT SECTION ONE

START – PLAN – FINANCE
LOCATE – DESIGN

TABLE OF CONTENTS - Section One

START–PLAN–FINANCE–LOCATE–DESIGN

THE BUSINESS
  STATE OF THE INDUSTRY   1- 1
THE CUSTOMER
  CUSTOMER SATISFACTION SURVEYS   1- 2
  SUSTAINED COMPETITIVE ADVANTAGE   1- 3
PLANNING AND ORGANIZATION
  CONCEPT   1- 4
  START UP   1- 6
    ORGANIZATION STRUCTURE   1- 6
  PROJECT MANAGEMENT   1- 7
  BUSINESS PLAN   1- 8
    PLAN FUNDAMENTALS   1- 11
FINANCE
  SOURCES   1- 12
  NEGOTIATING WITH INVESTORS   1- 13
  FRANCHISE   1- 13
PHYSICAL PLANT
  LOCATION   1- 14
    SELECTION OF GEOGRAPHIC AREA   1- 14
    SITE SELECTION   1- 16
      SOURCES OF DATA FOR DECISIONS   1- 16
    SITE NEGOTIATIONS   1- 17
DESIGN
  KITCHEN DESIGN   1- 18
    WORK FLOW IN THE KITCHEN   1- 20
    KITCHEN SIZE   1- 20
    WORK STATION DESIGN   1- 21
    THE KITCHEN DESIGN PROCESS   1- 22
    FLEXIBILITY AND MODULARITY   1- 23
    KITCHEN RENOVATION   1- 25
    BUDGET   1- 25
  CUSTOMER AREA DESIGN   1- 26
OPENING   1- 27
SUMMARY   1- 28

Appendix – Section One
  Break-even Analysis

THE BUSINESS

STATE OF THE INDUSTRY

Grow in a growing environment. Each person should attach personal growth to growing opportunities. The restaurant industry is a growing environment. Opportunity is rich in the restaurant business, despite well-known risks. Consider the consistent strong growth numbers.

Forecasts & Facts	2006	2011	2012
Total locations in the U.S.	925,000	960,000	
Historic 5yr average growth rate vs. 3.4 for GNP	5.6%		
Total sales this year ($ billions)	510	620	657
Daily sales ($ billions)	1.4	1.7	1.8
Consecutive years of growth	15	20	22
Percent of the total food dollar (25% in 1955)	47.5		
Food service sales as percent of GDP	4%		
Average household spending on food away from home		$2,620	
Food service growth is outpacing grocery store growth.			
Single-unit operations as related to total eat-drink units		70%	
Proportion of operations with less than 50 employees		93%	
Proportion of adults who worked in restaurants		1/2	
Proportion of adults who's 1st job was in a restaurant		1/3	
Partial source: National Restaurant Association			

The industry rate of growth continues to outpace the growth of the general economy, according to numbers from the Food Institute. The forecast is that growth will continue. Evolution of the demographic environment drives this growth. Reasons commonly cited include these lifestyle evolutions:

- Women growth in the workforce.
- Reduced time at home and inclination for home cooking.
- Baby boomers with higher disposable dollars for eating out.
- Two-earner lifestyles have increasingly become habit.
- High productivity through technology allows more time for eating out.
- The growth of the industry itself makes eating out ever more convenient.
- Dollars spent on food continue to be a smaller portion of total disposable income.
- Perceived value of eating out continues to grow.
- Demographic changes of the population encourage social interaction.

Consider, for instance, that at the turn of the 20th century 40% of the population were farmers, and they did not get out much. Now that number is 2%, and they generally have big dollars to spend on dining out.

Data says that the industry is somewhat recession proof. Certainly, hunger never goes out of style. The industry is less affected than the total economy during slow times.

It appears that, even when disposable incomes are reduced, there exists repressed demand to get out of the house for restaurant services. Yet, the business is complex, and delivered-value is so much more than satisfying hunger alone.

The industry is obviously robust. It is the largest employer of women, minorities, and teenagers. Still, individual restaurants continue the traditional high rate of turnover. The National Restaurant Association has calculated that fifty percent of restaurants fail in the first year. Thirty percent of the surviving-half fail in the second year.

The healthy units are those providing a compelling price/value proposition. Value is easier to deliver when your whole team has the knowledge and skills required to provide the exceptional customer experience consistently. Those who will succeed in the business will arm themselves with superior knowledge of how to best deliver value.

THE CUSTOMER

Be very clear: the customer controls all aspects of the health of this industry. They are knowledgeable and demanding. Many know the business intimately. Restaurants, as an industry, are the largest employer in the U.S. So, almost half of all adults either now work in the food/hospitality business or did work at some point in their life. Since they have been there, they know good-from-poor in regards to prompt and efficient service, cleanliness, product presentation, and value. Customers are going to notice details. They will only be impressed with proper and professional execution.

The customer wants to be: important and appreciated, entertained, relaxed, and comfortable at a price that fits a budget. Guests seek total satisfaction, and not just good food.

CUSTOMER SATISFACTION SURVEYS

Customer satisfaction surveys are popular and published often. As years pass, the surveys still appear similar, possibly illustrating the basic nature of the restaurants business. The results usually depend on the questionnaire design, and customer concerns vary depending on the type of operation. For fast food, the large concerns are speed and cleanliness. For sit-down dining, excellent service is first.

With "top ten customer complaints", the order of complaints is usually (1) poor quality of food, (2) poor quality of service, and (3) cleanliness. The balance of the complaints are usually related to atmosphere such as; (8) lights too dim, (9) music too loud, and (10) lights too bright. (Note "music too quiet" does not appear.)

One important point is: that quality of food usually appears as first and quality of service second. Do not always accept this at face value. People vote differently with their mouths than with their dollars or their feet. Feedback is necessary and surveys are always informative, but this is an illustration of why surveys are not always accurate. Human nature forces us to want to think highly of ourselves, and to want others to think highly of us also. We therefore usually give answers that present us in the best light. Our easiest answer is to knock the quality of the food rather than the service. We would rather appear as discerning connoisseurs of food not up to our standards and say for instance "the steak was overcooked" rather than admit we are snippy or impatient and "no one came around to refill my coffee".

Note that if something is truly wrong with the food we must learn it immediately, and the customer who gives us this valuable insight must be praised and thanked. However, it is relatively easy to maintain the high quality of food compared to the sustained high quality of service with its many human relations variables. Any customer who has been made to wait and feel ignored always looks around for a solid complaint that will not make them appear fussy. They will usually direct their feelings in a complaint about things rather than people.

Prompt and courteous service must be consistent throughout the dining experience beginning with the immediate greeting at the door. Do not ever make your guests wait unless it is clearly unavoidable to the view of your guest. Guests who must wait must be continually updated by your staff, because ignoring guests is the greatest sin. The importance of this reality will be repeated in several other sections of this manual.

Customers always give a complaint that makes them feel important, if at any time they have been made to feel unimportant.

SUSTAINED COMPETITIVE ADVANTAGE

We know that brand-new restaurants as a group are generally not as profitable as those two and three years old. We also see that restaurants over seven years old are less profitable as a group. There can be many reasons for this, including changing demographics and trends. However it is management's job to anticipate and adjust to external changes. Often, declining sales that are quickly attributed to external factors, such as competition or the economy, are really caused by internal deficiencies. Too often success breeds complacency as business begins to rest on its laurels. Steps can and must be taken to negate this cycle. Make adaptation to change a part of your culture.

When you start a business you will do anything to please your customer, and you are conscious at-all-times of exactly what the guests' needs may be. When you become successful, you have less enthusiasm for details and quality can slide. If you continue to coast, sales will begin to drop and you will blame external forces rather than yourself. When customer counts go down, a common mistake is to cut costs that affect quality of product and service. Customers then perceive reduced value, and counts erode even further. You will chase yourself down a hole with such circular reaction.

To ensure healthy trends, profit-planning projections should be on hand for each month. When operations surpass projections try to identify what specifically produced the good numbers and do more, including rewards to staff. When operations are low also find the cause. Trends require vigilance and early action. Great restaurants that evolve to mediocre are those that did not evolve with change.

"Management - almost alone- has to live always in both present and future". Peter Drucker

The way to maintain success is to see yourself through the eyes of your customer and continue special efforts to please and provide satisfaction. This may require sitting in every chair in your dining area and creating a checklist of problems to be corrected. That checklist will include the level of service from all staff as well as the physical view.

Remember, out -of change comes opportunity for profit.

RESTAURANT HANDBOOK – TOOLS & RULES

PLANNING AND ORGANIZATION

Before you step into this business do a personal assessment. Restaurant managers must have broad generalist skill-sets. The environment is dynamic with many variables in constant flux. You will deal with people, things, and processes. *People* include customers, staff, suppliers, professional services, and government regulators. *Things* include asset management: land, building, facilities management, equipment, raw materials, supply chains, inventories, and cash. *Processes* include systems, procedures, and methods, all of which must be smooth, speedy and efficient.

Restaurants deal with both products and services. In general industry, these job functions are separate, but you must cover both. You must do all this in conditions of constant unsolicited interruptions while reacting to many dynamic time-critical expedients.

Manufacturing characteristics of restaurants:
- Physical product output
- Quality easily measured
- Raw material inputs
- Inventories required (including highly perishable)

Service characteristics of Restaurants:
- High customer contact
- Intangible service quality output (not easy to measure)
- Short response time
- Small facilities
- Local market only
- Labor intensive

Complex events require quick informed decisions and actions. There is virtually no time for planning and organization during operations, so take serious time up front. Develop your concept, and perform all due diligence first.

CONCEPT

You would not be here without some basic concept in mind. The competitive nature of the business means that your concept must help you *differentiate* in some way. Some ways to differentiate might be:
- Menu breadth
- Concentration on limited type of cuisine
- Unusual and exciting menu items
- Type of service
- Imaginative approach to promotion
- Pricing strategy and flexibility
- Great location
- Rich décor
- Entertaining environment
- Convenience

The *one surest way* to differentiate will always be the quality of your people, their skills, and their strong motivated commitment to creating value.

Whatever ways you choose to differentiate, your concept must always start with a clear view of a customer need, and ways to deliver perceived value. Know why your target customer has incentive to bring their dollars and spend time with you rather than your competition.

What will be your *core competencies* to set you apart? Take a *resource based view* (RBV) of your special capabilities for sustained competitive advantage. A core competency is any special capability or skill that you can identify, nurture and use in daily operations. What unique bundle of resources can you employ, both tangible and intangible? Tangible assets are the physical means to provide value including building, location, facilities and finances. Intangible assets will be your reputation, knowledge, experience, and employee morale. Core competencies will include the ability to combine capital assets, people, and processes. Your greatest asset will ultimately be your staff. Human resource assets will be modified by how you measure and promote these characteristics.
- Management staff skill sets
- Total staff skill, knowledge, and morale
- Efficient and effective personnel policy
- Effective motivation to excellent performance
- Incentives
- Controlled labor costs compared to industry
- Low staff turnover and absenteeism
- Specialized skills required for your concept

Consider any resources that can differentiate how customer needs are met. Go beyond the menu and service value. Break down opportunities for special-customer-service into a list similar to these items.
- Ease of access
    - Turn lanes
    - Parking
    - Door positioning
    - Welcoming and informative external signs
- Ambience
    - Eye catching exterior
    - Décor/features
    - Wall/Floor treatment
    - Bar layout
    - Window treatment
    - Table configuration and presentation
        - Theme, Materials & Colors
        - Table top presentation
- Special welcome for first impression
    - Smiling, quick and cheerful greeting at door
    - Prompt friendly table service
    - Speedy and smooth service throughout
- Minimized waiting time
    - Transparent waiting lists
    - Constant feedback from host on updated status

- Ensuring an enjoyable experience
    - Provide atmosphere for social interaction for wait list
    - Entertain
    - Provide informative promotional material
- Special table service
    - Careful selection of quality servers
    - Continuous staff development
        - Customer awareness
        - Menu training
        - Sales training
        - Handling difficult situations training
- Menu Decisions
    - Breadth of offerings
    - Mix of offerings
    - Physical design and materials
    - Layout
    - Pricing
- Speed of service
    - Kitchen layout, queuing and coordination
    - Service standards and procedures

Any list of opportunities to differentiate is incomplete. You have unlimited possibilities. Most of these items are covered in more detail in other sections of this handbook. SWOT analysis; listing your strengths – weaknesses – opportunities – and threats, will always solidify your resource-based-view of your special competencies. Your concept should make your restaurant a vibrant, innovative and creative place for great people to serve and be served. So it will always be a good time to think different.

START UP

ORGANIZATION STRUCTURE - CORPORATION / PARTNERSHIP

PARTNERSHIPS

A majority of partnerships fail over time, an ugly statistic that must be faced. Partners generally start as great friends who recognize that their combined symbiotic skills are necessary for the project success. During the inception phases it is a great adventure, and everyone on the team is enthusiastic, energetic and ready to work long hours. All partners are hungry at this stage, and complimentary areas of responsibility are easy to define. Later when questions of distribution of duties, time, and dollars arise, resentments can also arise. The result can be a painful divorce, which creates bitterness, bruised egos, hurt feelings, and anger. The partnership arrangement can be subject to stresses not found in corporations. It is necessary, therefore, to have a clearly defined agreement, which anticipates disagreements even when the possibility of discord appears farfetched and is unpleasant to contemplate at the enthusiastic beginnings.

Some rules to follow in *partnerships* are:
- Meet and discuss capital requirements candidly and realistically.
- Share output equity in relation to input. Input can be in the form of dollar capital, "sweat equity" hours of labor, or skills brought to the mix. Shares in corporations pre-define this equity, but in partnerships there has to be understanding and agreement before operations.
- Complete a business plan with projected cash flows.
- Share formal letters of intent on duties and responsibilities.
- Have the partnership agreement include the clauses on dissolution.
- Meet early and often to discuss progress to planned benchmarks.

Partnership structure will affect success. Some suggestions are:
- Limit the number of partners to those who will contribute assets.
- Avoid partners with personal relationships. Do not automatically use current professional services providers such as: family lawyers, insurance agents, accountants, and bankers.
- Found the group based on measurable skill-sets rather than spontaneously.
- Avoid complete harmony at the expense of creative conflict.
- Do not give away equity or stock options without tying directly to performance milestones.
- Use outsiders for board of directors to avoid inbred strategy.

CORPORATE STRUCTURE

Incorporation is easy and relatively inexpensive. Often it can be done on-line. The corporate structure is valuable because it limits the liability of principals. Incorporation is important if you are seeking financing from several individuals. Issue of stock lends itself to simple finance decisions. Chapter S corporate structure seeks to avoid taxing corporate profits before again taxing dividends to the stockholders, with some tradeoffs. Seek advice from your attorney or accountant for that option.

One caveat is: try to avoid having stockholders, or coalition of stockholders, that can control 51 percent of your stock, unless you don't mind losing primary control in the case of huge success. Another consideration is that you might delay incorporation until approaching actual opening, since it seems to raise your profile and attract government regulation-attention earlier to complicate your progress.

Choose the structure that best fits your project, and create the primary tool for successful start-up, a solid business plan.

PROJECT MANAGEMENT

Restaurant start-up is a complex project that must be brought in on time, on budget, and on spec. A useful tool can be project management software to keep the tasks under control. Project management software is intuitive to learn and will likely have a high return on investment of your time.

The "right" to open a restaurant in NYC means working with demands of eleven municipal agencies, passing about 23 city inspections, plus gaining 30 different permits and certificates, all before the NY liquor license. You must prepare for ambiguous complexities and delay from self-important agents.

THE BUSINESS PLAN

You absolutely need a business plan before you enter business. When your business has no history of revenue, you have very little negotiating leverage beyond the power of your business plan. Further, you need an updated business plan every year that you are in business. It shows where you expect to end up and exactly how you will proceed. Those who proceed without a plan will be primarily those who are surprised by why they are not making a profitable enterprise. The business plan serves these vital functions:

- ✓ Financing is based on this tool
- ✓ Planning keeps project organization steps on schedule.
- ✓ The business plan forces attention to all elements of the business for complete preparation, and to avoid unpleasant surprises.
- ✓ Realistic goals set benchmarks for operations control and continuous improvement.

The *business plan* should contain some or most of the following:
- An executive summary
- History
    - Brief background of introduction to this business
    - Philosophies and goals
    - Why rewards outweigh risks
    - Special characteristics of the operations package
    - A brief two-year and five-year plan
- Product and services
    - Description of operation
    - Quality and content of the menu
    - Quality of service
    - Atmosphere
    - From the customers' point of view
- Market, targets and trends
    - Promotion policy
    - Customer profile
    - Special characteristics or niche differentiation
    - Charts of beginning volume with scenarios
    - Breakeven analysis (See Appendix Section One)
    - Survey of competition
    - Survey of complementary businesses
    - Strengths, weakness, opportunities, threats
- Projected financial statement pro-formas
    - Income statement
    - Statement of cash flows
    - Cumulative cash position with timing
    - Balance sheet
    - Organizational capital needs, start-up costs
    - Organizational time-lines with milestones, periods, dates
    - Ownership structure
    - Lease terms if applicable
    - Schedule of Non-departmental Expenses and Fixed Charges
    - Schedule of Salaries and Wages

- Location, Land, and Buildings
    - Trade Area Market Demographic Analysis
        - State of the Industry
        - The State and County as a Market
        - The selected local area as a Market
        - The specific site as a location
        - Map of area by density and income levels
    - Land
        - Description
        - Sketch of plot
        - Site Evaluation
        - Zoning Considerations
        - Summary of Site
- Building
    - Description
    - Functional Design
    - Floor Plan Kitchen, Dining, and Utility
    - Multi-use Contingency
    - Preliminary Building Cost Estimates
    - Financial Analysis of Land and Building
        - Cost
        - Income
- Personal profiles of management key figures
    - Experience
    - Knowledge and skills
    - Track record of success
    - Whys of symbiotic chemistry of individuals
- Appendices with all supporting materials
    - Back-up the executive-summary statements with details
    - Back-up all financial statement details and assumptions
    - Sources of statistics for market projections
    - Population demographics.

Conclude each section with the next action steps you will take to achieve results. Assign specific responsibility, dollars involved, and time targets.

BUSINESS PLAN LEGWORK

Do your homework. Take time to investigate *market trends* both in the industry and in your area. Your ultimate pricing is subject to these market forces and consumer demands. Market trends influence your sales potential and growth prospects.

Survey your competition. Do primary research by visiting restaurants in your area. Note their menu, their pricing. See if you can identify any special features that add or detract form their popularity. What do they do best? What can you emulate? What will help you differentiate? Fill out a report form for each. (See Section Six). Note that some restaurants near you can be *complimentary* rather than competitive. If they serve a separate market niche, their proximity can be a plus.

RESTAURANT HANDBOOK – TOOLS & RULES

Consider *area demographics* with your location. Visibility, positioning on the street in relation to other restaurants, accessibility, convenience and the desirability of the surroundings influence whether competition is good or bad.

Take special care with your *cash flow projections*. Here is where many planners come up short. Cash flow is much more important than profits. Profits are an accounting concept, and cash is how you actually transact business.

Construct a spreadsheet for cashflows. Be certain of your starting cash and the timing of any cash inflows. Be exhaustive with the listing of all cash outflows and the probable timing. Cash-flow-out will include administration expenses, rent, utilities, construction costs, leasehold improvements, purchases, materials, labor, starting payrolls, initial inventories, etc. Consider all possible expenses and allow a reserve for contingencies and delays. Note that unexpected delays from bureaucrats are normal.

Overruns happen. Use a standard construction costs estimation form to cover all likely items for construction or remodeling. Also, go on-line for current construction cost standards of materials and labor for over 34 construction categories for realistic expectation of outlays. Do not overlook special kitchen costs of electric, lighting, plumbing, mechanical, ventilation hoods, cooling, refrigeration, fire suppression, grease traps, stainless steel fabrication, etc. Dining area will need flooring, millwork, drywall, finishes, tiling, artwork, special décor, signage, POS hardware, etc.

There will always be some surprise of unanticipated need or cost, often in the form of demands by inspectors. Be diligent, inclusive and allow for surprises, to find probable actual cash outflows. Accordingly, plan a financial *reserve for contingencies*.

Calculate net cash flows and *cumulative cash position*. Use the spreadsheet chart function to give a clear picture. You want to delay cash outflows as long as possible until you open and generate revenue.

The time you spend getting these numbers realistic will pay off continually. Your business action plan will evolve as your business grows and faces change. The plan measures both what has worked in your operations and where you need new action to force sustained competitive advantage to ensure success.

The business plan looks like a lot of work. Well, yes it is, but you cannot take shortcuts, or defer the process of putting a good plan together. Do it properly. The first beneficiary is you. It is a checklist of all of the important steps to success. The plan covers all of the basics: objectives, concept, strategies, market target, décor, location, customer profile, competition, historical information, the management team, capital needs, cash flows, and why you will be successful at providing exceptional value in a tough business.

The business plan shows evidence of your drive, and your applicable business and technical experience. The plan must verify your integrity and show your ability to plan, communicate ideas, and build a team.

> "A goal without a plan is just a wish" – Antoine De St. Exupery

PLAN - EXECUTIVE SUMMARY

Finance sources will require a complete business plan that establishes your credibility. Bind the executive summary separately. The whole plan will be thick, so bind the sections separately. Few others will want to read the whole plan, so you will have to capture attention with the summary. Add, but limit, some arresting artwork or attractive photos. The summary should be less than six pages.

The main point is show why the net present value of the project is high enough to balance risks. Financers want to know exactly how and why projected cash flows will produce a good return on investment. Clearly demonstrate your economic viability; why, how, and when. This risk/reward assessment should fit on an opening page. A pro-forma income statement for a typical month should also fit on one page.

Include a table of contents of all of the separately bound sections and their scope.

The summary is necessarily brief, but you must be prepared to back up any point or question with detailed analysis. You must be able to turn to the exact page in one of your other sections to document your numbers and the sources.

Note: a PowerPoint presentation will work here. Provide nice illustrations, but do not let artwork or gimmick-graphics obscure the content pointing to why the project is worthy. The few summary slides will still have to be backed up by the separately-bound materials: data, charts, schedules, and graphics

PLAN FUNDAMENTALS

Here are some fundamental rules to use as guidelines to avoid mistakes and errors of omission.
- ✓ Start working on the plan now. The steps are lengthy and involved, and will need constant refinement. Start on the first draft and add relevant sections before urgent startup needs capture all of your attention and time. Once you have the framework, keeping it up and current will be easier. Planning for your business continued success requires constant update.
- ✓ Retain focus on priorities. Your plan will have a few main priorities that map towards the major goals. Especially in the executive summary, limit to three or four main points. The body of your plan will contain other priorities in a hierarchy. These will be in the form of mini-milestones with time lines.
- ✓ Limit verbiage and excess dialogue in your plan. It will be detailed enough as it is with documentation of the main points. Keep argument focused, cogent and persuasive. Use bulleted points where possible.
- ✓ Do not attribute dollar value to ideas. Ideas are largely worth what they are made of, thin air. Everyone has great ideas and they do not necessarily translate to great business. All ideas must be linked to probability of measurable returns from specific actions. Your credibility is on the line.
- ✓ Do not inflate sales, cash flows, or profits. You must have a solid basis for projections. Offer scenarios that are high, middle, and low-end expectations, all based on reasonable historical data from similar types of business. No one will believe sales projections with hockey stick shapes.
- ✓ Document the first year financials carefully. Do not fudge dates, responsibilities, or deadlines. Be clear on what is expected to happen, and who will make it happen.

- ✓ Five-year projections do not require details. If you reasonably match your first year numbers you can spend a little more time with longer-term projections.
- ✓ Move all details to appendix sections.
- ✓ Follow the KISS principal with formatting. Absolutely do use photos, charts, graphs, and other graphics, but keep them simple and limited. Present one main point per page. Do not allow art or graphics to detract.
- ✓ Remember your plan is only a structure for action. Implementation calls for strict timelines and personal accountability for each task to ultimate success.

FINANCE

Your business plan is the vehicle for finding start-up capital. When you demonstrate that you are credible in your knowledge and skills, and that your projections are based on reasonable assumptions, financing the project becomes much easier. You will be surprised at how many people would like to be part of a successful restaurant operation.
Those first contacts can introduce you to a network of possible finance sources, when they believe you can produce.

SOURCES

Options for the sources of funds are many. Family and friends are possible sources. Some mortgage the equity in their homes. A network of individual investors is a good source when you can demonstrate a likely track record. Note that banks generally are not financers of restaurants without extra measures of security in the form of assets that can be secured as collateral.

Seller financing is very common as part of a deal structure. Seller financing can give the buyer confidence that the seller believes the business can thrive at that location. Often the terms of seller financing can be more favorable than traditional financing sources, especially if it affects the sale price. The rate should never be much above the current bank rates for such loans.

The seller should determine the ability of the buyer to perform. Ask for written permission to see their credit record, especially when the buyer is an individual. Credit records can be queried via the Internet. The buyer should cover the query fee. Also ask for financial and business references.

Seller financing can provide benefits for both parties. Make sure both parties are comfortable with the other's ability to deliver what is promised.

Seek *credit terms* from vendors. Your cash flow projections will give you ideas on where cash outflow can be delayed, so that total capital requirements until opening are a small as possible. Suppliers of your equipment, supplies and initial inventories can be persuaded to offer credit terms.

Barter works well to conserve start-up cash as you approach opening. Much of your precious working capital can be preserved by trading for essential services. You can negotiate services for a meal account to be consumed after you are open. Many of your professional services are readily amenable to this type of arrangement, possibly from tax their considerations.

Assume you have a thirty percent direct food cost, then your total bartered cost becomes only the incremental cost of the food and beverage consumed. You effectively reduce your cost for the services to one third of the value. Try to stipulate that consumption of the food and beverage account will be at off-peak hours. If the consumption comes when you have a waiting line for seating, your cost is the opportunity cost of the full menu price. Otherwise, you have drastically reduced your cost for the services, and a deferred cash flow, at that.

NEGOTIATING WITH INVESTORS

Restaurant startups do not have strong negotiating positions. Investors will only advance capital if you present yourself with confidence in your numbers. Always draft investment terms before the meeting. Know how you will structure the investment options. Do not let investors with minority positions restructure your investment terms unless they plan to take a lead role in fundraising. Avoid negotiating special terms with individual negotiators because it will later raise resentments regarding inequitable treatment.

LEASE CONTRACTS

A lease will be one of the largest decisions an operator will ever make with long range consequences. Never take a commercial lease for granted. Review standard lease "boilerplate" to cue your attention to any and all future contingencies that could apply to the needs of your business. For basics to cover, see Section Six – Leasing Checklist.

FRANCHISE

Franchise is a logical path for food operations. A franchise has some obvious advantages, but also some challenges to consider before taking this path.

Potential *franchising advantages* are:
- You will start with a built-in demand.
- You reduce risk with a relatively known expectation of performance. Many food franchises have a track record of success over time.
- Financing is easier. The formula for the franchise finance is well known to traditional lenders. Potential lenders can have high confidence in the cash flows of established franchises.
- Franchisors lay out the proven systems and procedures to guarantee smooth operations. A major portion of your organizational work is done for you.
- The franchisor helps with on-going advice on best practices, as well as supplies of raw product.

Some *franchise disadvantages* to consider might include:
- The initial investment can be higher than a non-franchise start-up.
- You will have to do the legwork for *zoning and code compliance*, but this is required for any type of food operation, and the franchisor will provide proven guidelines.
- Turnover can be higher at franchises, so securing a conscientious *labor supply* can be challenging.
- Many franchises have relatively *low margins* because they operate in competitive environments that are very price sensitive. Franchise fees contribute to the narrow margins. Narrow margins are acceptable when high volume is relatively assured.
- Management hours can be long and tedious.

Before taking the franchise path, evaluate the franchise track record thoroughly. Make sure you can match your personal qualities to the demands of that kind of operation.

PHYSICAL PLANT

LOCATION

"Location-location-location" is trite but very good advice, and helps ensure success. Just be clear that a great location, by itself, cannot overcome poor execution of quality of product/service and atmosphere.

Site selection is obviously critical. A majority of selections seem made from intuition or convenience. Probability of long term success, however, is vastly greater when sites are selected using measurable defining criteria. Objectively match the market characteristics to your operation. Proper demographic evaluation is essential for site selection but also for your financing. It will also be an integral part of your business plan for your own peace of mind and for leverage in negotiations.

You want to provide your action where the action-is-happening. There is a systematic approach to finding where the action is, and maybe more importantly where the action is going to be. You must start with your target customer, which as we have noted, directs your menu and concept. Create first a customer profile (See Section Two - The Menu) then proceed to get a location profile. The location is a specific site within a geographic area, which breaks analysis to two primary steps; geographic area, and specific site.

SELECTION OF GEOGRAPHIC AREA

There are several indicators of optimal geographic area for locating. These include:
- Total population and per cent of the U.S. population
- Population growth rate of the State
- Population growth rate of the region or county
- Size of base or minimum total drawing population on which growth is calculated
- Is the state a right-to work state? Unions raise the cost of doing business to all.
- Per capita income of the region or county (defines expectations of customer)
- Per capita disposable income
- Employment ($1/8^{th}$ of households have 2/3 of disposable income)
- Per capita spending on food and beverage for the region
- Percent Urban
- Ethnic mix (need for tailoring to local expectations of menu and service)
- Average household size (important for family style operations)
- Age (cafeteria vs. French service)
- Sex (light dining vs. meat and potatoes)
- Economic base of area (multiple vs. single housing)
- White/blue collar mix
- Education level
- Home ownership versus rent
- Comparable crime rates for area

Select the indicators that may apply to your concept. Rank alternative geographic areas with use of a formula on a spreadsheet. The formula will take some of the above indicators and give each a weight, with the total of the weights adding to 100%. The weights will be your own, based on menu concept and ideal customer for that product. Rankings should also compare to a benchmark such as average U.S. numbers or ideal numbers.

Use a process similar to this example when you have not already selected the geographic area or are considering where to expand next.

Example: LOCATION – SELECTING GEOGRAPHICAL AREA

Characteristic	Weight	Area #1 Rank	Area #1 Value	Area #2 Rank	Area #2 Value	Area #3 Rank	Area #3 Value
Growth Ranking of County	50	10	50	8	40	9	45
Population of County	25	4	10	7	17.5	8	20
Percent Urban (SMSA)	5	6	3	8	4	5	2.5
Per Capita Disposable Income (SMSA)	10	7	7	6	6	7	7
Per Capita Spending on food and Beverage	10	8	8	7	7	9	9
Totals	**100**		**78**		**74.5**		**83.5**

Note: Rank areas against each other with 10 points being best and 1 point being poor
    Value is the (Rank * Weight)/100 - (SMSA) Standard metropolitan Statistical Area
Conclusion: Given the 5 variables selected and the weights applied, Area #3 looks best.

Give *growth rates* the highest weight. The reasoning is: growth of services always lags a dynamic population growth, thereby creating a strong service demand. Also a new population has fewer established habit patterns and has already shown a readiness for change. They are more likely to patronize a new restaurant. It is always great to open a restaurant with a big pop, and then see continued waiting lines for seating thereafter.

SOURCES OF DEMOGRAPHIC DATA FOR REGIONS

Free sources of data, including much available on the Internet, are:
- U.S. Census is primary. (Note: Census data can be dated - taken every 10 years)
- U.S. Department of commerce
- State economic development
- State Restaurant Associations
- Regional and city planning commissions
- Restaurant Growth Index by SMSA is published yearly in "Restaurant Business".
- Statistical Abstract of the U.S.
- Local Chambers of Commerce
- Google newspaper articles

SITE SELECTION WITHIN CHOSEN GEOGRAPHIC AREA

Again you are to use weighted variables to find a specific site. Among these are:
 - Area and direction of city's most recent growth, usually the last 3 years.
 - Area of highest income as indicated by housing, if this is your target
 - Traffic counts and patterns during the day, plus speed of traffic
 - Restaurant Row (complimentary v. competitive)
 - Population density (You can't sell a steak to a tree)
 - Number of subdivisions within 10 minutes (five miles) with average home sale price.
 - Have easy access near major arteries
 - Located away from the direction persons travel to work
 - Regional preferences
 - Rural versus urban mix

SOURCES OF DEMOGRAPHIC DATA FOR LOCAL DECISIONS

- Local chamber of commerce
- Traffic departments
- Newspapers
- Television stations
- City and county planning commissions
- County building permits
- Realty MLS listings
- State Statistical Abstracts

Now you are down to specific site location. There are several other critical factors to be examined.

- Sales estimate, can you afford the site buy or lease? (See Section Six - Valuation Buying Check List)
- Local zoning, sign restrictions, parking, building exteriors, hours of operation, access, etc.
- New construction versus existing structure, type of construction and method of payment
- Availability of financing
- Visibility (View amenity)
- Accessibility; median strips, traffic lights, turn lanes and parking space
- Environmental Planning
- Obstructive local residents
- Other local restaurant analysis, complimentary and competition
- Free standing versus shopping mall
- Easements; sewer and drainage
- Union restrictions to the free market sources of supply of goods, services and labor, adding to costs.
- Health codes
- Local Liquor ordinances
- Closeness of colleges and universities (source of staff as well as customers)
- Development plans for roads, schools, malls, hospitals
- Local road median strips, turn-through and turn lane changes
- Area crime rates published by precinct

Restaurant rows can be great for business. The atmosphere is not usually competitive. Rather it is complimentary. The grouping provides an end destination that can have greater market penetration than can individual operations. The draw may be the age-old desire to see and be seen. Rows may have nearby attractions such as; theater, a beach, antique stores, exclusive shops, art galleries, and strong foot traffic.

The opposite of a row location is selecting an unusual site such as a warehouse, or a hot new area where trendies are rehabbing old houses. Also, we all know of locations far in the country, which are a pleasant destination because of the drive.

Note this caveat. Often you may be shown a real estate parcel that is properly zoned but fronts on a side street 100 feet or so from the high traffic strip. The cost per front foot is dramatically lower and would save you tens of thousands of dollars. There is a reason for this: the 100 feet is 100 feet too far. To cut corners here would be an expensive mistake. When you compromise at the beginning of your decision process, you are starting a pattern that leads down a bad road.

ETHNIC COMPOSITION OF MARKET AREA

Ethnic compositions of neighborhoods are legitimate appraisal factors for any business decision. Blindness to ethic makeup is a luxury that is strongly felt by persons who are not betting their own dollars on the future of any enterprise. Clearly ethnic makeup will influence concept and menu decisions, so such information is relevant to the decision process. Personally traveling through the target neighborhood might be the best approach to assessing ethnic makeup to fit concepts.

> Example: Canvass the Richmond District of San Francisco for a fast food franchise. Find a majority of high-mean-age ethnic Chinese, and a solid community of Russian-speakers, along with a community of vegans and those committed to "organics". The local-draw is physically cut-off to the West (Ocean) and South (GG Park). High ground rent, high taxes and regulation push break-even targets (a challenging mix).

Geographic areas do not stay static with demographics. This includes the long-term life cycle of restaurant locations. Local and social changes require monitoring. Translating social change into forecasts of business-effects may be complex, however, informed estimates of geographic shifts and demographics are important to help the entity change to meet the changing external environment.

SITE NEGOTIATIONS

Be totally prepared for meetings with developers or landlords to sell your concept and your credibility. View negotiations form the potential landlords' perspective.

Negatives to your negotiating position are:
- Economics of prospective lease is risk/reward driven
- Restaurants have high failure rates
- Restaurants costs more in tenant build-out versus typical retail space
- Lease terms of over 10 years represent uncertainty
- Landlords prefer chains with proven records over single units

Positives for your negotiations are:
- Restaurants are demanded by the public as service to compliment other services.
- Restaurants generate traffic and volume for neighbors. Offered as amenities they can help entice other tenants
- If the developer participates with rent based on volume, return can be high or low

Have the business plan that includes all elements including drawings or photos. You must have a documented answer for any question. For rules of negotiation see Section Six.

"Always grow in a growing environment". Piggyback your personal growth rate upon the steeply rising growth rate of your surroundings, otherwise you swim upstream.

DESIGN

KITCHEN DESIGN

This handbook is about rules of thumb. We see some who violate the rules and still do well. However, one rule that should be kept faithfully is: *do not limit your capacity*. You are selling a product and service, but it is measured by your ability to fill in a customer area with people with dollars to spend. Square footage in your building is precious, and when dedicated to functional use other than customer-area use it is expensive. An old rule of thumb was that kitchen area should be 2/5ths of totals square footage. With good equipment and workflow design, this kitchen ratio can be vastly reduced. Versatile design allows the menu to be creative, exciting and fresh.

THE KITCHEN

The kitchen has been called the back-of-the-house and non-revenue generating space. But, obviously, the front can only exist with an efficient back food factory. When the workflow is good, front-of-the-house staff should have rare need to enter the kitchen. The kitchen layout will always consider speed as well as the ease of quality production.

PLANNING THE KITCHEN

A carefully designed kitchen is highly productive. You must provide an (1) efficient, sanitary, and people oriented work environment, (2) low direct labor and food costs, and (3) low initial capital costs. Your kitchen square footage will cost about twice as much as the space in the rest of your restaurant, and will require vastly more planning and attention to detail. The costs of developing the kitchen in: cash, time, energy and stress can be held low with careful planning. Planning also controls the on-going costs of kitchen operations.

You start planning of your kitchen; whether new or renovated, by looking at your intended customer and the menu to best please that customer, which defines your concept. The menu sets the theme and the décor, but dictates the kitchen layout. Each menu item should have a work order. This work order will say what will happen in the kitchen:
- Receiving (What raw products will come into the kitchen, quantities, and when)
- Storage (Refrigerated, Frozen, groceries, produce, dry goods, beverages, janitorial, and high security items, how much and where located)
- Prep (Food pre-processing and work surfaces)
- Cooking (What equipment will cook the easiest, quickest, and with best quality)
- Holding areas (The optimum temperatures of foods are basic both to the customer and to sanitation)
- Serving linear flow (The product should come out to quality spec, but also conveniently and quickly)
- Cleaning and Sanitation (Ease and speed are always factors)
- Ware and pot washing, and possibly laundry

All of the above functions, in turn, dictate the layout of workstations with the following additional constraints.
- Labor costs of production must be kept low by: considering workflow, reducing the number of kitchen staff, the number of steps and distances within stations, and eliminating cross traffic. Labor costs are one of the two parts of your prime costs where a line must be held for good profit outcomes.

- Cost-of-goods-sold is the other component of prime costs. Losses from: waste, spoilage, and pilfering can be controlled with proper design. (See Section Five - Control – Inventory)
- Organizational costs are the time and capital costs of getting the kitchen to a finished and efficient production facility ready for action.
- Utility cost-conservation needs design considerations, and new generation equipment.
- Flexibility and versatility must be built-in at the beginning since menus must and will evolve. When all of the business comes in at once or you have banquets, holidays, or special events, people and stations must be shifted, such as prep persons temporarily moved to the line. Space must be able to accommodate these movements. Make as much of the equipment and work surfaces as mobile as possible.
- Heating, ventilating, and air conditioning must balance throughout the building.
- Cooking fumes and grease exhaust must be handled with make-up air sources to avoid unbalancing air conditioning. Kitchen work environment temperatures should stay comfortable in any ambient weather.
- Fire safety and Sanitation must meet code, and be easy and automatic.

EXHIBITION COOKING

Part of the dining experience is entertainment and showmanship. Many opt to make the kitchen the stage for their theater. Functions that lend themselves to exhibition are: broiler, rotisseries, grills, pasta making and baking, attractive glass front refrigerators or ice bins, and display cases (tilt to 30 degrees). When a kitchen or portions of the cooking process can be shown off to the customer, several benefits can accrue.
- The customer is entertained as the atmosphere provides a more total experience.
- The customer can see, smell and get a feel for the food that they will enjoy. The appetite is sharpened.
- The average ticket can rise with the enhanced order.
- The customer can feel confident in the cleanliness and freshness of your facilities and the menu.
- Verbal exchanges between cooks and servers are entertaining.

Exhibition requires that the equipment, utensils, uniforms, and personal hygiene be neat and clean. Walls will be stainless-steel or of non-porous material such as decorative tile.

SELF SERVICE AREAS

For many years we have heard that salad bars are on the down cycle in popularity. Probably, however, a majority of persons will always enjoy the walk to see, and be seen, as well as the opportunity to customize the salad to their own taste. Buffet style dining enjoys a strong continued popularity, with value from lowered server costs.

WORK FLOW IN THE KITCHEN

Follow the product from two directions. Look at receiving and trace the menu product to the service pickup. Then follow the same steps backwards. What does the customer see and experience? Look at the workstations from the view of both the cook and or the guest. Input of experienced cooks at this stage of workflow design might be good at this stage.

Beware, however, of radical design of work spaced to fit an individual, because others will also eventually use that space.

- Storage should be closest to the back door with items most accessed closest to the prep and cooking work stations
- Workstations should flow linearly if possible. Always look for continuous improvement in the form of easier, faster, better, and less costly.
- Ware washing will be located to the side but requires convenient bus drop-off and uninterrupted flow to clean storage. Clean storage will be close to access by plate preparers. Pot washing will be away from busy areas.
- The finished product workstation will be closest to pickup.

KITCHEN SIZE

Architects and restaurant design consultants use formulas for kitchen size in relation to total square footage, with 1/3 for kitchen being common. Kitchen space includes preparation, receiving, storage, walk-ins, and other storage and support functions for all consumable products. Note: exclude liquor storage, linen storage, condiments, guest checks, and other paper goods from kitchen planning footage, and plan for that storage elsewhere that is closer to final consumption.

Menu breadth and complexity dictates kitchen size. Differentiation by menu can call for extensive production capacities. Obviously, limited menu uses less space.

An older standard of 40 percent of total square footage for a dining facility devoted to kitchen must now be considered a rare top limit reserved for kitchens that must adapt to flexible volumes and menus. If you have limited capacity, it may take almost as much kitchen to serve 50 as it does to serve 150. With advances in equipment efficiency and multi-use versatility, the target range for kitchen size might be 20 to 35 percent of total square footage. Limited menu operations can go below 20 percent, and full menu and service over 35. Limited kitchen size that slows production with bottlenecks is an expensive mistake, but smaller can usually be better.

Small kitchen footprints can be a key to profit potential as they deliver lower prime costs. Small and efficient layout can deliver both lower food costs and lower direct labor costs. 20 to 25 percent is a size formula that often works very well.

Small is healthy for several reasons.

- Construction costs go down for substantial initial capital savings. New kitchen construction can easily exceed $150 per square foot, about twice the cost for dining room space. Lower capital expenditure will have a large influence on your total financing needs. Note that under-capitalization, whether true or not, is the most-often quoted reason for restaurant failure.
- Customer areas can be larger for additional seating and revenues. Restroom sizes are relatively fixed for any given number of seats, but can be more flexibly positioned for least impact to the diners.
- Workstations can be multi-use, which allows better use of kitchen staff, thereby holding costs and turnover low.

- Kitchen consciousness rises with well-defined space. Working station relationships will force closer interaction with staff as long as we follow the rules to avoid constrictions, bottlenecks or cross traffic. Physical distances are shortened and micro motions reduced which gets more product out quicker at lower labor cost. Teamwork and cross training become easier. Fewer people delivering productive levels of work product can command higher wages to the benefit of all.
- Inventory turnover becomes more efficient. Limited storage increases inventory turnover, and reduces pilferage and storage. High inventory turnover is a profitable strategy that assures more freshness and quality, as it reduces food costs.

STEPS TO REDUCE KITCHEN SIZE

Each workstation must be analyzed for efficiency and space use.
- Consider cubic kitchen volume rather than footprints.
- New modular stackable multi-use cooking equipment creates space and versatility.
- Refrigeration can be located to serve both pre and final prep. Reach-in refrigerators can serve both sides for linear input and output. Go for glass doors and shallow depth for visibility and inventory ease.
- Cutting boards can be placed over sinks and cart tops for temporary work surfaces.
- Under-counter refrigeration and warming saves steps.
- Use a standup office with clipboards, and remove most off-line clerical tasks to a remote site.
- Walk-in interior shelving can be on ceiling suspended rails for saving isle space.

WORKSTATION DESIGN

The cook and prep staff should not have to stray far from their stations. This means: product supply, equipment layout, work surfaces, delivery surfaces, and communications are located within short reach and few steps. Note that wireless technology, headsets, and flat screens make communications more flexible to the workflow.

A workstation can be as small as six square feet with proper traffic flow. Much of the work is done in the classic *work triangle* isle space with cooking equipment, refrigerators, and sinks or other work surfaces at the points of the triangle.

To layout the work triangle measure from the front of the equipment to the centers of where the hands will be employed. The sides of the triangle should be from 42 inches to six feet. This gives three side totals ranging from 10.5 to 18 linear feet. Corridor space should be about 40 inches, but where two people pass infrequently this can be reduced to 36 inches. If possible, circulation paths should not break triangles. Consider door handles and hinging for the correct handed opening depending on location to either side of the equipment of work surface/station.

An adjoining work triangle can face 180 degrees and use one or two of the common points of the triangles. Utensils on ceiling racks can serve several work triangles as they maximize vertical space. Also consider wall mounted and below-work-surface placed equipment for the three dimensional station.

Interleaved Triangle Workstations

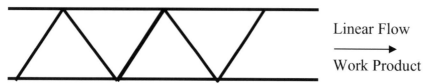

Linear Flow →
Work Product

Note: The increasing consumer interest in "fresh and healthy" eating has also had a significant impact on layout. Because fresh fruit, vegetable, and seafood ingredients have relatively short shelf lives, they require extra amounts of preparation and handy storage space in the kitchen.

THE KITCHEN DESIGN PROCESS
- Determine the customer, the menu, the concept, and the style of service. Business plan pro-formas should already exist, or in the case of remodeling, numbers on net present value (NPV) of the capital expenditure. You will have an idea of the expected hours of business, the peak loads, the number of covers, and the expected table turns.
- Look critically at the total space both horizontally and vertically with an eye to full and efficient employment to reduce total size.
- Define the space with utilities, doors, windows, ceilings and bearing walls.
- Try to list all equipment and storage needs. (Your equipment suppliers will help you with these decisions, and often will draw up plans for your space.) Allow for flexibility as systems and menus will evolve. Arrange equipment in workgroups or zones.
- Computer assisted drafting and design (CADD) software is powerful, inexpensive, and easy to use. Alternatively, you can copy many sheets of the raw floor space for rough and preliminary layouts with pencil to view options.
- Get copies of building codes and health codes for review. Underline all section that will apply to your space
- Locate adequate sources for electric power, water, gas, and drains. Your plumber and electrician can advise. A central utility nerve center can monitor for peak loads.
- Check on space and route of ducts for fans, exhaust and return air.
- Consider refrigerated space needs, and possible placement of external compressors.
- Consider the workflow of the product in, the product through, and the product out. Look at each workstation for integration into a smooth process.
- Put yourself in the chair of the customer to see the view of access/egress to the kitchen. Lighting, noise, and traffic will affect ambience.
- Arrive at a tentative floor plan for pricing and installing the kitchen. Adequate hood exhaust, lighting, ventilating and air conditioning will be on this plan. The floor plan will contain dimensions for functional areas.
- Create elevations for each wall surface with equipment and dimensions.
- Think about sloping floor surfaces to a central drain for easy power wash.
- Design for chilled water lines and large conduit for remote beverage lines where appropriate. Place conduit sub-floor with new construction.

- Include a schedule of equipment to purchase and be fabricated, to accompany your layout. The list will include written descriptions and specifications. Specifications include warranties, delivery, installation, and training.
- Double check mechanical and electrical specifications. Allow for future expansion and modification.
- Create working plans. Local planning departments might require an architect or engineer's stamp for the approved plans.
- Solicit bids for the working drawings. Ask for time frames and penalties for time overruns. Time is always of-the-essence, since cash flows only outward until you can open and operate.
- Award contracts. Determine time for completing of contracts. Get contracts in writing.
- Construct and install using modern project management tools. Use a critical-path scheduling plan. Do as many steps in parallel when possible because time frames are always uncertain. Delay delivery of expensive equipment that is in stock at the dealer until closer to opening.
- Work on a punch list as construction and installation proceed.
- Test equipment and train personnel.

Ray Kroc used chalk to layout workspaces and flows on his tennis court for his early McDonalds units. He had employees walk through the flows to test alternative layouts for speed, convenience, and efficiency.

DESIGN PRINCIPAL – FLEXIBILITY AND MODULARITY

Time brings change that requires constant adjustment. Keep design as flexible as possible.
- Choose simplicity when possible.
- Consider workflows, both materials and persons.
- Engineer ease of sanitation.
- Ensure that water, electric, gas supplies and drains are strategically located
- Use space efficiently both horizontal and vertical (See work triangle).
- Plan for control of temperatures and humidity.
- Plan adequate lighting and controlled noise levels.

AISLE SPACE

Traffic flows and equipment dictate aisle space. The number of people using common space and the frequency of passing are factors. Try to design workstations and back bars to limit crossover traffic.

- Single person	Limited equipment	2'-6" to 3'-0"
- Two persons	Limited equipment	3'-6" to 4'-6"
- Single	Protruding equipment	3'-6" to 4'-6"
- Double	Protruding equipment	4'-6" to 5'-6"
- Aisle	Little traffic	3'-0" to 4'-0"
- Aisle public	Major traffic	4'-0" to 6'-0"

STORAGE

Stainless steel wire shelving is ideal for most storage, including walk-in cooler storage. Try to label sections for each item so that staff will not spend time looking for lost items. The most used items, naturally, will be closest at reach. Group similar items when possible. The labels will ease the taking of inventory and the rotation of products when deliveries arrive. The bottom shelf must be high enough off of the floor level to allow easy inspection and cleaning. Do not allow product to get lost in deep shelves.

Stainless steel wash racks can be wall mounted for efficient space use.

A guideline is: one cubic foot of storage holds about 28 lbs of food product.

For checklists of kitchen equipment and supplies to consider for your operations see the Appendix.

KITCHEN VENTILATION AND HOODS

Hood area should be large enough to cover cooking areas that will produce smoke and heat. Cooking equipment to cover includes broilers, grills, and stoves. Hood design will include filters and grease curbing. Exhaust fans should have multiple speeds to handle varied levels of activity. The air exhausted must have make up air sources designed in to avoid negative pressures on air conditioning for people. Hoods are usually fabricated from galvanized steel. For exhibition cooking, consider facing the hood with copper or stainless steel. Have the electrician include a feed to the exhaust fan for an electrical generator, for inevitable power failures to avoid filling premises with smoke.

KITCHEN LIGHTING

Kitchen light should not glare into customer areas. High efficiency bulbs are now available in natural warm colors. Cover bulbs with protectors including wire guards to avoid breakage from mob handles.

WALK-IN COOLERS AND FREEZERS

Options include pre-fabricated modules in standard or customized sizes starting as small as 5'x 6'. One-piece units come as pre-wired, energy efficient, seamless walk-ins that only need hook-up to the power source. These are good choices for external units, which will require heavy locks and security.

Walk-ins can be built into almost any pre-existing space with the addition of proper insulation, smooth cleanable interiors, and properly engineered compressors and condensers. Prefab panels are easy to ship and assemble. They come in standard sizes of 1', 2' and 4' widths with heights from 6.5' to 9.5'. Standard corner panels allow easy configuration to fit your existing space. R-30 insulation uses 4-inch thick walls. Higher R-values are available and will require thicker walls.

Walk-ins can be laid out as combination freezer-refrigerators. Have the freezer door open into the refrigerator rather than to outside air to reduce heat loss and minimize chances for product degradation. Add air curtains or vinyl door strips mounted above walk-in doors to make sure proper temperatures are maintained, as well as to protect units from insect infestation.

Locate inside the kitchen or, if space is a problem, external to the building. Locate compressors remotely considering heat release into interiors or external to the building. Roof mounted compressors work well.

Plan for walk-in energy sources. Typically they use ½ horsepower compressors for coolers, and 1-hp compressors for freezers, depending on size. Larger refrigerators, over 170 square feet – 8.5'x 20', will require 2-hp and 208-230/60 voltage.

KITCHEN FLOORS
Quarry tile is a durable surface that is easy to clean. For high traffic areas consider non-slip tiles, but keep tiles under equipment smooth since the non-slip tile abrades the mop heads. Plan for a central drain where possible.

KITCHEN WALLS
Kitchen walls must be smooth and impervious to absorption. Options include fiberglass or stainless steel panels.

KITCHEN CLEANING
Mount equipment on wheels. Wall-hang equipment and shelves where possible. Slope floor to drain.

KITCHEN RENOVATION
Renovation goals are: to make the kitchen more efficient by reducing labor, improving storage, smoothing workflows and handling, and to create a more organized and easily supervised plant. Upgrade of equipment can improve energy efficiency and processing times. You may need to upgrade to meet sanitation and fire codes. The main reason, though, is always to better serve the customer. A capital budget, cash flow projections, return on investment, and payback period analysis is a prudent precursor of renovation.
A working kitchen will always call for update and evolution as times, menus, and chefs change.
- Sink drains and water supplies can be run in walls with capped stubs, on four foot or greater centers, for flexibility in relocation of sinks.
- Electrical outlets, both single phase and three-phase, can be located on close centers.
- Mount equipment on wheels for easy cleaning and flexible repositioning.

BUDGET
Construct a spreadsheet for expected capital costs - before startup - with a column that calculates percentages of the total. Look at each category for possible ways to save or delay cash outflows. Some items that belong in your major heading are:
- Design
- Carpentry
- Labor
- Walls, framing lumber, drywall
- Plumbing
- Electrical
- Masonry
- Tiling
- Finishes
- Lighting fixtures

- Hood, ductwork, and exhaust fans
- Grease trap
- Floor safe
- Remote soda/tap lines (get advice from suppliers
- Miscellaneous allowance

Refer to published construction estimator's guidelines for updated costs. Such guidelines will give you a complete list of current-actual construction costs to consider and you will avoid unpleasant surprises for unseen construction costs or unrealistic costs.

Restrooms and dining areas will have separate costs for construction, furnishings, fixtures, and artworks.

Starting capital overhead might include insurance, professional services such as legal, and licensing.

CUSTOMER AREA DESIGN

An interesting exercise as you dine in restaurants across the country is to look for restaurants that are full, and have been popular for over 20 years. Ask the locals. Observe what these perennials have in common with other favorite places and where they differ. One thing they all have in common is customer space where the customer feels comfortable.

How people feel about the comfort of your restaurant depends partly on the dining space and the proximity to other tables, walls, traffic, doors, and the view of what else is going on. With freestanding new units, space planning can be a luxury. Many successful restaurants, however, inherited space that is constricted by bearing walls. Traditional urban retail space had a narrow front width, but was extended in depth. This "shotgunned" space required that customer area space be compressed below standards that most would consider optimal. Surprisingly, these cramped-space restaurants often become perennial popular places to be. People are forced to be in close proximity with apparent lack of personal space. We are forced to assume that this forced social situation, this appearance of being crowded, is sometimes sought out by the basic human psyche, especially if your market target includes singles. Therefore, even with planning guidelines for optimal space, we must reserve room for alternate strategies.

The Hilltop Steak House near Boston grosses over $25 million per year and has been the perennial top server of meals in the U.S. for an independent unit. It occupies a sprawling building with many square feet. They had the luxury of carefully planning space as rising volumes dictated need for more dining capacity.

FLOORS

Dining area floors must deal with high traffic, wheeled carts, spills and food detritus smeared by foot traffic. Spots and spills will be common. Options are tiles, including the new porcelain stone designs, and carpet. Use washable area-matting in high traffic areas near food production to avoid transfer of grease to customer areas. Keep lobby brooms handy at wait stations.

Carpeting decisions deserve several specifications beyond beautiful styling and vibrant colors.
- Protection against stains, including probable frequent coffee spills
- Durability to high traffic
- Easy maintenance and acceptance of frequent extreme cleaning

START – PLAN –FINANCE – LOCATE – DESIGN – Section One

- Exposure to high temperature steam and chemicals
- Color retention
- Resistance to fuzzing and pilling
- Resists fray or sprout when cut lengthwise or crosswise
- Easy seaming and pattern matching
- Easy repair of burns and minor damage
- Minimizes odors from spills
- Ergonomically soft while tough

A popular carpet choice would be with a relatively busy pattern to camouflage spots and spills. Also consider polyurethane backing that provides barriers to liquids and dirt deep penetration, while preserving the overlying carpet.

TABLE SIZES

One good size for square 4-tops is: with sides approximately 34 inches. Then, make the deuces about 24 inches wide with the 34 inch length to exactly match the 4-top sides and surface height. This allows easy flexibility to quickly match up table combinations to handle various party sizes.

DIVIDER HEIGHTS

Your guests might seek relative privacy, but most come to see and be seen, which is part of the decision to come to a public restaurant to dine. Make divider heights near shoulder level. Design the top of dividers with lattice or décor that allows guests to see surroundings when seated close to the divider, but protects privacy from those a greater distance from the divider.

Dining area table layout left us with a seemingly least desirable table location from the customer point-of-view. The table was near kitchen traffic, salad bar traffic, and subject to the broiler staff hollering "order up" for waitstaff attention. Unexpectedly, that table became to be a requested first choice for non-peak periods. Go figure.

RESTROOMS

Maintenance of cleanliness is always primary in restroom design considerations. If possible, design with hall space to avoid door openings directly to dining areas. Doors usually open inward, but doorknobs for exit are not sanitary, so consider door placements near walls that allow push of the door for exit.

OPENING

Have a grand opening. The problem is: no one knows when that will be. Opening is often delayed by miscellaneous demands of bureaucrats, and licensing. When you are fully licensed, staffed, trained, and provisioned to operate, you might have a quiet opening by invitation-only to iron out opening kinks. Ask your local contacts to help you create the invitation list of the type of potential guests that would best fit your desired market target. Those guests will best promote your initial word-of-mouth that will always be your most valuable source of promotion. Be candid that you are still learning and sincerely ask for feedback from all your brand-new guests

Later - as you see you are ready - have a grand opening with a high level of promotion, including mailed invitations. Invitations ensure a strong start. Start full and stay full.

RESTAURANT HANDBOOK – TOOLS & RULES

SUMMARY

Numbers show that the restaurant business is robust and growing as an industry. The social and demographic trends seem to indicate that the future will be even better. However, the problem of high fatality of individual units persists.

Customer perceptions define success. The customer is discerning and demands value. Restaurant mangers and staff must arm themselves with superior knowledge and skills to drive value in service.

Organization and planning is a critical part of getting ready to provide superior service. Planning will impact all daily operations that follow. Business plans are an essential tool for both startups and on-going operations. Take adequate time for the business plan, the return on investment is high.

Planning includes location, and you already know how critical location can be. Site selection and market area selection should both be based on objective criteria. Use the detailed checklists to ensure all relevant questions are considered. Pilots always follow checklists, and you are similarly in command of a vehicle with many passengers.

Planning includes careful design of all space including the kitchen and customer areas. Follow guidelines of proven design concepts to ensure that space is put to its highest and best use within your operation.

Open with a vibrant and exciting splash to start full and stay full. Do not remain static while basking in success. Change of your internal and external environments will always dictate continued evolution for competitive advantage.

APPENDIX – Section One

BREAK-EVEN ANALYSIS

The *break-even point* is amount of revenue (usually sales) required for zero loss or profit. Include it in your business plan, and as a tool for alternative scenarios. Managers use it as a minimum daily target of dollars and customers, without needing to think of *contribution margin* or *fixed expenses*. The break-even benchmark is a clear metric for daily sales as determined by the point-of-sale accounting system. Here is a simple example of break-even analysis to easily set up on a spreadsheet.

Break-even analysis		Month	Daily (Mo/30)
Selling Price per unit (average customer ticket $'s)		$12	
Cost of goods sold (COGS) as % of sales price	33.33%	$4	
Direct Labor per Unit	$4		
Variable Expenses per unit (direct costs at given volume, =COGS + direct labor)		$8	
Per Unit – Volume - Total - %			
Contribution per unit (price less variable expenses/unit)		$4	
Contribution margin (as percentage of sales price)		33.34%	
Fixed Expenses (fixed + non-departmental charges)		$20,000	$667
Revenues at Break-even (Fixed/Contribution Margin)		$59,994	$2,000
Break-even number of Units/period (Revenues/Price) (# customers - covers) = zero profit or loss		5000	167
Estimated number of units sold per period (Volume)	6000		200
Profit or Loss at estimated Volume		$4,002	$133

Of course, you want to operate above zero profits to survive and grow. Plug in your numbers and use the spreadsheet to alter numbers and watch how profits change. Keep elasticity of demand in mind when playing with the menu-mix-prices that influence your average customer ticket. (See section 2 - Menu Science)

CHECKLIST OF POSSIBLE SERVICE NEEDS – Make a phone list
- ✓ Locksmith
- ✓ Fire and intrusion alarm
- ✓ Dishwash chemicals
- ✓ Knife sharpening
- ✓ Sanitation services
- ✓ Restroom chemicals
- ✓ Parking lot services – snow/clean
- ✓ Plumber
- ✓ Electrician
- ✓ Hood degrease
- ✓ Exterminator
- ✓ Plant maintenance
- ✓ Outside landscape
- ✓ Janitorial
- ✓ Coffee equipment

RESTAURANT HANDBOOK – TOOLS & RULES

- ✓ Soda and beer systems tap
- ✓ Ice cream
- ✓ Florist
- ✓ Linen
- ✓ Music
- ✓ China and silverware
- ✓ Kitchen equipment repair
- ✓ Refrigeration equipment parts and supplies

CHECKLIST OF POTENTIAL KITCHEN NEEDS

- ✓ Exhaust hood
- ✓ Exhaust fan and ducting
- ✓ Fire suppression and extinguishers
- ✓ Lighting fixtures
- ✓ Storeroom and walk-in shelves
- ✓ Walk-in coolers and compressors
- ✓ Refrigerators reach-in glass faced
- ✓ Freezer
- ✓ Ice machines
- ✓ Yogurt machine
- ✓ Fryer
- ✓ Steamer
- ✓ Mixer
- ✓ Convection oven
- ✓ Cook and hold low temp oven
- ✓ Burner stove
- ✓ Work surfaces
- ✓ Kettle cookers
- ✓ Tilting skillet
- ✓ Char broiler
- ✓ Slicer
- ✓ Sandwich units
- ✓ Bun Warmers
- ✓ Microwave
- ✓ Toaster
- ✓ Sinks 3 compartment
- ✓ Video monitor
- ✓ Plate dispenser
- ✓ Clean dish racks
- ✓ Hand sink
- ✓ Mobile carts
- ✓ Ice bins
- ✓ Disposer
- ✓ Spray rinse
- ✓ Ware washer
- ✓ Stainless steel tray slides for dish racks
- ✓ Bus box rack
- ✓ Wall shelves

- ✓ Waitstaff pickup counter
- ✓ Filing cabinet
- ✓ Desk
- ✓ Phone

CHECKLIST OF POTENTIAL KITCHEN SUPPLIES NEEDS
- ✓ Scales – ounces, pounds, and heavy
- ✓ Thermometers for pocket and all refrigeration plus oven calibration
- ✓ Bus trays – gray color for food, and dark for bussing tables
- ✓ Sets of dry measures
- ✓ Sets of liquid measures
- ✓ Stainless steel mixing bowls
- ✓ Rubber spatulas
- ✓ Whisks – two sizes
- ✓ Mixing spoons
- ✓ Slotted spoons
- ✓ Rolling pin
- ✓ Pastry blender
- ✓ Mixer
- ✓ Cutting boards
- ✓ Knives – paring, chefs, butcher, serrated, boning, cleaver, roast
- ✓ Sharpening steel and hone
- ✓ Shears
- ✓ Vegetable peelers
- ✓ Graters
- ✓ Colander
- ✓ Strainers – 3 sizes
- ✓ Sifter
- ✓ Timer
- ✓ Spatulas – metal and soft
- ✓ Ladles – sizes
- ✓ Tongs
- ✓ Meat fork
- ✓ Basting brush
- ✓ Bulb baster
- ✓ Citrus juicer
- ✓ Ruler
- ✓ Bottle openers
- ✓ Can opener
- ✓ Skewers – metal and wood or bamboo
- ✓ Saucepans – sizes with lids
- ✓ Stockpots – sizes
- ✓ Double boiler
- ✓ Skillets – sizes
- ✓ Steamers
- ✓ Baking sheets
- ✓ Baking pans
- ✓ Additional items dictated by menu.

RESTAURANT HANDBOOK – TOOLS & RULES

RESTAURANT HANDBOOK

TOOLS & RULES

Roderick A. Clelland

FUNDAMENTALS OF RESTAURANT MANAGEMENT

PRINT SECTION TWO

QUALITY - MENU SCIENCE

RESTAURANT HANDBOOK – TOOLS & RULES

TABLE OF CONTENTS - Section Two

QUALITY – MENU SCIENCE

VALUE - QUALITY
  QUALITY OF PRODUCT   2- 2
MENU
  MENU DESIGN – PHYSICAL   2- 4
  MENU CONTENT   2- 5
  MENU MANAGEMENT – SCIENCE   2- 6
  MENU PROFITABILITY ANALYSIS   2- 6
  MENU ITEM - RECIPE COSTS   2- 7
  DIRECT FOOD COSTS   2- 8
  MENU STRATEGIES   2- 8
    PORTION SIZES   2- 9
    MENU BREADTH AND VARIETY   2- 10
    MENU HEALTH AND NUTRITION   2-11
  CHANGING THE MENU   2- 11
    PRICING STRATEGY   2- 12
    YOUR TARGET MARKET   2- 12
    CUSTOMER PERCEPTIONS   2- 13
    PRICING AND VOLUME   2-13
    PRICING DECISION CONSIDERATIONS   2- 14
    COMMON SIMPLE PRICING METHODS   2- 14
    PRICE INCREASES   2- 15
    PSYCHOLOGICAL PRICE BARRIERS   2- 16
  WINE MENU   2- 16
QUALITY OF SERVICE
  DELAY OF SERVICE AND THE CUSTOMER   2- 18
    THE IMPATIENCE CURVE   2- 18
    THE POINT-OF-NO-RETURN   2- 19
  REGISTER CONTROLS   2- 20
  CUSTOMER COMPLAINTS   2- 21
  COMPLAINT CORRECTION   2- 22
    NO EXCUSES   2- 23
  COMMON COMPLAINTS   2-23
  TEAMS
  TEAM STRUCTURE   2- 25
QUALITY OF ATMOSPHERE
  SOCIAL   2- 27
  PHYSICAL   2- 27
TOTAL QUALITY MANAGEMENT
SUMMARY

VALUE OF PRODUCT/SERVICE - QUALITY

VALUE

Your customer is constantly seeking value. Since the needs of individuals are different and changing over time, that value is more accurately described as perceived-value. To ensure value, and to have the highest probability of meeting perceived-value, the safest policy is to always adhere to the basics of quality delivery and quality control. Quality must be part of your organization's ingrained culture. Quality resolves to delivery of value in three basic areas: quality of service, quality of product, and quality of atmosphere. Each of these three areas of quality has layers of sub components.

Quality is even more important to the restaurant as a part of a fractionated industry, where no entity controls overall business aspects. The entity must compete solely on value to the customer. Quality is how you deliver value to differentiate for long-term competitive advantage. Every restaurant manager must be a quality fanatic.

WHAT YOU ARE PROVIDING

You are selling a package of value to satisfy a set of customers. You do not necessarily need to provide the highest quality food or the lowest price, as long as you satisfy a market. You may have more than one customer set, but you must know who they are. Why do they come to you? What reasons and times do they not need you? You will have a niche or market segment based on opportunities and particular strengths.

You must always start with your target customer and a concept that you believe will deliver differentiated value to that customer. Your concept must be well researched. Any concept must also be flexible, since the customer will tell you quickly how the concept must be constantly modified. Note that sales will always be market driven rather than product driven. Profits, therefore, depend on how your customers see your menu value.

The product/service mix of your concept has three parts. (1) You have the product, the combination of food & beverage as defined by your menu. You can be creative, but there are a finite number of basic foods that customers want on a regular basis. You can be trendy, but trends wane by definition. Further, uniqueness that succeeds will be copied. Quality and quantity, however, can set you apart. (2) You have the delivery mechanism, the level and quality of your service. With your staff you have an infinite number of variations. Delivery is your greatest opportunity to differentiate. Personal and friendly interaction with your guests can be the single strongest addition to their perception of value. Pride and team spirit are readily noticed by your guests and will deliver immeasurable benefits. (3) You also have the customers' needs and expectations. The combinations of service and customers-needs, people and concepts, like a musical score, are infinite.

QUALITY

Quality is usually thought of as quality of the product served. This is the manufacturing view of: materials, specifications, inspections and adjustment. Actually quality needs to be seen as a package as perceived by the customer. Ray Kroc described it as, "good food, quick and cheerful service, and cleanliness". A four star description implies: elegant entrees, unobtrusive total service, and ambiance. It is relatively easy to serve quality food and beverages (things). To serve good food consistently, quickly, cheerfully, at a good price in pleasing surroundings over time is vastly more difficult. The customer is looking for the whole package. If any component slips even for a moment the customer is quick to notice and the whole package is damaged. Your guests are knowledgeable and demand value for their dollars.

All quality control is driven solely by customer needs. Carefully designed quality practices and procedures ensure getting quality right from the beginning and avoiding the large cost of error correction. We will try to give you good examples. Good operations management will put written procedures in place to affect the methods that lead to total quality. Quality is a package but we will break it down into the components of: product, service and atmosphere.

Quality of service requires the greatest attention. However, style of service derives from the menu, so we will look at quality of the product first.

QUALITY OF PRODUCT

The value of the food and beverage is seen from the customer's eye. It has two components: (1) high standards, and (2) efficient production.

High standards have these components.
- Purchasing specifications
- Handling methods
- Recipes

To meet standards *efficient production* requires:
- People with practiced knowledge and skills
- Good procedures
- Efficient layout of production facilities
- Proper equipment in good functional condition
- Constant awareness of waste

To *ensure standards*, inspection involves:
- Checking and measuring products against specifications by preparer
- Checking and measuring finished product with specifications by server
- Checking with customers

Analysis of high standards and catching non-standard production calls for:
- Providing early feedback
- Adjustment mechanisms
- Rewards for meeting high standards
- Help, or negative rewards for poor quality

All of the above requires constant measurement and periodic review with staff teams actively involved. The specific steps are discussed throughout this handbook. Standards are defined below with the menu development process.

MENU

The menu ties your concept to your target customer, and is a primary way to differentiate for competitive advantage. It drives your profit and therefore your survivability. Every menu is an offer for a contract. When a customer orders from your menu it is an acceptance that completes the contract. Your end of the contract offer says; "We have it and it is good". This has always been true, and how well you keep the contract over the long run is a major measure of your job. Menu management requires more attention than most managers give. Some of this required time and attention to the menu can be made routine, and with the proper approach we can avoid common errors.

Menus from the last two centuries show that they have actually changed very little. Except for price, and the availability of new fruits and vegetables, we see similar kinds of fare. Also, except for modern materials, we see similar kinds of menu design. It appears that, despite some popular and trendy surveys, basic tastes change very little over time. The foods that tasted great to your grandparents are largely the items that will taste great to you and your guests. Your menu will provide some of the same basic quality fare, as it appeals to your own special market. Differentiation comes only in presentation and combination, and that is where creative art comes in. Your whole operation will accommodate to this menu.

One claim for the first luxury restaurant, according to Jean-Anthelme Brillat-Savarin, was La Grande Taverne de Londres (1782), said to be the first to combine the four essentials of "elegant room, smart waiters, a choice cellar, and superior cooking."

The menu is so powerful that it dictates:
- Kitchen design and layout.
- Kitchen equipment
- Purchasing, inventory, handling, storage
- Use of seasonal items
- Speed of service and table turn
- Hiring and direct labor costs
- How you will grow as a business

The look and feel of your menu, as well as the content, sends a signal to your customer that is part of your restaurant's personality. It is the vehicle for prices and sets the tone of your commitment to excellence. In addition to simple listing of your bill of fare, it ultimately controls your operations net performance. The menu must be functional, creative, and individual to your niche and image. Your target customer, as usual, directs your sense of identity and market strategy, which in turn rules both your menu format and the content. Your menu creates your niche.

Give your customer a sense of something memorable that sets you apart. Appearance sets and sends that message. There are no hard rules, but we will try to supply some standard guidelines for effective and efficient presentation.

RESTAURANT HANDBOOK – TOOLS & RULES

MENU DESIGN - PHYSICAL

The menu appearance immediately tells your customer what to expect about your level of service and expense. Design includes; size, shape, color, size of script, font, materials, binding, inserts, number of pages, number of items offered, manner of printing or silk screen, and use of graphics including your logo. For instance, leather binding or embossing will convey upscale, while laminated menus may convey bargain value.

First, think of your customer and then proceed to look at your own decor. This includes: the exterior, your sign, logo, carpeting, lighting, wall colors, napkins, fabrics, table top surfaces, size of tables and chairs, dishes, silverware, style, and niche. Match your menu to the image, or vice versa. You can be wildly creative since there are few strict rules.

Some menu design considerations, however, are:

- Avoid use of script or italics in dim light.
- Start each item with a capital letter.
- Upscale restaurants usually use smaller menus.
- Consider novelty shapes or materials consistent with your image.
- Bright colors invite family and fun, if that is your target.
- Flexibility may be important and is recommended for continual menu evolution.
- Simple printed copies or souvenir menus can be distributed outside or mailed for promotion.
- Complement the menu with: listings on a blackboard, table tents, clip-ons, and prompting from well-trained waitstaff, if it fits your particular image.
- The menu must be user-friendly and easy for customer to make a decision and enjoy the outcome.
- Balance the menu with (1) basic fare, (2) some middle of the road comfort, and (3) items not available elsewhere.
- Use a back page to describe the history of the restaurant or name, describe rare antiques, or promote your high quality standards. The back page space is valuable space for directing attention to positive perceptions with entertainment value.

One approach that eases menu upgrades and flexibility - for breakfast and lunch menus - is use of high quality heavy or gloss paper pre-printed with your logo, composed with your computer word processor/graphics, and printed on your new color printer. Use the menu for 4 to 12 sittings then throw away if soiled or tattered.

Menus for my restaurants were silk-screened in white ink on small slate chalkboards from Portugal. They were unique and inexpensive to reproduce, and walked out the door as customers collected souvenirs. When we put toll-paintings of fruits and vegetables on the back, the menus walked almost instantly. That was expensive. They still appear on kitchen walls all over town.

MENU LAYOUT

The order and manner of layout directly affects sales as it influences choices.
Layout suggestions include:
- Give prominence to the most profitable items. Move highest contribution items (rather than highest priced items) to top of menu. (See Menu Profitability Analysis). With a 2-page menu, place most profitable items at the top right of second page. Some other emphasis options are: place a box around the item, add the item to a clip-on, repeat the item in other parts of the menu, use bolder or larger type, bullets, asterisks, different borders, or color highlights.
- De-emphasize popular but low margin items. Place them on lower left side.
- Try to avoid listing items in order of price. Rather go from higher towards lower in the middle and back up at the bottom.
- It may be easier to have your customer focus first on items rather than price by placing the price at the end of each item's copy rather than lining up prices in a column.
- Description can push a favored item, but some feel lack of description allows the server to actively promote. Also printed descriptive dialogue can be overdone.

MENU CONTENT

You select the initial concept. That concept largely revolves around the menu content that will target your planned customer.

Menu content considerations require attention to these items.
- Superior quality and consistency is easy to achieve?
- Ingredients are available year around with relative price stability?
- Items affordable and demandable by clientele for perceived value?
- Offerings fit the cook staff and current systems in use?
- Raw materials easily portioned by weight for control?
- Consistent cooking results easily achieved?
- Shelf life fits?
- Similar cooking times?
- Inputs fit adequate storage?
- Creative items not readily available in other restaurants?

Specializing with the menu is an opportunity to build a solid customer base. The substance of your menu is a mix of offerings that requires balance. When you change one item, the change will impact all of the other items as alternative choices. This means that the menu requires monitoring and adjustment using objective analysis described below. Attention to the science of menu management will drive superior profits with balance.

MENU MANAGEMENT - SCIENCE

Menu management means optimization of long run profits through increased sales volume and controlled costs. Note that cost control is not the same as cost reduction. Cost control means staying as close as possible to a pre-determined cost/price ratio over the whole menu. This ratio is the average of each item's costs weighted by the sales mix. Most managers use shortcuts to pricing. They use either (1) a simple markup over direct food costs to establish a price, or (2) they price to the competition. Both of these simple methods allow them to avoid thinking and stress, and they can wash their hands and move on to other important jobs. Use of these simple methods for pricing is a huge mistake, which may account for the large number of marginally profitable operations. In fact menu management is one of the more vital aspects of your job. Menu management uses numbers that do not lie, but never let numbers come before attention to people,

MENU PROFITABILITY ANALYSIS

There are two main reasons for menu analysis, (1) to make it more profitable, and (2) as a base reference for evaluating the balance of your operations. Menu analysis will flag your cost/volume/profit relationships so that you may focus on areas for improvement in a systematic patterned-search for customer-wants, efficiency, and profits.

Your menu must not be static. It needs to periodically evolve to ensure profitability for several reasons.
- Supply availability and costs always change
- Tastes and trends will change
- Menus need excitement. Bored customers erode your base
- Product mix needs adjustment for maximizing cover count by item.
- You can adjust to seasonal values and quality
- Design and layout can be improved to guide choice
- It may be good to periodically test elasticity of demand for an item

Evolution of the menu must be: carefully thought-out, prepared for, executed, and served well. The proper approach will be more involved than the cost-markup formula that most use, but it is a mandatory starting point. Excellent menu preparation may seem complex; however you will see - once your spreadsheets and formulae are set up - that the way to study and improve your menu can be done quickly, easily and routinely. You then can review and revise often, such as quarterly or even monthly, but certainly review objectively before any contemplated change.

To prepare for change you must capture a database over a period of at least one month. (Later adjust this period for seasonal or unusual business). This data actually should already be accumulating automatically as a byproduct of your other on-line controls and POS systems. (See Section Five - Control)

The object of this data analysis will be to calculate marginal contributions for each item on the menu for each of your menus. Mix/price decisions require knowledge of those marginal contributions. To calculate this contribution you will need three points of data: (1) dollar sales figures, (2) up-to-date direct food and preparation costs for each item, and (3) menu item order-counts as percentages of the total items ordered. We will start with menu item costs.

MENU ITEM - RECIPE COSTS

Create a menu recipe on a spreadsheet for each item. The sheets represent the work-order and describe the plate presentation. A picture can be included. Sheets should have a protective cover and stored in a loose-leaf binder handy to all. It will contain (1) the specifications and quantities for the ingredients with serving portion size, and (2) the method of preparation. The recipe cost sheet should have a key field for ingredients so that it can relate to an ingredient file. Review the sheets periodically with your staff to control quality and uniformity, and to avoid costs of deviation. The spreadsheet will also include (3) the cost of the ingredients, (4) costs of labor and times for preparation, and (5) miscellaneous allocations to direct food cost including a waste factor, portions of management overhead, and makeup costs.

QUALITY – MENU SCIENCE – Section 2

Let us look at each of these five components.

(1) *Ingredient specifications* need to be complete and accurate. This may require such tests as yields (See Section Five – Operations), cooking yields, and batch yields for fruits and vegetables. Serving ladle sizes are important. Portion scales must be handy for both pounds and ounces.

(2) The *recipe method* for the finished product should identify serial and parallel steps with time standards for each step.

(3) *Direct labor costs* are those incurred with preparation, but not usually including the labor after the item is ordered. The costs of cooks and broiler-staff are generally fixed so we are looking for kitchen prep duties that take time from alternative jobs. How labor intensive is this prep work? You can use a stopwatch to measure the time to produce a unit, and then multiply time spent on prep by the appropriate wage standard. Alternatively, you can capture the total time for the batch and divide by the number of servings in the batch before applying the wage standard.

(4) *Costs of ingredients* are from your purchase orders or your inventory database. Review purchase prices (See Section Five - Purchasing). Remember to try to allow for normal fluctuations and be alert for future prices and supply problems.

(5) Miscellaneous costs may need to be added. Sometimes management time - which is normally a fixed-cost to be spread as overhead - may need some percentage of its cost applied directly to the product. Often there can be a waste or shrinkage factor for some items especially for those with poor shelf life. The waste factor is added as a percentage of the total costs. Also, makeup-costs are items that accompany the entree that are not ordered a la carte. Examples can be bread and butter, condiments, salad bar, coffee, etc.

DIRECT FOOD COSTS

You now have an accurate measure of your menu direct food costs for each item. We are looking for a planned direct food cost over the whole operation, not each item. The National Restaurant Association publishes typical direct food cost for type of operation. Are your direct costs where they were planned? If high, there are many potential causes. A systematic approach to cost control is to look first at direct costs, and then follow the steps listed in the section on Control (Section Five – Prime Costs)

> I once had a new bartender open a $ 90 bottle of Dom Perignon to make a $3 champagne cocktail.

MENU MIX ITEM COUNTS

Your point-of-sale (POS) system sales reports should tell you how many of each of your items are ordered in relation to the whole. If not, you must take your guest checks and make a manual count for the period of study. Remember to look for unusual patterns such as holidays or special business.

RESTAURANT HANDBOOK – TOOLS & RULES

CALCULATE MARGINAL CONTRIBUTIONS

Armed with the above data we can now proceed with a spreadsheet to the object of our calculations, which will tell us about our menu performance. Contribution is the amount of dollars left over from sales after subtracting the direct (variable - or out-of-pocket) costs. This left-over amount must cover the fixed expenses (overhead) and produce a profit. Marginal contributions are the amounts of contribution from each separate item of the menu mix.

RANK MENU ITEMS BY CONTRIBUTION

A popular mode of analysis for improvement of profitability, by those who have followed the analysis necessary to learn their marginal contributions, is to rank each menu item in order of marginal contribution. After ranking, find the average contribution by dividing the total contribution by the number of items. Next get the average item count. Now place each item in to one of four groups for further action depending on whether they are above or below average for both item count and contribution. The four groups are, (A) high volume - high contribution, (B) high volume - low contribution, (C) low volume - high contribution, and (D) low volume - low contribution. To rank items do as follows.

MENU STRATEGIES

After placing the items in the quadrants (A, B, C, and D), according to popularity and costs, look at each item separately. These categories call for alternative strategies.

(A) High volume – high contribution
   These signature items with low costs are both popular and profitable. Strategies are:
   - The items may be less price sensitive for small price increases, otherwise leave alone

(B) High volume – low contribution
   These are popular items but also high cost. Strategies are:
   - Review portion sizes. (Be careful not to crash customers' perception of value)
   - Review costs for alternative supplies or ingredients. (Do not lower quality).
   - Review price increase. (Again, be careful since price changes alter your whole menu mix).

(C) Low volume – high contribution
   These items are not popular but have a high dollar contribution. Strategies might be:
   - Review possible price decrease. (Remember influence on mix).
   - Possibly promote through menu emphasis or salesmanship.
   - Consider replacement with a new item (but leave Dom Perignon on wine menu)

(D) Low volume – low contribution
   These are items not often ordered and also less profitable. Strategy is:
   - Consider elimination and replacement.

Obviously the strategies are not all that simple. C and D items may be a key part of your image, but if they are labor intensive, or take extra storage with poor shelf life, consider change. All price changes should be done carefully using the guidelines below.

PORTION SIZES

The key to high long-term profitability is: consistent high volume of customers. High customer volume usually requires high repeat business. In turn, high repeat depends on perceived-value by your customers. As we have seen, perceived-value depends on the many variables of quality of service, product and atmosphere. One variable, however seems to have a very large influence on perceived value, and that is the portion sizes delivered. Many of your guests will see quantity as part of the quality in value.

No doubt you have observed restaurants, one with fabulous décor and friendly servings of petite portions but with mostly empty tables, while a neighbor with modest décor serving overflowing plates of food has a waiting line out into the street. The stark difference appears to be portion size as it affects perceived-value. Often the portion size of the busy restaurant cannot be consumed at the sitting, but will require a take-home container. Possibly the customer feels that they are getting two meals for one.

Portion size obviously affects your direct food cost, however, larger portions generally can support a higher menu price and therefore give the high marginal contribution that so strongly affects cash flows. Direct food cost can easily have room to go up when your marginal contribution and your total volume also go up.

If, indeed, portion size affects perceived-value, so that total volume rises as customers are inclined to talk-up your value-provided, and return with their friends and relatives, then your operation will flourish, given other qualities as being equal. Keep in mind that, whenever you have a waiting list, you are no longer selling product/service but seating capacity.

Be aware of the difference between incremental costs and total costs. Since ingredient-costs - direct food/beverage costs - are only a part of your total cost structure, adding to portion size can be effective strategy. Note that preparation costs of the menu offering may not go up substantially as portions sizes go up, including batch processing. This means that the extra ingredient portions have only their incremental costs to add to your direct food costs, not total direct costs including labor. The small incremental costs of larger portions generally give a positive cost-benefit payoff. Super-sizing is controversial as regards health of people, but not for health of profits.

"An egg still only costs 8 cents." – Bruce Nelson – Lone Bull - Lake George, NY

MENU BREADTH AND VARIETY

Often it may be better to do a limited menu superbly than full menu items moderately well. Here are some potential *advantages of a limited menu*.
- Kitchen size is reduced allowing greater seating (income producing) space.
- Kitchen equipment is reduced lowering initial equipment costs, utilities, and maintenance.
- Food prep time is reduced lowering direct labor costs.
- Food prep skill level is lowered giving greater staff flexibility and avoiding chef's temperament and high fixed-cost salary.
- Purchasing is simpler and less time consuming.
- Dry and cooled storage space is reduced making better use of square footage.
- Inventories are smaller and easier to control, tie up fewer dollars, and lower spoilage, pilferage, and stock-outs.

- Cooking times are consistent, which can help table-turn.
- Staff can be expert on menu.
- Quality is easier to assure.
- Knowing in advance what to expect can draw customers.
- Customers do not want to be forced to think, and may not plow through a long menu.
- Long menu reading times slows table-turn, and slows service to others as order-takers wait for decisions.
- Wait staff trip numbers and distance are reduced allowing less waiting time for service.
- A higher direct food cost can be sustained, bearing directly on quality and portion size, where the customer perceives value for dollar spent, prompting repeat and word of mouth related volume.

Disadvantage of a limited menu: some guests may be in a mood for more variety.

MENU HEALTH AND NUTRITION

There has been widespread disagreement over whether emphasis on nutrition and health helps or hurts volume. However, at least with the fast food segment, recent evidence is clear. When emphasizing healthy offerings on the menu, sales tend to drop. Conversely, when emphasizing delicious and decadent mouth-watering taste, volumes go up substantially. Indeed, menu item-counts for high calorie offerings have proven hugely successful, with dramatic rises in volume and competitive positions. The popularity of the 1,420-calorie burger sold a Hardies starting in late 2004 is measurable. In one survey 74% of people chose fruit for next week, but for today 70% chose chocolate

You cannot tell consumers what they want. They will tell you. They may say they want health for appearances sake, but the only thing that counts is what they say with their dollars. When your customers come to you, they want delicious, not health or nutrition. Americans have intent to eat healthy but may not always have the will, especially when eating out. Julia Child often indicated that when in doubt "use more butter".

In a large metropolitan area your niche can be a small segment of the population that feels good about a particular atmosphere or kind of menu such as vegetarian or "organic". "Healthy" whole foods make people feel good about themselves, and perception is always reality. To illustrate niche menu, a minor portion of the population prefers lamb as an entrée, but some really crave it, so it can be a profitable part of the menu but only as choice among other items.

Surveys say we are all eating healthier. Obesity stats say that we are not. Discrepancy comes from respondents' need to appear informed to the questioner. They lie. We know what is healthy and we vow to comply "next time". Today at the restaurant we want what we want. Allow your guests to be healthy at home.

CHANGING THE MENU

NEW ITEMS
- Look at production capabilities.
- Check sources of continuing supply.
- Do prep times fit current personnel?
- How is shelf life?

QUALITY – MENU SCIENCE – Section 2

- Be aware of time to deliver to table after order.
- Do not let menu changes bog down the POS system with adjustments

DELIVERING THE CHANGED MENU

Follow these steps to execute:
- Train production staff allowing for learning curve.
- Introduce newness gradually, if possible.
- Review all items with the waitstaff. Ask for input.
- Staff tasting sessions may help them sell the new item.
- Get early staff feedback on customer reaction.
- Talk to customers who comment on change.

PRICING STRATEGY

Pricing is critical to profits and therefore the success or failure of any restaurant. The aim is to optimize pricing for profits with prices acceptable to the market for high volume over the long run. Price is determined only by the market over time. Your customer, not you, will ultimately determine your prices.

Pricing influences the following within your operation:
- Net profitability
- The kind and number of customers to be attracted
- The menu items that will move most in relation to others, and in what total quantities, and therefore, menu balance
- The average time of wait for meals and, therefore, table turnover
- The volume of purchases to be made and when
- Storage needs
- The operating equipment required
- Labor costs incurred and at what level (direct costs of production)
- Cash flow and financial liquidity
- Where sales efforts should be directed
- Return on equity

Commonly pricing is treated as an art, a process influenced by gut feeling about you and your competition. Yet, only guest's subjective feelings about price determine perceived value. Perceived value depends on the moods and expectations of diverse persons. The knack is to determine the broadest expectation of your target customer and cater to that. Given the number of independent variables listed above and people variable listed below, this is not easily quantifiable. Social sciences with endless human variables are always inexact sciences. The rational or science part of pricing uses formulas, and the pricing of your competitors. The art approach requires balancing all the variables from the rational to match guest perceptions. Balance, however, is always best achieved when based on science. Technology allows easy objective evaluation so that you can treat pricing more as a science, and get measurably increased cash flows for your efforts.

Pricing strategy, as with most all strategy, must again begin with your customer. You must (1) establish your target market, and (2) try to see your customer's perception of you through their eyes.

YOUR TARGET MARKET

Your desired customer can be identified by several profile characteristics. Some are:
- Age group peak purchase power in 30's and 50's, but aging.
- Income range (usually defined in geographic area)
- Gender mix, males order meat dishes more often
- Family vs. couples
- Casual vs. dressy
- Persons on salary versus wage (flexible lunch hours)
- Business persons meeting clients or business partners on expense account or sales commissions
- Residential drawing area, or local convenience walk-in
- Tourist or local
- Special events such as anniversaries and birthdays
- High use of credit cards
- People who like alcohol with food
- Budgets for food, entertainment and recreation
- Distance they are willing to travel to get to you

"People will climb barbed wire if you have what they want", Joe (Big Daddy) Flannigan

---

CUSTOMER PERCEPTIONS

How your customer views you depends on the total mix of your location, decor, service level and on your menu and it's pricing. For example, for an upscale operation some guests may see you as expensive. Others bringing guests who they want to impress such as; relatives, clients, or dates may expect high prices and perceive a direct price-quality relationship. Direct price-quality moves the classic elasticity of demand curve upside down. For example if you have Lafitte Rothschild on the wine menu, does it convey "quality" to the rest of your menu without conveying "expensive"? The answer is yes, as long as there are balanced alternative selections on the wine list. Raising the price of a usually ordered item such as a baked potato by 25 cents can raise the average customer ticket by 15%, but raising the price of a rarely ordered dessert might add only a penny to the average customer ticket. Do guests notice the difference? How does it affect their perception, at what return on margin and net operations? Do they perceive a fair and reasonable value, which will generate future increased volume?

PRICING AND VOLUME

There is the old story of the Brooklyn wholesaler who complained that he was being beaten down so low on price that he was being forced to sell below cost. When asked how he could stay in business, he replied, "Wolyoom". High volume can cure all ills as long as price is above all costs. Any price increase contributes to net profit only by the incremental dollar amount of the contribution (the non-prime cost) of the menu item. (See break-even analysis - section one) It only takes a little extra (or less) volume to overwhelm this hoped for increased net.

We learn in econ 101 about elasticity of demand, which says; "as price goes up volume generally goes down and vice-versa. For example how much will volume decline with a 5% increase for a particular menu item in your location? The classic direct price volume curve is a downward slanting straight line.

In practice the curve is almost never a classic straight line or simple curve. Since it is based on perception of value, it is usually curved or stepped, and it may even be upward as noted above with the perception of direct price-quality. Your optimum target pricing is to operate at the end of the flat area before the steep curve down.

PRICING DECISION CONSIDERATIONS

- Try to list your target customers and define in specific terms their perceptions of your operational concept.
- Look at competition and the market.
- Relate each menu item to your planned total direct food cost. (See Recipe/Cost Sheets)
- Modify price with direct labor for each item. Some recipes are more labor-intensive. Also consider whose labor. Is it a chef, or is it line-prep? (See Menu Analysis)
- Lower the margins on high contribution items, and raise on low contribution items (See Menu Analysis).
- Keep in mind that the price of each item affects the total menu mix.
- Employ some loss-leader types of pricing if called for.
- Price by-product items to move in proportion (example if you produce hamburger from cutting primal cuts for steaks, price the hamburger to move the whole amount).
- Have a range that includes higher as well as moderate to low prices.
- An excessive price spread between the lowest and highest prices will drive volume to the lower.
- The highest priced entree should usually not be over two times that of the lowest.
- Have your staff promote highest contribution items. Apply incentives.
- Price for contribution, rather than margin, to maximize long-run volume
- Keep in mind psychological price barriers.

COMMON SIMPLE PRICING METHODS

Long-term success requires that customers perceive value. Menu pricing, obviously, is key to value determination, and is a critical part of your integrated market strategy. Pricing plays a significant role in your competitive positions, and can exploit profit opportunities. Two common approaches to pricing are:
- Cost based pricing
- Market determined pricing.

Both of these approaches can only provide a starting point for pricing strategy.

Cost based pricing is the scheme that uses your direct cost of materials and production as the predominant factor in determining menu prices. Historically this has been a multiple of direct food/beverage costs. Direct food costs vary by the type of operation and menu.
Typical direct food costs run from the high teens for pizza to near 50% for steakhouse operations. Many planned overall direct food costs targets are in the mid to low thirties.

The level of labor intensity for production of menu items will also influence costs and therefore the target. Advantages of cost based pricing are: it is simple to use and intuitive since demand forecasts are not involved. Also cost based pricing can appear as less risky. Cost based pricing should, however, only be a tool to guide ultimate menu prices.

Market determined pricing sets prices by apparent demand, as well as prices of expected dominant competitors. The market ultimately sets prices, and cost-based pricing can only be a starting control point. This market approach may require canvassing or a survey of restaurants in your market area. Use a map and an evaluation form to rank the restaurants by relevance to your menu. Look for those that are perceived to have the most similar menu item types. Then modify these observed prices with other contributing variables, including the current perceived popularity and level of business in your area and particular location. The science part of your pricing will require addition of some level of art, or intuition, since many of the variables will have subjective components hard to measure.

Note, however, both cost based pricing and market determined pricing suffer shortcomings and require objective analysis to fine tune for profitability.

PRICE INCREASES

Pricing and price increases are critical and, because of the number of variables that are largely subjective, can create stressful decision making for the operator. Our purpose is to help you make the best decisions here, and avoid the simple and wrong shortcuts of a basic markup formula.

Price increases are dictated by normal inflation over time, and by unusual influences upon supply. You do want to keep prices stable through a period of over five guest visits, which means not necessarily reacting to temporary fluctuations in supply. A balance should be found between the size of increases and the frequency of increases.

Price increase questions must always consider the expected elasticity of demand for an item and how it will influence the total mix. The best long-run strategy is volume, even if gained by price reduction. Therefore, proceed to price increases with caution. Look at previous price increases to see if they put any downward pressure on volume. Test and measure elasticity at regular intervals.

Generally consider the following with price increases:
- Raise prices of most popular items by small amounts rather than large increases on less popular items.
- For items with a fluctuating supply, do not list prices; rather use something similar to "Priced daily".
- Use odd cents for the first digit to the right of decimal. (Example: a raise from $5.75 to 5.95 is subtle).
- Do not raise all prices uniformly at once. (Rather, see Menu Analysis for selective increases).
- Avoid crossing out or pasting over prices.
- Avoid price increases with a new menu layout. (Rather, increase on old menu before new design)

PSYCHOLOGICAL PRICE BARRIERS
- Generally round your final digit to 9 or 5 for items below $8.
- Never round to the nearest penny as dictated by a rigid food cost.
- Final digits for items under $8 can be to $.99, which seems to be accepted by all.

- Use 5 or 0 as a final digit for items above $8 and below $20
- Price raises of $.50 can be large for menu items under $5.00 (lunch & breakfast)
- Raises from 3 to 4 digits (from $9.99 to above $10) can be significant in the mind of your guest.
- Crossing $20, $30 and $40 are also psychological barriers.

Targeted direct food costs, as we have seen, are only a component of pricing strategy. The direct food cost formula is important only as a guideline to be maintained (not necessarily reduced) over the whole menu mix in the long run. As noted, it is composed of total direct food costs plus food preparation costs divided into price. The food cost component must include all costs down to the cost of condiments and paper supplies. The labor component must include any and all time spent with preparation before orders from the menu. You as operator must know the relative contribution which each menu segment adds to the profit structure. (See Menu Analysis) Finally, best price does not mean beating competition prices if you are giving better quality and quantity of product and service. Non-price differentiation allows higher prices.

WINE MENU

The key to a good wine list is balance. You need a wide variety of prices, and a reasonable variety of wines based on the fit to your food menu. Balance with reds, whites, domestics, international, Bordeaux types (high shoulder bottles), burgundy types (sloping neck bottles), and local regional products (if available with quality). Include champagne, including a high price offering. A good guide is "Wine Spectator" magazine. Your wholesale reps will also give you free advice. Just remember that their job is to promote their particular products, and your job is to create balance.

Wine pricing mark-ups can be 300 percent, but mark-ups towards 200 percent are more normal. The higher priced offerings can have lower mark-up, since they also have a high contribution. For instance, Dom Perignon with only a 50% markup will have a $50 contribution, whereas Beaujolais with 200% mark-up will only contribute $20.

Always include some high priced items. Some guests will always be in a mood to impress their friends and order the most expensive item on the list. Also, because of the human nature bias called the *Anchoring Effect*, the high priced items on your menu make the lower priced appear more reasonable.

QUALITY OF SERVICE

The triad of what you provide is still always: quality of service, quality and quantity of the product, and atmosphere. However, the one overriding determinant of either your prosperity or your demise is: service. The product and your decor are "things" with a finite number of variables. The number of variables with the service to your customer is vastly larger, with a corresponding opportunity to grow or be hurt. Quality service is your surest competitive weapon. Always attend people over things.

There are many motives causing persons to bring their dollars to your place.
  - Hunger and the desire for something delicious
  - Convenience/time
  - To be pampered, to relax
  - To be entertained
  - For business meetings
  - To see and be seen
  - To be made to feel important
  - Romance
  - To impress others

The main reason they all come is to be served.

The main components of service are (1) courtesy and (2) promptness. There is an old restaurant, Durgin Park, near Boston's waterfront where the staff repartee often borders on being rude as matter of long-standing understood atmosphere (entertainment). They can be grumpy, but they try always to be prompt.

PROMPTNESS IN SERVICE

The one key element of service is not making people wait. It is wait-staff's job to wait. The occasions for a customer to wait are many. Waiting for:
  - The host to greet after entering the door
  - A table after greeting
  - The waitstaff arrival after being seated
  - The order delivery after being placed
  - Re-orders
  - Check presentation
  - Change from the check or credit card
  - Refills
  - Coffee, ketchup, etc.
  - Ashtrays to be emptied
  - Empty dishes to be removed

Often when your staff is busy (and we hope they are, as long as you are not understaffed) customers must wait. There are two radically different kinds of customer wait. One is when the customer sees that you are busy and is promptly informed of a delay with frequent updates of the delay status, and (2) when they are ignored.

DELAY OF SERVICE AND THE CUSTOMER

We know that service is your one overriding key to long-term success, and that promptness of service is the most important component of service. Making persons wait is not always bad (unless they are on a tight schedule), especially when they see you are packed with happy customers. They can enjoy the social atmosphere while waiting. They will never-ever tolerate being ignored. The quickest way to go out of business is to let even a few of your guests be ignored. The following chart "The Impatience Curve" shows the effects of delay of service when the customer feels ignored.

QUALITY – MENU SCIENCE – Section 2

THE IMPATIENCE CURVE
This chart may be the one most important lesson for your staff to memorize in your initial and continued training.

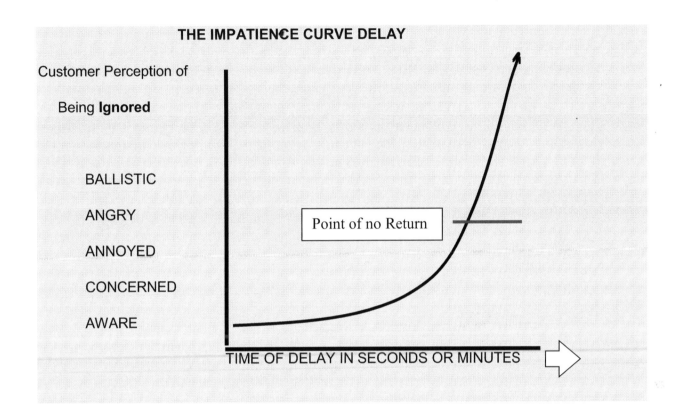

The horizontal scale on the impatience curve is the actual serial passage of time. Often this time is a matter of seconds and not minutes. An example is when a party walks in your door and no one acknowledges their presence. After 30 seconds they likely will be annoyed (and may walk out). This initial tone may set the whole stay, and be a long downhill experience for your guests and staff alike.

THE POINT OF NO RETURN
The impatience curve concept should be easy to understand, since we have all been there. Looking at the chart you see a point-of-no-return. This is when your guests have lost their temper. It is infectious to the whole party. Their brains begin to dump volatile chemicals into their bloodstream. At this point you are lost. You can "comp" the dinners and drinks, but it is too late. They don't like your service, they do not like your food, they probably don't even like your ceilings, and they certainly don't like you. They can barely wait, unsolicited, to tell many other people exactly how they feel about you.

AVOIDING THE POINT OF NO RETURN

You can make many mistakes (we hope you don't) and still fix problems. Your customers can leave feeling happy, if you do not allow the point-of-no-return. This point is reached more quickly by some, depending on their day or mood and consumption patterns before reaching your door, but it always comes from a feeling of being seen as unimportant. The point can come from (1) an interminable wait or (2) a cumulative pattern of neglect. This flash point must never be reached. Luckily there is a way to head it off, and that is: simply never ignore any customer.

When your staff is hard pressed, they must still keep their eyes moving as well as their hands and feet. They must be aware of guests that are experiencing a wait, and guests trying to catch their eye. Staff must constantly let the customer know that staff is aware of the delay and is doing their best to "be right with you". This may take the form of a quick word, eye contact while raising a finger to indicate "one moment", and mouthing the words "I'll be right with you" from across the room. Constant reassurance that your staff knows the customer is waiting is the only way to temporarily slow the steepness of the impatience curve.

IS EVERYTHING OK?

How many times have you heard your server ask, "Is everything OK"? First, customers did not come in for an "OK" experience. Second, the implication is: that everything might not be OK. Better queries might be:
- What else might I bring you?
- Are we all happy?
- Is your steak cooked the way you asked for?

Look at plates for unconsumed items, and ask questions that might give positive feedback to improve the guest's experience of improve overall product quality control.

Do not allow staff to ask "Would you like change?" when presenting the bill.

CUSTOMER SENSITIVITY

Some customers are aggressive when angry. Others might not speak up, but will never return. Staff needs to look for and be sensitive to subtle signs. If a plate is not finished, someone might ask something such as, "Not hungry today?" or ask a specific question to gain feedback on the unconsumed item. Avoid the question, "Is everything alright?" with its negative implications. Find if there is a real problem. Feedback is valuable.

To illustrate alertness to sensitivity, envision a hypothetical ideal, an impossible but perfect service: A guest begins to desire some form of service and the server appears instantly to provide that exact need. It would be nice if the guest's wish appeared as a screen that begins to glow above their heads pointing to the specific wish. This telepathic scenario is not possible, but we must in theory try to approach it with our service. Instead we must observe and try to sense moods.

Each guest has a different package of needs that create their mood. Some want unobtrusive service, and some want cheerful interaction with the server. When considering their needs, never be supply driven rather than demand driven.

REGISTER CONTROLS

Great service will employ all of our senses and capabilities. We face the guest. We use our eyes, ears, speech, facial expressions and body language. We use our knowledge and skills. We use our hands, our feet, our smile, our wit, and good nature to deliver great service.

One component of service is providing an accurate and clear guest check to the customer quickly at the time they desire it. A second component is settling that guest check promptly.

Creating the guest check and accounting for accurate sales is a necessary part of control, but consider the steps. A bartender, for instance, to record an order for a beverage, must first turn their back on the customer and proceed to the cash register. Depending on the register system and the procedure, the whole process to final bill settlement can exceed 25 separate steps. Possible steps for the register system might be these:

1. Turn away from the guest
2. Walk to the register
3. Reach for guest check
4. Place check in register printer
5. Enter server number
6. Enter item
7. Continue several steps to enter proper data to register system
8. Create a preliminary bill with the order for menu item
9. Miscellaneous steps that lead to printing a final bill and presenting.
10. ....

20. Pick up guest check with form of payment
21. Turn away
22. Walk to register to begin final processing
23. Place check in register
24. Enter proper data to close the check
25. Process credit card, or make change
26. Walk back to the customer to deliver change or credit card slip to sign.

Two of the steps, presenting the final bill and settling the final bill, involve serving the guest directly. These two steps are the only "do" operations. All of the other steps are overhead chores that require time and attention away from the guest's presence. Technology can rescue us from this detraction from serving the customer directly. Off-the-shelf technology to help us includes: wireless networks, Bluetooth, remote processing, remote slip printers, remote flat panel screens, wireless headsets, and reliable voice recognition software and hardware.

CUSTOMER COMPLAINTS

Be wary of any customer complaint survey that puts quality of food ahead of service, unless of course the food is truly poor. When customers are ignored they become angry and begin to notice any fault that can be found. The complaints that are actually articulated are usually driven by being made to feel unimportant. The complaints registered (as in any survey) are more likely influenced by how the customer wants to be perceived by you, rather than what accurate and helpful feedback they can give to you. Customers who are annoyed because they had to wait an extra minute to order another round are not going to say that this was what bothered them. They may not even be aware themselves. Instead for instance, they are going to notice that a bite of their steak is somewhat chewy and therefore that the steak is tough and inedible.

When polled, persons vote with their emotions. They vote with words differently than they vote with their actions or dollars. When customers are happy they may tell others of the pleasant experience at your place. This word-of-mouth is your one most important source of growth and prosperity. When customers are not happy they also tell others about their ordeal. Different studies have determined that the bad experience will be related to between 5 and 13 other parties.

Quality surveys lie. People don't mean to be dishonest, they just cannot help themselves. When respondents say that the quality of food was not good, often they were put in a snitty mood because of late and poor service. They focus on food quality only because it is not seemly to be seen as impatient of people rather than things.

COMPLAINT CORRECTION

Complaints from customers can be very valuable and must be treated as such. Although "the customer is always right" even when a small percent is actually very wrong, Murphy's Law will impose itself. Your staff must be trained to respond quickly and consistently.

- First, don't keep customers waiting for a manager. They are already unhappy. Empower the server to be generous on-the-spot. Just ensure that the problem is logged for future analysis.
- Second, the customer is always right. Admit immediately that you are at fault, not anyone or anything else. If you did nothing wrong, apologize anyway. The important idea is the customer's perception of wrongdoing. Do not explain why there is a problem. The customer does not care.
- Third, tell the customer how you are going to correct the problem and how quickly
- Fourth, offer appropriate and reasonable amends. In some cases this may require comping food and/or beverages. Sometimes a gift certificate is necessary for the customer to have a chance to see that the error was a fluke.
- Last, thank the person profusely for bringing the problem to your attention, because (usually) they have in fact done you a great favor. Explain that most persons would not have done such a favor by speaking up. Treat all complaints as a valuable opportunity to move all service towards excellence.

There are good reasons to *empower the server* to make "complimentary" adjustments to correct customer reaction to delivery of inferior value with product or service. *First*, always delegate authority downward when possible. Those with the most immediate knowledge of the situation can cure the problem best. The fix is quick to avoid escalation of bad feelings. Manager attention is not diverted from other valuable tasks. *Second*, the one-time cost of correction is small compared to the compounded costs of bad feelings.

Note the true cost of complimentary items is lower than most perceive. Costs are incremental costs only, that is: direct cost of the item plus any incremental direct labor cost for production. For example to replace a tough steak, the only cost is the net cost per pound of the steak with negligible direct labor costs. Overhead expenses are already in-place, so those costs cannot be charged to an additional unit of production.

EXCUSES

Automatic excuses are often the quickest reply during service lapses. An example is: a customer might mention that their order was placed quite a while ago. A wrong response is to say something similar to, "Oh, there were two large orders that went in just ahead of yours". A better response would be, "Oh, I am sorry. I believe it is coming right up, but I will double check". Never make excuses. They never help. The customer does not want to hear about your personal problems. The guest comes to you to avoid problems and be served. Any excuse or explanation will always have a negative effect.

You can log and later brainstorm these typical problems with teams, and discover best responses for creative solutions and lasting reinforcement.

COMMON COMPLAINTS

There are many lists of customer complaints compiled and published. Top 10 complaint surveys are popular but are influenced by how questions are phrased and what kind operation and level of service is studied. Most surveys show food quality as the number one complaint and service as number two. We believe this is erroneous and misleading information. Empirical evidence shows that service is the number one problem, but is commonly expressed as food quality problems, because the explanation is simpler and more direct in an angry atmosphere. We do tend to believe the studies that show *service* derived complaints are about two thirds of all complaints. The balance of most items, after quality of food and service, are usually miscellaneous items related to atmosphere and cleanliness.

Following is only a partial list of reasons customers do not come back with their friends and their dollars.

- Being ignored while waiting
- Regular patrons not recognized by name
- Being put on hold for more than 30 seconds
- Acts that cause the guest to feel clumsy or ignorant
- Service staff with; "I'm doing you a favor" attitude
- Not being met with eye contact and smile immediately
- Too-long dissertations on menu specials
- Waiting in line when empty tables are visible
- Service staff asking; "who gets what?" (auctioneering)
- Service staff who talk to their order pads
- Staff not listening when spoken to
- Service that appears disorganized or rushed
- Staff consuming food/beverage in view of guests
- Appearance of poor personal hygiene
- Soiled or ill-fitting uniforms
- Staff who cannot answer questions about the menu
- Service not provided in order of arrival
- Inaccurate estimates of waiting time
- Lost reservations
- Ordering an item described and not getting it
- Running out of food/beverage items on menu
- Orders arriving incomplete
- Items arriving at disparate times
- Food checks that are sloppy or calculated wrong

RESTAURANT HANDBOOK – TOOLS & RULES

- Food sitting visibly in a pickup area and not picked up
- The feeling of being processed rather than served
- Failure to promptly resolve complaints (in guest's favor)
- Paying top prices for food and not getting it
- Hot food/beverage on cold plates/cups and vise-versa
- Hot food and beverage not-hot and cold items not-cold.
- Salads not chilled
- Water glasses and coffee cups not filled automatically
- Dried out fruit garnish at bar
- Running out of china, silver or glassware
- Chipped dishes
- Salt and pepper shakers not clean or full
- Streaked glasses (hold up to light as you pour)
- Poor cleaning, dust, dirt, grease stains, spills
- Untidy table tops, wet/sticky
- Linens with holes or stains
- Unclean chairs or booths with crumbs
- Wobbly tables or chairs
- Untidy sugar bowls
- Cloudy water in flower vase or wilted flowers
- Restrooms not spotless
- Lighting to dim to read menu
- Opening late or closing early contrary to posted hours
- Music too loud
- Not being sincerely thanked upon leaving

The service staff is not responsible for all of the items listed above, but they must be trained to be continually on the look-out for each and inform the person responsible quickly.

Cover these poor practices periodically in floor-staff meetings. It is easy for staff to lapse to these bad habits with normal entropy at work.

Remember someone in your guests' party made the decision to come to you. Your service is a reflection upon their judgment. Do not make them look foolish in front of their family or friends.

If a customer feedback system isn't already part of your operation, use the staff meetings to elicit reports from the servers on what their customers want and think. This valuable tool starts with listening, and should be fine-tuned to pick up customer perceptions and biases, attitudes, and preferences that will help you serve more effectively.

TEAMS

The restaurant environment is necessarily a team environment that will define the organization's culture. Required team skills are not necessarily instinctive and must be guided with structure and discipline to organize for high effectiveness.

One value of structured teamwork is to allow decisions to be made at the level closest to the customer for most effect service quality. This is especially important to restaurants since the decisions with the customer must be made on the spot and without delay.

TEAM STRUCTURE AND CHARACTERISTICS

- Team members must agree on, and have input regarding, a clear set of goals as to benefit the team, the members, and the organization as a whole. The initial guidance for restaurant goals, however, should come from a manager. Also a manager will initially structure the team's working conditions, training needed, access to shared information, and incentives. Some examples of goals that are easy to define and measure might be:
    - Sales related to the same period last year
    - Sales divided by server hours equals level of productivity
    - Lowered number of customer complaints
    - Individual sales volumes related to total sales
    - Amount of pooled tips in relation to sales
    - Number of table-turns in a given period
    - Percentage of high contribution menu items related to average counts
    - Success of promotions such as suggesting wine with dinner

- Team members must be directly accountable for the outcomes of their actions toward those goals in defined and measurable terms. Members should have some power to monitor and modify goals, and reap rewards for achievement. Some regularly scheduled path for timely feedback, input, and communication is important. Group based forums for diagnosis and problem solving can be very healthy. Fortunately, the evolving information-technology environment can produce some important feedback in near real-time for quick decisions on adjustment strategies.

- The culture of the team requires mutual trust and spirit of cooperation with a mechanism for solving inevitable conflict for positive outcomes. Further, the culture should allow for creative change management, as all restaurants need to evolve through sustained competitive advantage. The team performance can inspire, integrate and energize the whole organization toward competitive excellence. Team smoothness will impact performance, employee satisfaction, and profitability.

TEAM NORMS

The culture will evolve with direction of top management. Formal guidelines in the form of job descriptions and employee manuals are very desirable. Team members reinforce performance related norms. Members will cue each other on expected behaviors including: best work processes, expected levels of output, boundaries, channels of communication, and appropriate dress. Norms allow the team to express and differentiate values that define the group identity. Peer group pressure regarding norms will have a very powerful influence on performance and productivity.

TEAM PROBLEM SOLVING

Continuous improvement is always the team's target. The ammunition is the problems encountered during operations that slowed or otherwise diminished the quality of product or service perceived by (1) the customer or (2) the internal clients in the supply chain to the customer. Staff should get in the habit of recording and reporting each problem in a written

format when time allows. Later in scheduled group meetings the problems will be covered. Provide a template for a clear problem statement. It can be a standard form that includes:
- What specifically was observed
- How rare or frequent is the problem
- Where did the problem occur
- When did the problem occur
    - Time of day
    - Day of week
    - Level of activity in shift
- What contributed to the problem
- What are costs and potential harm from the problem
- What are some suggestions to avoid the problem
-

Reward those team members who provide specific examples of service problems with praise and possible defined dollar incentives.

The agenda for each problem-solving meeting should reserve a few minutes at the end to reflect on the effectiveness of the meeting. Were the right issues discussed, and were the proposed solutions considered in an inclusive manner with complete information leading to good policy? Are we agreed and actually committed to better outcomes policy? What specific steps are we each personally pledged to in order to improve. How will we measure changed behavior?

Ground rules for team meetings might include some of the following.
- Listen attentively
- Wait to consider alternatives before conclusions
- Avoid personal attacks
- Participate actively
- Ask questions when more information is needed
- Allow all others to participate equitably
- Do not interrupt when others are making a point
- Focus on fixing for the future rather than assigning blame
- Be specific about problems rather than generalities
- Do not react defensively if ideas are criticized
- Understand need for confidentiality

TEAM REINFORCEMENT

Reinforcement builds cohesion and homogeneity, but can also breed complacency. Developing group norms adds to cooperation towards mutual goals, but to avoid loss of team energy it is important to stretch task goals with creative processes. On-going shared education and operations-analysis frees thinking for creative change management.

GROUP DEMOGRAPHY

There has been much study suggesting that team shared-demographics affect overall performance and co-operation. Group demographics are: length of service in the organization, education level, age, race, and sex. Similar age levels, for instance, for kitchen-staff or for wait-staff can engender cohort behavior, or a peer-group camaraderie. People seem freer with constructive talk when there is demographic homogeneity.

QUALITY – MENU SCIENCE – Section 2

Research suggests that turnover will be higher when group demographics are dissimilar, as communication is more restricted and power struggles more likely and more severe. (O'Reilly, Caldwell, and Barnett - Work group demography, social integration, and turnover)

We must, obviously, avoid illegal discrimination while considering individuals and common attributes for team cohesion. Further, cognitive ability or level of intelligence is almost always correlated with both job and team performance, whatever the job or team role. We may not administer IQ tests for most restaurant jobs, but there are indirect indicators of cognitive ability such as the short essay question approach to selection.

CONFLICT
Conflict within teams is normal and unavoidable. How that conflict is resolved determines whether natural conflict reduces productivity or releases positive competitive energy.

QUALITY OF ATMOSPHERE

Atmosphere has the two subcomponents of social atmosphere, and the physical surroundings. Your guests are generally looking for what they cannot get at home. The surroundings are part of what they cannot get at home. (1) Social interaction is part of that need, and that is why people often prefer crowded space, but (2) their surroundings also include the décor and cleanliness.

SOCIAL ATMOSPHERE
One subcomponent of atmosphere is entertainment. Showbiz has always been a part of the popularity of certain restaurants. How the product is presented on the plate, and with what flair the product is delivered, adds value. The entertainment element can greatly add to your word-of-mouth promotion. Entertainment is a basic need of your customer, along with relaxation and convenience. The product, service and exterior decor are all elements of entertainment. Of course all of the activity occurs within a given physical environment also part of the package.

PHYSICAL ATMOSPHERE
Physical atmosphere has the two subcomponents of surrounding décor, and absolute cleanliness. The interior decor adds essential value to the customer experience, but cleanliness throughout is absolutely critical.

Have closing task checklists for all job functions. Cleaning can be the responsibility of all personnel. The actual off-hours cleaning should also have strict checklists for kitchen, bathrooms, and dining areas.

A manger should take time frequently to sit down in each dining area. View the atmosphere from the eye of the seated customer. Look at walls, floors, ceilings, doors and the furniture and fixtures. Remember that your guest will have much time to be seated at that same spot and notice details.

It has been said that the worst restaurant decor is empty seats or un-bussed tables when you have a waiting list.

TOTAL QUALITY MANAGEMENT

McDonalds' founder, Ray Kroc called it QSCV, quality, service, cleanliness, and value. It is often referred to as QSC for quality, service, and cleanliness.

TQM, Total quality management approaches value by involving everyone in the organization in continuously improving quality for competitive advantage. Quality management is a staple in operations management of large organizations as a matter of survival. The same quality concepts apply to restaurant operations for the same reasons. Competition is based on delivery of quality of product, timeliness of delivery, and cheerful personal interaction and attitudes. Your customers demand it.

Customers have many opportunities to evaluate the quality of your service. A key is to empower the staff at the main interaction level to make decisions, both preventative and corrective, without the delay of management approval.

TQM stresses three principals: customer satisfaction, employee involvement, and continuous improvements in quality. TQM involves:
- Benchmarking
- Product and service design
- Process design
- Purchasing
- Problem-solving tools
- Process control using techniques for appraising and monitoring quality in operating systems.

All quality programs deals with competitive priorities of: designed high standards with consistency of delivery, and continuous improvement. These priorities characterize an organization's competitive thrust, and involve everyone in the organization. Strategic plans that recognize quality as an essential competitive priority must be based on definitions that include input from those ultimately responsible for delivery. A culture of quality forces operating capabilities to meet consumer expectations of value.

Your mission: provide best long term value to your customer at a good profit.

SUMMARY

Restaurant prosperity depends solely on customers' perception of value. Restaurant management must be quality fanatics to build a culture of continuous improvement. Customer *perceived value* involves the product, the delivery, and the total atmosphere.

There are many specific steps throughout the whole operation that ensure value.

The *product quality* is a function of proper menu management. Most restaurant mangers do not take advantage of the objective *tools and rules* to get the best profits from the menu. Specific proven strategies will maximize menu performance. Once menu profitability analysis and rules are established, monitoring menu quality and performance becomes relatively easy.

The *quality of service* is your surest competitive weapon to help you differentiate. Follow proven tools and rules to ensure that your customer will be eager to return with their friends and dollars. Make sure all staff is aware of the impatience curve concept. All quality is ultimately delivered through your most valuable asset, your people.

RESTAURANT HANDBOOK – TOOLS & RULES

RESTAURANT HANDBOOK

TOOLS & RULES

Roderick A. Clelland

FUNDAMENTALS OF RESTAURANT MANAGEMENT

PRINT SECTION THREE

TEAM EXCELLENCE

RESTAURANT HANDBOOK – TOOLS & RULES

TABLE OF CONTENTS - Section Three

HUMAN RELATIONS – TEAM EXCELLENCE

MANAGEMENT
- MANAGER PERSONAL CHARACTERISTICS AND SKILLS   3- 2
- MANAGER JOB REQUIREMENTS   3- 2
- TIME MANAGEMENT RULES   3- 4
- FLOOR MANAGER   3- 5
- PRAISING STAFF   3- 7
- CORRECTING STAFF   3- 7
- STAFF MEETINGS   3- 8

HIRING STAFF
- FINDING STAFF   3- 10
- SELECTING   3- 11
- APPLICANTS   3- 12
- INTERVIEW TECHNIQUES   3- 13
- WAITSTAFF PERSONALITY CHARACTERISTICS   3- 13
- HIRING YOUNG PERSONS   3- 14
  - ORIENTATION CHECKLIST   3- 15
- HIRING FOR THE HOST/HOSTESS FUNCTION   3- 16
- EMPLOYEE TERMINATION   3-16

MOTIVATE
- ATTITUDE AND EXCELLENCE   3- 17
- CULTURE   3- 18

BUILDING MORALE
- ASSESSING MORALE   3- 20
- MANAGEMENT ROLE   3- 21

MOTIVATORS
- COMPENSATION / PAY   3- 22
- ACCEPTANCE BY PEERS   3- 22
- STATUS – GROWTH & ACHIEVMENT   3- 23
- INVOLVING STAFF   3- 24

STRATEGIC GOAL SETTING
- MEASURING PERFORMANCE   3- 24
- INCENTIVES FOR MEETING GOALS   3- 25
- PERFORMANCE REVIEWS   3- 26
- DELEGATING   3- 26
- RESOLVING STAFF CONFLICT   3-27
- CORRECTING STAFF WITH PEER REVIEW   3- 27

POLICY
- MISSION - GOALS - POLICIES – PROCEDURES   3- 27
- MOTIVATION FOUNDATIONS   3- 31
- TEAM DYNAMICS   3- 35

SUMMARY – MOTIVATION

HR - TEAM EXCELLENCE – MANAGEMENT - STAFFING

MANAGEMENT

Restaurant management is uniquely a very tough job. It is not like other management where there is a relative luxury of planning and organizing time. Most management deals with either a product or a service, whereas the restaurant manager must do both. Managers in general industry are specialists. Operators have a division called sales, where a sales staff does all of the customer interaction. General industry management also usually has a personnel division. The restaurant manager, however, has to be proficient with and perform all functions without specialization or divisions.

Restaurant operations require attention to so many diverse details. The number of variables with plant, product, staff, and customers is almost unlimited. Almost no problem is fixed permanently, so continuous vigilance is imperative. The manager must see a potential problem before the customer does. The whole job might be the most stimulating, creative, and demanding to be found. The day-to-day interaction between server and end user creates an endemic need of immediate problem solution, an environment hard to match. The duties and skills are extensive, including both personal skills and technical abilities. The restaurant manager, then, obviously must employ a broader range of skill sets.

Often the job requires longer than 40-hour workweeks, and unconventional hours of duty. The work environment is complex and dynamic. Unsolicited interruptions require quick thinking and action. This constant flux removes the option of sustained concentration. For all of these reasons, a restaurant manager must be a special type of person with rounded knowledge and skills. Such workloads can strain a manager's domestic relations. Finding and holding qualified managers is always a challenge.

MANAGER EQUITY

An agent often has different goals than a primary business owner. Managers need reward for meeting common goals and specific milestones. A major problem can be: that the total waitstaff often makes a higher hourly income with tips, but with less responsibility and hours than the manager. This can make it hard to recruit and promote from within.

For these reasons a manager has to have an incentive to stay alert to all details. The incentive should be tied to both volume and profitability. Either bonus or equity (stock ownership) can be spelled out using clearly defined numbers based on realistic projections. If the manager hits or exceeds the numbers, the cost of the bonus will be easily borne. No one watches details better than an owner. Note that any bonus targets must be set with the managers involved, with agreement on outcome metrics.

MANAGER PERSONAL CHARACTERISTICS AND SKILLS

Too often prospective managers look forward to the prestige and power, and not the responsibility. They want to flog the galley slaves. They believe the manager is someone tough who can give orders. They seem not aware that a manager is a coach who guides by example to extract team productivity. An effective leader must be a caring person rather than self-centered. When searching for a good manager look for these skills and personality traits.

- Public relations skills both for customers and staff, tact and diplomacy are difficult to teach.
- Ability to influence others without the use of power defines good leadership.
- Good communication skills both written and verbal require sensitivity.
- Ability to conduct several kinds of effective meetings with proven methods.
- Effective training skills can be learned. Training never ceases. Use checklists. (See Section Four - Training)
- Planning and organizing skills for the big picture balanced with eye for detail.
- Crisis management can also be learned, but ability to handle crises smoothly and without stress might not.

MANAGER JOB REQUIREMENTS

- The manager will help establish and maintain the overall philosophy of the operation. This may be something on the order of: To provide a total value of customer experience so your guests will tell others and return often. The philosophy will include providing this service in a thriving atmosphere of growth and good cheer for all employees. Without this effort there will be no profits, no jobs, or future for staff and the business
- The manager is the captain: responsible for smooth operations from open to close.
- The manager sets an example for the tone of all staff to follow, including a manager's own dress code. Ethics, communications, and fairness must prevail.
- Time must be employed efficiently so that the manager is available to douse incessant fires. Staff must have needed access to the manager at busy periods for: advice, assistance, and control.
- The manager will establish standards for policies and procedures for each task, and ensure adherence. Set all procedures with input from those who do them, first.
- Written standards must be created for: job descriptions, recipes, labor schedules, purchasing, forms, and all areas of operation where rules are needed to ensure quality. Assign staff input for all standards. (See Section Four – Motivate)
- The manager will communicate effectively in writing and in person to aid adherence to standards.
- The manager must know when and how to delegate, and move any task to the lowest level at which it can be competently done.
- The manager is the primary trainer and orienteer. Much of training should not be delegated. (See Section Four – Training)
- The manager is invested with the care and respect of the staff. An atmosphere will be provided where they can build confidence, learn good habits and skills, gain a sense of pride, and bond with team members.
- Planning is a function of the manager. Good projections help the operation serve the greatest number of guests at the lowest cost in terms of labor and waste.
- The menu requires periodic profitability analysis and adjustment.
- Control of quality to the eye of the customer - both of product and service - requires unceasing care.

- Control of costs in all of its many aspects is the responsibility of the manager. (See Section Five - Control)
- The manager has to have a sense of critical timing for every job aspect from service delivery to the guest's departure.
- Staff scheduling for productivity includes: seeing that scheduled staff is actually on hand, personal greetings and appraisal of conditions to arriving staff, continual and effective feedback, and proper thanks at end of shift

MANAGER PERFORMANCE EVALUATION

No part of operations should go un-audited. The manager evaluates staff to identify areas for improvement, so there also needs to be a periodic mechanism for evaluation of management. A good tool for this is the anonymous evaluation form for management job performance. This form will include good management practices to be rated as performed regularly, occasionally, or rarely. The form is handed out to all staff. Since only check marks are required it stays anonymous, unless staff cares to write comments on the back. Tally the results for scoring each manager. An example follows.

The following is an evaluation form for the performance of Sue and Jay
Check the boxes that best apply and leave the form in the drawer below the front register

You:	Regularly		Occasionally		Rarely	
	S	J	S	J	S	J
1. Clearly define our philosophy and mission.						
2. Provide achievable written standards and procedures.						
3. Are genuinely helpful to those with whom you work.						
4. Set a good example.						
5. Assign reasonably responsibility & clear accountability.						
6. Give constructive criticism in bite-size amounts.						
7. Reinforce good job performance.						
8. Give co-workers a say in decisions that affect them.						
9. Give adequate support.						
10. Are fair.						
11. Communicate clearly.						
12. Are open in your communications.						
13. Are decisive.						
14. Give objective performance appraisals.						
15. Have realistic expectations for co-workers.						
16. Acknowledge individuality of co-workers.						
17. Treat all team members with respect for dignity.						
18. Are a total Jerk.						

Please feel free to add to this list, or expand with comments by number on back of form.

TIME MANAGEMENT RULES

Another glaring difference between restaurant managers and general management is the high number of interruptions. A classic study from Cornell shows that the typical restaurant manager has more than 4 desk sessions, 2 scheduled meetings, 58 unscheduled meetings and 22 phone calls per day. A personality type is required that can handle this constant interruption.

The *unsolicited demands* are of many types.
- While walking around the manager will see items or situations than need correction immediately.
- Some customer complaints are best referred to a manager.
- Walk-in job applicants must be seen at least for courtesy sake.
- Cold-call sales reps occur often.
- Your regular supplier reps must always be met.
- Plant or equipment can fail.
- Stock-outs must be precluded.
- Personnel always demand audience.
- Overloaded staff functions need temporary bailout.
- Security and bookkeeping often need attention.

Constant *telephone solicitations* are a regular source of interruption. The manager will need a policy for screening. Often the true statement "The manager is not available, may I take a message?" is the best policy.

One type of continuing phone interruption is *requests for donations*. If the requesting cause is local, such as high school promotions or nearby charities, the donation can be some of the best-spent part of your advertising budget. Most phone requests for donations, however, are done from "boiler rooms" where the organization members are not volunteering their own time. Inquire if the person calling is local or a volunteer member of the organization making the donation request rather than a professional that will take a majority of your donation dollar for sales effort. If the person is a volunteer, you might volunteer your cash. Also do not necessarily be intimidated by the many police and firemen's type funds. Consider if your donation will actually help needy persons or worthy local groups.

Sales representatives will arrive at your door regularly. The sales function is important. It is legitimate and necessary to keep you informed. Try to establish a good time of day for your regular supplier reps to meet with you on a weekly basis to discuss quality, prices, and new products. With cold callers give them only a minute to get your interest for a real cost/benefit need. If they do, ask them to make an appointment, otherwise explain that you are in the middle of a very busy job and cannot as a matter of policy see sales reps. Always be gracious and thank them for their time.

Responsible time management requires successful delegation. Follow these steps to *delegate*.
- Set clear goals for the subordinate. Tie the outcome to organization objectives and philosophy, with clear data-points for success
- Reiterate current policies that affect the process and the outcome.
- Define the job in terms of steps or tasks that lead to the best outcome. Give guidance with details.

- Balance authority to the responsibility. Name the person to turn to if there are problems with authority.
- Set limits to authority in terms of dollars and personnel.
- Set communications channels for two-way flow. Tasks can be delegated, but not ultimate responsibility.
- Establish controls, including reports at progress milestones or time intervals.

FLOOR MANAGER

The manager is not "The Boss". Your customer is the boss. Your customer gives orders through your staff. If you have selected staff well, and trained properly and continuously, then you should be receiving more instructions than you give. Your personnel become your boss as they apprise you of operational procedures that need fixing. Management styles range from dictatorial and autocratic to the laissez-faire. The style that appears to work best is to look and listen and act as coordinator and coach as a co-worker. Firmness can be achieved and direct orders can usually be avoided.

Peter Drucker long ago advocated management by walking around. It is especially vital in the restaurant business. Benefits are:
- You get primary and timely feedback from customers versus secondary through the pipeline.
- It affords you visibility to customers and staff.
- It facilitates communications.
- You are exposed to production and delivery problems first hand.
- It allows personal implementation of fixes.
- You can directly observe the culture of your organization at work for needed adjustment.
- Customers react positively to personal interaction.

The *floor manager* must keep moving. This means primarily cycling through the customer area but also throughout the kitchen. It is good to have a 3x5 card and pen handy. There are always many chances to observe and capture events and items that must be done differently. "There is always a better way". Notes should be made often during operating hours. Directives to personnel should be kept to a minimum as they are already busy and their mood in relation to customers may be fragile. Rather, transfer the notes by function/category to the master floor log. Areas for improvement can be discussed at the end of the shift or at scheduled meetings. Situations that must be corrected immediately should be addressed with a minimum of autocratic management style. It is often better in the short run for the manager to jump in and correct the problem with sleeves rolled up. The problem can be brought up later in a private or staff meeting and discussed in a reasonable forum, agreed to in principal, and incorporated into standard operating procedures. The S.O.P and checklists should be brought out and checked off often. The checklist is a good tool to remind personnel of duties and standards as already outlined, trained to, agreed to, and expected. Entropy is always with us, and must be fought.

MANAGER DAILY LOG

Combine a floor managers daily log with a daily manager checklist. The daily lists can be kept handy in a three ring binder with the checklist on the front sheets and room for daily observations on the back. Use the checklist at the start of the shift. At the end of the shift, transfer notes from the 3x5 cards – or handy voice app - about observations made in the heat of the battle. One example of a checklist follows.

RESTAURANT HANDBOOK – TOOLS & RULES

Example: EVENING FLOOR MANAGER CHECK LIST

S M T W T F S

Consult with each prep persons, bussers and food - give shift expectations

Guest checks supply to: Waitstaff, Cocktail, Bar

Let chef and broiler see projected sales volume.

Check general appearance of plant: Exterior - parking, sign, landscape, front
                                 Interior - cleanliness of dining and bar
                                 Bathrooms, lighting, music, walk-in

Inform waitstaff of night's prep needs

Review early bus function check list for performance and compliance

Check on any/all stock that may be below pars for alternative source.

Check regularly through shift: (Keep on the move)
- Dining rooms for help with customer service, note tables due to turn
- Salad bar for full and clean
- Broiler-staff and cut meat supplies
- Bartender, Waitstaff, Cocktail for any assistance or supplies
- Host waiting list and lounges
- Kitchen
- Bread, coffee, register

Responsible for customer reactions, complaints and repair

Optional: If slow do inventories Sundays and Wednesdays

Close: Collect notes on function areas
- Check broiler area & walk-in as broiler checklist is completed
- Set thermostats
- Dollars to safe
- Review K-staff checklists prior to release of staff
- Follow lock-up check list

Notes to Day Manager:

PRAISING STAFF

Praise can be given formally at the employee performance review. Day-to-day praise helps ensure good habits and should outweigh criticism of bad habits. Here are some guidelines.
- Praise a good performance when the person has struggled with the particular job aspect.
- Be genuine, sincere and un-begrudging.
- Do not flatter. The praise must be authentically related to specific performance.
- Save praise for measurable accomplishment rather than minor tasks to avoid dilution of impact.
- Do not make or imply guarantees of future rewards to induce performance.

CORRECTING STAFF

Always approach correcting individual staff members with sensitivity to their own feelings. When time permits you might say; "I noticed (occurrence of condition that needs improvement). Did you notice the same? What is your opinion about that?" This will allow the staff member to think about how conditions affect the team and the total operation. It allows consideration of whether established standard operating procedures were sidestepped or whether the staff member can help you draft improved S.O.P. Have the controlling S.O.P. handy.

The effect of criticism may be more powerful than it appears. Conflict not properly handled can lead to resentment that engenders greater future problems. There will be, however, occasions when you need to turn up the heat. Follow basic rules when timely correction is expedient.
- Do not criticize staff when they are busy with customers or already under pressure.
- Do not criticize staff when you are angry. Don't raise voice.
- Do not criticize staff in front of other staff or customers. Wait until the person can be consulted in a quiet relaxed and private atmosphere.
- Plan what you will say. Take a little time to ensure you will be clear in your language and intent.
- Ask questions about the behavior. Effective communications is an exchange process. The person may take the criticism less personally. You may learn some reasons for altering policy.
- Make the criticism specific as it relates to the job and overall objectives. Cite written standards. Stick to the issues and do not wander to far-ranging condemnations. Distinguish facts from feelings and opinions.
- Avoid general criticism of the person's integrity or abilities.
- Do not inject humor, sarcasm, mimicry, ridicule or flippancy.
- Do not dilute the subject with insincere praise.
- Summarize and repeat key points of agreement. Ask for a meeting of the minds on future behaviors.
- Do not linger on the subject once both parties have achieved apparent understanding.

STAFF MEETINGS

Meetings should be scheduled on regular basis. They can be for all staff, or broken down to front and back of the house, or further by job function. Special meetings must be called for special problems or organizational changes such as the menu. For general staff meeting you will have many subjects for improved staff performance. These subjects will be gleaned from your daily manager log of observed problems. Often a particular problem with an employee can be described in general terms without naming individuals. The offender will recognize the discussed behavior, and therefore direct criticism can possibly be avoided. Good meeting outcomes require preparation.

Follow these steps.
- Schedule meetings for times convenient to your staff.
- Write an outline of the meeting goals and key points to cover. Hand out outlines.
- Rehearse critical parts out loud - to a mirror if necessary.
- Start by putting the meeting participants at ease. Reduced tension aids participation.
- Keep the meeting time as short as possible to adequately cover the planned ground.
- Use physical or visual aids where impact can be much more memorable.
- Ask questions that cannot be answered "yes" or "no" to coax participation.
- Be positive. Better results come when you concentrate on dos instead of don'ts.

- Relate the subject to how performance affects their own long-term income.
- De-emphasize your own presence to direct focus to the subject at hand.
- Use the outline to get the subject back on track when topics stray to the unproductive.
- If negative subjects arise, ask that person for their own recommendations for solution.
- Plan time for Q&A
- Close the meeting by closing the sale; ask for agreement on specific actions or behaviors.

When soliciting input from staff you will get many very thoughtful ideas. Unfortunately, most suggestions will be how to make improvements by spending more dollars or management's time rather than what the staff themselves can do. You do not want to stifle suggestions. Never criticize suggestions. However, you may want to say in advance that dollars and time are precious resources. Challenge them to offer solutions that are not expensive, and where they have direct control.

Meetings for all staff might be scheduled for Saturday mornings with plenty of advanced notice. Frequency of whole staff meetings might be quarterly, but not more than monthly since their time is also valuable. Persons who have a legitimate schedule conflict will have time to let you know and can be given a personal follow-up meeting. Have one staffer check off a roll call from the roster this will convey the importance of the meeting attendance in the future. The attendees can be rewarded either with pay for the hour or lunch. Saturday morning meetings can be coupled with food, beverages and post activities such as softball.

AGENCY ISSUES
Delegation of responsibility is healthy and necessary in restaurant management. However, separation of owners (principals) and managers (agents) creates potential for the wishes of owners to be ignored. This potential, with the knowledge that agents are expensive, drives study of a complex set of ideas known as agency theory. Whenever owners (or managers) delegate decision-making authority to others, an agency relationship exists between the two parties. Agency relationships such as those between owners and managers can be very effective as long as managers make decisions with goals that are consistent with the overall goals of the organization (usually to maximize long-run value). However when the interests of managers diverge from those of owners, then managers' decisions are more likely to reflect the managers' preferences than the owners' preferences."

Self-centered manager preferences can diverge from owner-optimal strategies when personal payoffs are considered such as dollars, relative status or friendships. Agency costs have two elements: (1) the costs of the direct benefits to the agent that detract from the organization and, (2) the controls required to reduce agency problems. Together these agency costs have a negative influence on the organization.

Potential Agency Problems arise when managers can have access to more information than owners. Managers can be aware of more operations details, but less likely to act to correct details. Managers might act to optimize personal rewards. Managers can act to protect their personal status rather than team performance.

Solutions to agency problems might include stock options for long-term goal achievement, to align manager and owner needs. Bonus incentives for performance, with trend analysis, may help for shorter-term goals. Emphasis on, and regular review of, organizational goals and the specific milestones towards them will help ensure focus.

HIRING STAFF

The manager has responsibility to three main groups (1) owners, (2) customers, and (3) personnel.

If we do not take care of customers we can forget about one and two. If we do not take care of personnel we will not be taking care of customers. Your personnel are the only vehicles through which your customers receive their valued product/service. Happy-employees insures happy customers, low turnover, reduced supervision, lower labor costs, and bigger profits. To have happy employees it is vital to hire the best, train properly-and-thoroughly to motivate and retain. People are your most important asset.

Quality production requires the selecting of the very best staff. First take time to select very carefully. The best people hired require less constant attention to training and motivation. Remember, turnover applicants, not employees.

Keep in mind that hiring employees is an expensive proposition. Beyond salary, payroll taxes, employee compensation and possibly health insurance, you will have an on-going investment in time and attention to their knowledge, skills, and general happiness. Also, each employee opens your company to risks of lawsuit for discrimination, harassment and other workplace issues.

Before hiring then, be sure several questions are answered.
- What exact job specifications do I have to fill with a new person?
- What specialized skills are required?
- Can existing staff perform the job?
- How many hours per week do I need this job function covered?
- What exactly are the costs of a new hire both initial and on-going?
- Are proper resources available for initial orientations and training?

Further:
- Have a clear description of the position and attributes needed.
- Hire only those that have a potential to grow with you.
- Do not hire the first candidate until you consider at least three applicants.
- Always check references.
- Never promise dollars or benefits that you cannot deliver.
- Avoid questions on race, gender, age, family or health.

FINDING STAFF

The restaurant industry is slightly different in that it traditionally provides many part time jobs. For some in the business, staffing can be a problem. The continuing aging of the population reduces the pool. Annual staff turnover typically can be near 200%, and often goes over 400% in fast food and tourist (seasonal) sections. Most of staff lost are turned in the first 30 days, possibly due to poor selection criteria. After 60 days staff is typically lost because of poor training, poor motivation, and lack of perceived growth opportunity. Costs of turnover are hard to quantify, but can be well over $1000 per person turned.

Following are some of the *costs of turnover*:
- Reduced customer satisfaction, counts, sales, and profits
- Higher direct costs of food, beverage, and supplies
- Lowered moral
- Recruiting costs up
- Training costs up
- Termination costs up
- Increased management time and stress
- Disgruntled ex-employees are sources of future problems

The good news is: that by following good practices and policy, turnover can be low. A good reputation as an employer will ensure a hopper full of good applicants.

SOURCES

Start four weeks before projected opening and let all persons that you may contact know that you are looking for staff. Continue to ask as you get inquiries. A favorite source for kitchen staff is high schools and trade schools. Call the school and ask about on-the-job training and bulletin boards. A list of *sources* is:
- Referrals from suppliers
- Current staff and friends
- Customers
- High schools and Trade schools
- College placement/ deans/ bulletin boards/ Fraternities/ Sororities
- Public employment agencies/ career centers
- Walk-in applicants. Keep a file with coded score for first impressions.
- Professional sales and business organizations/ conventions
- Community organizations

Left off this list are newspaper *classified ads* and help wanted signs in your window. Those using classified ads generally report time-consuming responses from unqualified sources.

Help-wanted signs in or on your premises should be avoided except in extreme cases. They advertise directly to your patrons that you are unable to gain and retain happy employees. The subconscious reaction can be that the dining experience will also be unhappy.

For the high schools, draw up an on-the-job training outline (See Section Four - Training)

One popular national chain hires about three times the expected staff need. New-hires are on probation and are given minimum starting wages. Floor staffers are given small stations. Competition and attrition weed out all but the strongest candidates. This staffing- policy is not necessarily recommended, but seems to work for this chain.

There are several ways to find the best staff candidates. First, always use your current staff to help recruit. When they like their jobs, it is evident to their peers. Have them recommend and refer friends and contacts. If you interview "friends or family", make it clear that you will not relax objective selection criteria for the sake of friendship. Once you have a solid foundation of excellent staff, building on it becomes relatively easy. "When you have a winning team there will always be a backlog of good applicants."

SELECTING

Excellent staffing starts with the careful selection process. Due diligence, here first, will save much downstream time and attention. Take time at hiring to avoid more time spent later on employee maintenance. It is very important to distinguish the difference between skill levels that can be hired and skill levels that can be trained. Before the interview- process, be clear on skill-sets required. One study found that the first few minutes are spent on why or why not to hire and the balance on justifying the decision. Front-room jobs will rely on initial appearance and natural ability for a smile and direct eye contact.

We all hope for employees that are highly motivated, loyal, and willing to work irregular hours. Our goal is to hire the best with the lowest cost of recruitment in time, dollars and stress. Screening to avoid turnover due to person/job mismatch requires a clear definition of job requirements. Job descriptions should be written in advance listing the major skills necessary for success. Job descriptions for those working directly with your customers will include people skills. Serving customers is more a sales than a service function, so look for applicants that easily sell themselves to you.

APPLICANTS

It is always wonderful to have a backlog of current job applicants for staff voids which can then be cherry picked. Walk-in applicants, however, can be a time consuming interruption for the manager. Pre-screening reduces the time lost. It is important not to waste the time of the applicant, or to give any false hope that would slow their continued search for employment. One quick approach is to provide a paper and pen and ask for some basics: name, address, SS number, phone, and ask for a short paragraph on what kind of work they are seeking, and paragraph on what they are doing now. Explain early and clearly that you currently have no openings, but that you will keep them on file.

First impressions count. The initial sight-screening avoids wasting time for all parties. If you progress, ask for past employers name and number and take time to check. You cannot ask others of the most specific personal questions, but do ask, "Would you re-hire this person".

Never discriminate for wrong reasons. Screening for a best hire, however, is discriminant by definition. We are trying to fit the skill sets to the particular job function in order to gain the highest productivity. In short, we are looking for the best person for the job. We are looking for staff that is efficient, conscientious, cheerful, easy-to-train, honest, anxious to show skills with job performance excellence, eager to work smoothly with a team, and get along with peers.

By law, we are not allowed to test prospective employees for intelligence unless it can be shown that intelligence is a direct requirement for the particular job function. It might be argued that the job function of "dishwasher" does not require high intelligence. The dishwasher function, nevertheless, needs a person that can be easily trained, can plan and think ahead, work in a quick and efficient manner, who can work with other regarding inputs and output, and can crossover functions when needed. All this is done better with staff who are relatively intelligent. Indeed, it can be shown that there is a high correlation between efficient productivity and intelligence with almost any and every job. Note that persons labeled as handicapped very often make efficient workers.

Microsoft does test for cognitive ability and it seems to serve them well. To avoid discrimination challenges, you must ensure that all testing and educational requirements are job related and necessary for the business.

THE APPLICATION

Keep the application form short and simple. You will need only essential information on how to reach the person, and information on job history and references. Later, use the personal interview and the requested essay type questions for the rest of decision-compelling input to drive the hire decision. Ask behavior-based questions that elicit sales skills responses.

INTERVIEW TECHNIQUES

In-depth interviews require a prepared structure. Have a list of well-framed questions. Follow a written guide to avoid drift and repetition. Questions asking "why" are best at exposing false claims and inconsistencies and give the best clues to predict ultimate performance. Look for significant departures from fact. Cover all key points such as:

- "Why do you believe you are qualified for this job?"
- Honest and consistent answers throughout?
- Verbal, do they have verbal communication skills?
- Writing, do they show organization and neatness in their written communications?
- Public relations, how do they appear to relate to others?
- Selling, are they persuasive?
- Creativity and flexibility, will they adjust to the new and unusual?
- Stress resistance, do they tolerate uncertainty?
- Planning, do they show skills?

WRITING SKILLS

Recent research shows a strong correlation between cognitive ability and writing skills. A quick evaluation technique for busy managers for culling before commitment to any deeper interview is the simple exercise noted above of asking answers to two one-paragraph essay questions.

> "Calligraphy is the physical manifestation of an architecture of the soul" - Plato

WAITSTAFF PERSONALITY CHARACTERISTICS

Select for people who already are of the following types to aid probability of success.
- Some people enjoy interaction with people versus others who like to work with things.
- Workers can be energetic and fast paced versus methodical and leisurely.
- Some can allow the customer to be the center of attention versus self-important.
- Sense of role and ability as salesperson contrasts with a purely mechanical server.
- Servers must be flexible to demands of customers and conditions versus dogmatic.
- Find those who can allow the customer to be always right versus argumentative.
- Are they ready to learn and grow versus believing that they know-it-all?

Personality more than skills is important in this business. If they can sell themselves, they can sell the customer. Sincerity, selling skills, and attitude can be learned, but genuine interest in people is harder to induce for those not naturally inclined.

HIRING YOUNG PERSONS

Teenagers are a prime source of many jobs in our industry, such as kitchen staff and bussers. Here you are charged with a solemn trust. You have a special and strong moral obligation to provide a best learning atmosphere from the moment of hiring. Often, this job with you will be their first real working experience. The attitudes, skills, and work ethic you install will be carried by them the rest of their lives. They need extra structure and patience. You have an opportunity and obligation to provide special training and guidance.

Start by providing a comfortable atmosphere for learning. Most are quick to learn if you provide primary training. (See Section Four). They will require feedback in a friendly and constructive manner. Peer pressure will push them to compete to do an excellent job. The camaraderie of the group will ensure a supply of friends and schoolmates for your rare staff vacancies.

Some young persons will learn slowly and generate frustration for both you and for themselves. You may not terminate such young people for the appearance of incompetence; rather it is your job to make them competent. In fact, there are few good reasons to fire teenagers, with exceptions noted below.

Your best training with younger staff is when you roll up your sleeves and do the jobs with them. Break the job components into micro-motions and provide philosophy and overall goals as well as providing details. The details of each job step will include why this particular way is best in terms of efficiency, why it saves time and energy and how it fits total operations and the value chain to their team. You should also develop an on-the-job training manual; indeed some states require it, for the hiring of teenagers. This manual can come from your employee handbook job descriptions and, as noted, can help you with sources from the local high school.

Tolerate no dishonesty. Firing of a young hire must be done quickly and visibly in case of theft. This hard lesson needs to be learned immediately for all. Also, we have noted over many years, that there is a small percentage of new hires who just don't quite get it. After much patience it is clear that they will never make the connection that they are trading their time and productivity for dollars. They feel entitled to an automatic paycheck. This kind of person may never be an asset to your staff. Further, they may be infectious to other staffers. You must cut your losses with such persons only after long and hard proof that you cannot help them improve. You will find that forced terminations will be few over your lifetime. Most young hires are bright, energetic, quick, eager, conscientious, honest, and fun to have as co-workers

You must provide the following in concert with primary training:
- The on-the job-training manual outlining what they will learn for:
  - General restaurant operations
  - Food handling
  - Inventory Control
  - Proper health and sanitation procedures
  - Delivery & receiving
  - How to coordinate with other job functions to get teamwork
  - Kitchen equipment use and maintenance
  - Safety, fire, cut and burns procedures.
- A clear written and oft repeated theft and drug policy
- Flexible part time hours
- Respect for their study hours and homework
- Schedules that do not keep them late into the evenings and early morning hours.

You may lose some of these staffers only when the go away to college. Possibly some of your greatest rewards in life will come from seeing these young charges mature and move on carrying your work ethic. Do not miss this thrill.

ORIENTATION CHECKLIST
For new hires use a checklist that includes most of these items.
- ✓ Welcome employee
- ✓ W4 form with social security number and green card if required
- ✓ Overview of the company
- ✓ Work schedule
- ✓ Job assignments and direct supervisor
- ✓ Training schedule and contact
- ✓ Punctuality and shift reliability and their importance
- ✓ Business hours
- ✓ Health card requirements and source information
- ✓ Pay procedures – pay period, payday, overtime, deductions
- ✓ Tip declarations policy
- ✓ Employee benefits – group health/life, accident, vacations, performance bonuses
- ✓ Emergency/accident/injury/fire procedures – locate first aid, extinguishers
- ✓ Attendance policy
- ✓ Theft and zero drug policy
- ✓ Smoking rules

- ✓ Personal phone call in and out – cell phones
- ✓ Dress code and personal hygiene / uniform maintenance
- ✓ Employee parking
- ✓ Employee entrance/exit policy
- ✓ Standards of behavior
- ✓ Grievance procedure / encourage early communication
- ✓ Outline of training program or syllabus
- ✓ Probation period and evaluation procedures
- ✓ Time and attendance clocking procedures
- ✓ Tour of facility
- ✓ Introduction to co-workers and mentors
- ✓ Starting hourly wage and increments
- ✓ Equal opportunity employment statement
- ✓ Answer any of the employee's questions
- ✓ Have person sign and date the checklist

HIRING FOR THE HOST/HOSTESS FUNCTION

This position requires the most care in selection. Persons in this job represent the first impression with service in your establishment. It is absolutely essential that you find people who are pleasant, who naturally smile, who can remember names, and who are competent to coordinate seating with all other staff members. Give weight to initial impression of appearance. Personality type will be key.

EMPLOYEE TERMINATION

Our industry traditionally provides jobs not careers. This is healthy for the employee who can learn skills and ethics and move on to a career elsewhere. You will turn-over some personnel, but employee turnover should be maintained in the low double digits for efficient operations. The laws of entropy say: that after some years, persons can lose their enthusiasm to provide a high quality of service to your customer. Use the motivation tools and rules to re-inspire performance to excellence, rather than lose to turnover. Note that it is always a mixed event when you lose valuable people who are moving to higher aspirations such as being accepted to an advanced school.

One estimate of the cost of turnover - to hire and train- is 150 times the hourly wage.

Firing of personnel is a very expensive action, and must be avoided if possible. The long-term ill-will created may have large costs hard to measure. We all are only too aware of the term "disgruntled ex-employee". Firing is painful to the person and stressful to the manager. The exception, as stated before, is violation of theft or drug policy. Staff who become mediocre performers must be given attention towards finding a cure, or moved to a less public job function.

The manager's daily log is the place to document the specific areas of failure. Poor performance must be documented before fixes can be tailored. You owe the documentation to help your total staff adhere to a high level of service, but it is also important feedback to the employee involved. A terminated person should be able to see clear and specific reasons for the firing.

An alternative to termination is: reduction of staff hours and prime shifts so that the person improves or is left with the need to seek employment opportunities elsewhere. Good practices should allow you to look back on long management periods where persons you actually fired were few.

Unfortunately, the popular attitude about firing is being defined by reality TV. Most public personalities were never forced to build an organization that depends on people for survival, and learn that firing should be a rare event.

Note: No one should ever be fired for making a mistake. We all learn from mistakes. Repeated gross incompetence and malfeasance are serious reasons for firing.

MOTIVATE

Every person deserves a job that is enjoyable. What a total blessing it is to get paid for going to work where the experience is pleasant and the atmosphere is conducive to learning and growth. Conversely, what a particular purgatory is a job where the boss is hated, the co-workers are not friendly, and customers are abusive.

People will always be your most valuable asset. The restaurant's path to success is only through excellent staff. Excellent staff is the easiest, most essential, and surest way to differentiate for competitive advantage. Selection, training, motivating, and retaining staff will always have large associated costs. Managing this asset well is very involved, but is never as expensive as having poor staff. The manager's job is to ensure high levels of productivity and job satisfaction with low turnover of valuable staff. One important staff quality, conscientiousness, must be a target we strive to develop.

Conscientious-culture develops when your people match their own needs with an awareness of the organization's clear mission. The conscientious employee manifests this trait by applying speed, quality, efficiency and flexibility to help meet overall organizational goals. Conscientiousness includes placing oneself in the shoes of the customer, including both the internal customers of fellow team members, and the final consuming customer that comes to you for value. The culture of continuous-improvement drives the conscientious staff-person. Motivation to conscientiousness can be complex, as any manager must discover, but it is vital to high productivity and the pursuit of excellence.

The pursuit of excellence, according to Charles Murray, requires three elements: (1) cognitive ability, (2) zeal, in the form of true desire to succeed, and (3) persistence over time, and in the face of temporary setbacks. You will select, train and motivate to maximize these three elements.

Motivation might be defined as the interactions and incentives that drive each employee's direction, intensity, and commitment to excellent value-added productivity with continuous improvement. *Direction* in the form of clear current goals drives these attitudes. *Intensity* is the level of effort to meet those goals. *Commitment* deals with the duration of the level of intensity, or persistence needed for success. Motivation deals with the conscientious effort to meet the organization's goals.

ATTITUDE AND EXCELLENCE

You have already hired the best that you can find using objective criteria. You have already trained properly and thoroughly using guidelines (See Section Four). Now you must get the high consistent productivity that pleases your patrons. Productivity means efficiency. All jobs have that dual component of quality and quantity, which defines efficiency. This means speed combined with smooth, working quickly with no error or wasted motion, all in an atmosphere of congeniality and conscientiousness. Efficient production is pulled by enthusiasm for doing a job well. Note that it is always better to be pulled by co-workers than pushed by bosses.

The key to high productivity and low attrition is high positive morale. Morale is: the attitudes, mental and emotional, of a group member towards the tasks expected by the organization and the loyalty to it. Positive morale adds to the quality of life of the whole team and can provide a family feeling, but is essential to your quality of service. Morale includes the awareness that the value of the individual within the organization is important. Note: Everyone is motivated in some direction; however, positive motivation to do assigned tasks both quickly and well requires high morale.

How do we create enthusiasm and the high morale necessary for good service? Creating positive morale is done through relationship building within the company environment, which requires a sensitivity and communication of the needs of individuals. The process takes time and authentic effort, since superficial steps are transparent and will create cynicism.

CULTURE

Organizational-Culture is the set of important assumptions, both explicit and assumed that members of an organization share in common. Every organization has its own culture. Culture, similar to an individual's personality, is an intangible yet ever present theme that provides meaning, direction and the basis for action. Shared assumptions (beliefs and values) influence opinions and actions within that firm. Shared internalized values shape content and account for the strength of the organization.

Note: You cannot motivate any person. You can only provide a motivational environment. Everyone is motivated, but not always by the same thing that motivates you. Some motivations are positive, and some not, but whatever motivates people comes from their own forces, not from you. People do things for their own reasons, never for ours. With all interaction, try to understand why a person will like a particular course of action and frame your negotiations accordingly.

Francis Bacon 1561-1626 AMBITION "[I]f they find their way open for their rising, and still get forward, they are rather busy than dangerous, but if they be checked in their desires, they become secretly discontent. And look on men and matters with an evil eye, and are best pleased when things go backwards, which is the worst property. ...[F]or if they rise not with their service, they will take order to make their service fall with them.

Primary motivational factors are: fear, incentives, and attitude. Effectiveness of *fear* is an overblown belief, and is a poor motivator. Fear can only play a role if one participant has a great deal to lose. *Incentives*, both positive and negative rewards, involve assessment of outcomes based on actions, but are marginally effective for most behavior change. The best motivator is *attitude* that derives from a positive sense of self in the current environment.

WORD ABOUT WORDS

High morale is about human thriving and human realization. These topics stir emotions, but we must make hard choices. In order to discuss intelligent options for decisions about people, we need to employ words that have useful and exact descriptive value, but lately seem to carry negative connotations, making them currently non-politically correct.

Your most valuable asset is your *human capital*. The word "capital" has emotional connotations that are left over from 20th century populism. Linking humans with capital implies exploitation. On the contrary, decisions about this precious capital asset will always require making individuals as happy and healthy as possible. People are assets just as your other capital assets of: dollars, time, talent, knowledge, information, technology, real estate, and capital equipment. All of these capital assets must be employed to their highest-and-best-use for long run optimization. One difference is: that long run optimization of people might cause temporary discomfort for individuals who have needs and emotions, whereas your other capital assets do not. You have contractual and moral obligation to this one class of assets. However, much of human asset decisions follow similar rules of logic for employment of all capital to the highest and best use.

Motivation is what drives all human behavior both positive and negative. The word "motivation" implies inducement from management. On the contrary, motivation-to- excellence means: providing the optimal environment and opportunity for rewards that make it easy for persons to be self-motivated.

Control connotes autocratic imposition of external rules and procedures by management. However, controls are best when people who actually have control can carry out their duties with clear support, knowledge, and proper tools. The metrics for control are also best when defined by those who have actual control at the operational level. Control works best from bottom up.

Discrimination, Judgmental, and *prejudice* are words that have strong negative connotations. Good outcomes, however, require decisions that are based on reasonable information. Since information is never perfect, decisions must also be guided by probability and judgment when necessary. The process of making superior decisions is always an exercise in discrimination.

Equality is a word that causes much mischief. It is not "fair" that all persons are not equal in their abilities and energies. The real world has never been fair, and human nature cannot be engineered. Forcing equality that overrides free behavior always does damage in the long run. Our job is to create opportunity for each person to develop abilities to their maximum in the real world. Blame that villain Rousseau for our unrealistic hopes for the virtues of equality-of-outcomes versus opportunity and fair-treatment-equality.

TEAM EXCELLENCE – MANAGEMENT –STAFFING - Section 3

BUILDING MORALE

Positive morale is worth more than can be bought with money. When it is poor, the cost to the operation is overriding. Morale must be created with a nurturing culture.

- Dollars alone cannot buy morale. Wages, up to a reasonable level above prevailing rates, are important but do not define the personal relationships required for high morale.
- Task clarity is important to job effectiveness. Clear accomplishment motivates powerfully. Clarity bypasses frustration and barriers to accomplishment.
- Morale is based on trust that management and the team have common goals that will benefit all.
- Positive morale requires employee feelings of security. The knowledge that hard quality-work will be met with resultant long term reward builds security.
- Morale requires a direct relationship between reward and the effort to earn it. When persons are given favorite treatment without earning it through competence and effort, then we create the unhealthy sense of office politics. Nepotism must be handled carefully. Staffers must know that they control their own destiny and can advance on the basis of their energy and skills.
- Positive morale creates a strong emotional bond to the organization, and the reverse is true. Both positive and negative morale once established have inertia, and are then hard to change.
- Positive morale is contagious. Co-workers communicate among themselves and their feelings reinforce the feelings of others.
- The organization must hire and promote people-oriented managers rather than numbers-oriented types.

SOP - Marriott Corporation (MC) was the 12th largest employer in the U.S. in 1992. J.W. Marriott Sr. started with a root beer stand, and then began to sell food to begin a record of long-term growth and success. MC had a reputation for quality and reliability of service through careful attention to detail using standard procedures. (MC also used careful site selection criteria). MC strengths included unique corporate culture built around personality and values, and attention to customers. However, the organization itself was focused on the employees. "People are No. 1 – their development, loyalty, interest, and team spirit", J.W. Marriott. If you take care of employees, they will take care of customers.   Partial source: Robert O'Brien, The J. Willard Marriott Story (1977)

ASSESSING MORALE - METRICS

Numbers provide clear bright lines for goals and feedback, and are preferable to vaguely worded goals. The more specific the goals, the easier it is to measure performance. Fortunately, in this electronic information age, measurement can often be an automatic byproduct of other essential functions such as recording sales, purchases, and time. The tools available for timely and relevant numbers from databases are now easily attainable with small effort and low cost. A list follows.

"If you can't measure it, you can't manage it."

Diagnosis of morale levels and direction requires awareness of indicators.
- Look at your rate of employee turnover. If it is above the levels normal for your area and type of service, you have a problem.
- Do people fail to show up to cover shifts on more than rare occasion?
- Notice if tasks are done according to spec with energy and good attitudes.
- Be sensitive to complaints or gripes. Since grumbling is contagious, the dissatisfactions will grow and show.
- Look for humor within the organization. Healthy upbeat joking and smiles among staff indicate a camaraderie. Cynical humor indicates low morale.

MANAGEMENT ROLE – VALUES - BEHAVIORS

Key management roles are high standards, compassionate control, and healthy involvement of all levels of management. Morale cannot be generated directly, but only by establishing an atmosphere over time.
- The first essential step for motivating staff is to set a good example with management's own commitment to hustle and ethics. This includes manager's dress code.
- Commit to integrity throughout the operation. Dishonesty in any form cannot be tolerated and must be publicly exposed before it spreads.
- Respect the value of employee's time. The golden rule applies. They have their own lives to live outside the operation. Do not make unreasonable demands with scheduling. Be sensitive to the balance for weekends and holidays. Allow staff procedures and channels for adjusting the schedule.
- Listen at the bottom level. Be accessible. Take all complaints and suggestions seriously. Staffers need feedback on a frequent and personal basis. Beyond keeping an open door policy, communications must be initiated from management downward. Ask opinions. Let them know you value their views.
- Support creativity and innovation. Remember there is always a better way. Do not let managers' pride of authorship stifle improvement. People can develop their own sense of style as long as it does not detract or deviate from good form and results.
- Stay flexible. Recognize that all events have unique variables that call for individual judgments.
- Complement and otherwise support good work. Reinforce the value of good work and the employee's own value in relation to good work.
- Criticize constructively. Explain solutions and demonstrate why a given way is a better way. Ask if the person agrees.
- Limit paperwork where possible. Clerical functions are necessary for control of overhead, whereas quality customer-interaction is your actual business.
- Work hard with staff having problems. Proper support can overcome the areas of difficulty. However, when staff persons show no willingness to hustle or make efforts to fix clearly defined problems they will infect others. Cut your losses.
- Promote the "We are winners attitude". Everyone needs to be part of something special. The operation that acts with class is one that everyone wants to enjoy. The feeling of excellence comes through teaching and training that gives opportunity to achieve above norms. Personal pride attracts other healthy recruits.

MOTIVATORS

Basic needs for your staff can be:
- Dollars, prestige, power
- Peer acceptance
- Status and personal recognition
- To grow and achieve
- Expanded self esteem
- Security
- Freedom

DOLLAR COMPENSATION / PAY

Every survey of motivators tells us that people are primarily motivated by factors other than money. This may be true but is grossly misleading. These surveys results are based on hypocrisy and naiveté. Remember persons always respond with answers that make them look best in the eye of the surveyor. Mention of dollars as a motivator in our society is taboo. Feeling of self-worth may be our most driving motivator, but it depends on the perceptions of peers, and achievement recognized by others that builds self-esteem. But for both self-worth and peer-esteem dollars are the most visible way of keeping score. Dollars are partly interchangeable with power and prestige.

There is a limit to your allowable labor costs. Industry averages are in the high twenties as a percentage of gross. As we have seen, labor costs and direct costs (food and beverage) comprise your prime cost, and if this strays much over 65% of sales then you are probably in serious trouble. Fortunately you can pay higher wages than the prevailing rates if you get higher productivity from your staff. This brings us back to motivation.

Dollars are always a motivator. As the whole team learns that efficient production and service to the customer raises their income they are motivated to do their best. Customer counts go up so that pay can go up, while staff turnover goes down. The relationship between pay and productivity is circular and self-reinforcing. Dollar influences include:

- Tips, and tip allocations when shared
- Benefits/Bonuses
- Pay differentials are necessary to equate jobs by intensity and responsibility.

ACCEPTANCE BY PEERS

"There is a power among peers that bosses can never approach". The need to be part of a group is a basic need, especially for younger staff endemic to this business. People need a sense of belonging, a feeling of proprietorship and participation. Providing a family type atmosphere has direct influence on morale and team performance, and drives low turnover. Provide an atmosphere where team members can demonstrate the value of their contribution to the team. For instance, if general staff meetings are called for a Saturday morning, keep them short and provide a picnic to follow. Staff softball teams scheduled against other restaurants, and captain's choice golf tournaments for staff and customers foster this team or family spirit

STATUS

Status is the strongest overriding motivator for all behaviors. Of course the trappings of status are often bought with dollars. Beyond this, each person must have the conditions where they can show their talents and skills. Management style must not diminish a persons' status in the eyes of fellow workers, this will require courtesy and respect when issuing directives. Delegating responsibility and authority, when possible, always helps.

GROWTH AND ACHIEVEMENT

People need an opportunity to learn and advance. Primary training will add to their library of skills and knowledge necessary for upgrading their lives. The job cannot be seen as a dead end, so achievement must be rewarded with expanded opportunity. Standards must be checked and enforced for proper feedback to aid the quest for each person's own personal excellence and status.

SELF ESTEEM

Essentially your people are co-workers and will be treated with respect. Respect allows them to earn self-esteem. They actually "work with" rather than "for you". This will become evident as the team meets the common goals. Their orders to you as manager probably will exceed the orders flowing to them. Refer to them as co-workers and not employees. You have the privilege to work with them. Do not, for example, refer to bussers as busboys. The bus function can be rotated through the kitchen staff as "K-staff job #3" with its own checklist of duties for that shift. Give praise for good work. Always listen with attention.

The dress code must allow staff to wear apparel that makes them feel comfortable with how they appear to others and to peers.

SECURITY

Staff must know that as long as they work well that the will be rewarded. There must be a clear connection between raises and specific performance. Avoid unmerited favoritism.

FREEDOM

After persons are trained well, they need the room to get the job done without excessive oversight. There must be some flexibility and atmosphere for creativity. The job still must meet or exceed the spec as detailed in the job description and daily checklists, but performance feedback should be with scheduled reviews rather than micro-managed.

Let floor personnel know they are de-facto independent contractors with the ability to give themselves raises by improving personal productivity.

EFFECTING CHANGE

Remember that workers can resist change when they feel pushed. They embrace change when they are asked for input on positive change specifics.

INVOLVING STAFF

People can more easily gain their own personal best performance when they can see and identify-with clear organizational goals. Meetings should usually cover both; problems that staff will have concern for, and profits that they can be proud of. This means sharing profit and loss results while covering each elements of contribution. Review objectives in detail, making sure they reflect the immediate short- and long-range needs of the organization. For floor staff this will include sales data. For kitchen staff this will include overhead quality and cost controls. There are three steps: (1) set reachable goals with input at the operative level, (2) provide tools to measure the goals for quick feedback, and (3) provide incentives for meeting goals.

STRATEGIC GOAL SETTING

The company mission statement defines the major goal. Other major goals are: customer-count increases, average customer ticket sales, and cost reductions. Each of these goals can be broken down into sub and mini-goals. Goal setting is often best when done with the ideas of the persons responsible for implementation. Discussion by all parties ensures the setting of reasonable goals for each area of pursuit, and those goals are more readily pursued and more clearly in mind when self-set. Reasonable goals must start from a historical base, so operating details must be provided. It may be easiest to set mini-milestones toward a larger goal with specific time frames for completion of each step. Always encourage participation from the bottom up.

MEASURING PERFORMANCE

A satisfied worker is not always a productive or a motivated worker, especially if no one is asking for growth. Growth cannot be demanded without measurement of performance towards goals. The goals once set should be clearly defined in measurable terms. There must be a numeric standard base-line for plotting growth against a calendar. Determine how progress can be measured without excessive additional input and analysis. This feedback has to be timely and should come as an automatic byproduct of other essential functions. For example, individual server sales should come from your point-of-sale register system, cost of goods numbers will come automatically from your ordering process, and overhead figures will come with actual accounts payable.

Server sales can always be improved with detailed information of the sales record of individual servers. This will require a database from your computerized system. Daily figures are captured but are subject to random variation. Therefore accumulated sales for weekly and monthly sales totals by individual give a better base-line for performance and improvement. One necessary background for sales analysis is: the sales for the same period last year and the sales forecast derived therefrom.

Weekly sales analysis should be posted. Posting of number-of-covers increases pride, awareness and responsibility. If numbers are low, everyone should ask why. When your software is set up correctly, a weekly spreadsheet printout with percentage changes from norms should be only a few mouse clicks away. Review the weekly and monthly sales analysis with server staff. Chronic under performers will be asked to take specific steps to bring numbers up. Hold clinics to sharpen suggestive selling skills.

Sales component breakdown is important because total sales by server can be misleading. Obviously high sales coupled with high customer complaints are not good. Sales must also be related to customer counts by average dollar ticket per cover. High total dollar sales can be driven by suggestion of the highest price menu items without regard to high- contribution menu items which looks good on paper but lowers profit margins. Measure total side-item sales: a la carte items, desserts, wine, liquor and appetizers per customer. Warning, do not measure wine sales without considering total alcoholic beverage sales per customer since they can be mutually exclusive.

For non-server staff, measure progress towards saving goals for each area of overhead (See Section Five – Control). Always, though, be careful that quality is not compromised in pursuit of lower costs.

INCENTIVES FOR MEETING GOALS

Consistent individual top-server sales performers can be rewarded with; recognition, pay-raises, choice of shifts, choicest stations and other favoritism. Rotate best staff through the best waitstaff stations. When persons show that they will be a continued drag on averages after much re-training, you must look for alternative areas for their employment. Rewards to top performers can be low cost because (1) they have earned it and (2) they certainly help you afford it.

One caveat: you must be careful with your server sales incentives. You cannot afford for your staff to be too pushy with guests. Raising sales through pushing expensive items over high contribution items can also be expensive. Remember your guest will want to return if the perception of value is there. When their bill exceeds their planned budget expectation, that perception can be depressed.

Communicate that personnel will themselves be measured on a regular basis to learn where they stand on defined norms of productivity, service, quality control, cleanliness, and safety. Create a highly visible way to keep score on performance. A merit system can let persons know when they need to strive harder before differences become irreconcilable.

An *incentive program* should have these guidelines.

- Determine a budget for the program and show that it will pay for itself.
- Find a base indicator against which measurable change can be documented.
- Establish doable improvement by discussing with staff.
- Provide highly visible management support.
- Share information on progress daily.
- Specify rewards commensurate with the effort and achievement.

When the incentives work, the cost/benefit will drive pleasant outcomes.

TEAM EXCELLENCE – MANAGEMENT –STAFFING - Section 3

MANAGEMENT STYLE

Style of management can range from hard authoritarian to laissez-faire. Authoritarians can be abrasive, such as the "smiling cobra" that issues edicts and punishment. Then there is the passive manager who fails to motivate at all, but just want to be friends. Both extreme styles can produce dysfunctional stress. There is a style in between where management is a coach and mentor to provide staff guidance and the tools to produce to the fullest potential. The manager must reduce dysfunctional kinds of stress, but some type of push helps staff reach higher. Some short-run stress may provide opportunity for pride and the feeling of accomplishment. Delegation, feedback, and counseling can produce positive stress. Stresses that may produce greater satisfaction and results are:

- Having a large clearly-defined workload with achievable goals
- Heavy responsibility in decisions that affect others
- Perception that job qualifications and skills can be improved
- Being pushed by peers towards perfection

Bad stress sources to try to reduce are:

- Poor job definition clarity & Insufficient training and tools
- Inadequate support from superiors
- Too little authority in relation to responsibility
- Unreasonable pressure for improved performance
-

Caring is essential, which is: visible sensitivity to needs of persons and the group.

PERFORMANCE REVIEWS

The employee performance review is a valuable tool for applying positive pressure. Feedback related to baselines is important for continuous improvement and growth. When communications are good, performance review frequency can be delayed. An objective form-checklist guides the process. The process must be done carefully in order to avoid the disgruntled employee who feels unjustly criticized.

Know that no one likes criticism. Reactions to criticism are usually negative and lasting. A great tool to evaluate and avoid criticizing is the employee self-evaluation checklist. When the employee does the rating, they can honestly consider and understand where they need improvement. You can either agree or disagree with their scoring during review, but you can always positively reinforce their strong points one-by-one while objectively discussing areas for improvement.

At the end of the review the employee must clearly agree on what the next targeted behaviors are to be.

DELEGATING

Increased responsibility can raise employee job satisfaction. Therefore, another valuable tool is delegation, even before considering the need to reduce the never-ending pressures on the time available to managers. Usually any job task should be delegated downward to the lowest level of competence needed to perform the task. Keep a log of all tasks encountered during the days. For each task ask, "Am I the only person who must do this"? When the answer is "no", look to your staff members who might have the time, skills and disposition to take on the task. When the staffer takes this task off your hands, they must be equipped with all the information and support to do it smoothly. For a checklist see time management rules earlier in this section.

Instead of seeking a manager, servers should be expected to use their judgment about how to please customers. Look to the server staff to anticipate potential problems and proactively deal with them at that primary level rather than react after a situation has become serious. They are the closest to the problem. Acknowledge that servers are customer service experts and are trusted to handle special situations. Clearly, people do best and prefer to work where they and their decisions are respected.

RESOLVING STAFF CONFLICT

On occasion personalities will not get along. This will affect team morale and service. To resolve, follow these steps.

- Listen to both sides taking an objective and detached role.
- Meet with each party separately to get in-depth perceptions. (Often the stated problem has deeper roots)
- Bring the two together to explain the nature of the differences. Listen for new information when the two are together for additional insight. Look for undercurrents.
- Define differences and discuss in the contexts of how it affects business and how they can be overcome. Stay alert for sensitivity and conflicts of personality.
- Provide guidelines for fairness as shaped by norms to get parties to see unwarranted behavior.
- Get parties to agree on specific points for future interaction.

CORRECTING STAFF WITH PEER REVIEW

Staffers with poor attitudes require help. Mediocre performers can fail to get along with others, fail to hustle at peak loads, not help co-workers, or just be poor team members. Such people drag on morale and everyone's income. The manager can have a hard time getting the person to accept honest criticism for needed change. Younger staff especially can resent authority. Peer pressure however is very powerful in modifying behavior either good or bad. To elicit change take these steps.

- List the specific poor behavior.
- State your thoughts on how this behavior affects business.
- Third, explain how the behavior affects co-workers.
- Cite peer feedback regarding the behavior while keeping sources anonymous.
- If necessary have the person fill out the self-evaluation form to discuss differences in perception regarding every aspect of performance.
- If still no improvement, have the co-workers do a rating using the same form. The person will probably respond to the team's view of the level of performance and improve dramatically.

POLICY

MISSION – GOALS – POLICIES - PROCEDURES

All personnel must work toward the clear *mission*. That mission, however worded, will seek to serve quality to customers so that the perceived value will compel them to return, and to provide good word-of-mouth about that value experienced. Value involves our trinity of quality of: product, service and atmosphere.

Policies communicate guidelines to decisions. They are designed to control decisions while defining allowable discretion within guidelines for efficient action at all operating levels. Policies empower in several ways:

- Policies establish indirect control over independent action by clearly stating how results are probably best achieved. Policies define discretion to effectively control decisions, yet empower staff to proceed with activities without direct intervention by top management.
- Policies promote uniform handling of related activities. Coordination of work tasks eases friction arising from disparate handling of common functions.
- Policies ensure quicker decisions. By standardizing answers to previously encountered questions that otherwise would recur and be referred to a manager again and again. Speed of resolution is especially important at the server level of operations.
- Policies institutionalize basic aspects of organization behavior to build the culture and norms. Norms minimize conflicting practices and establish consistent patterns of action to raise probability of successful outcomes. These pattern guidelines free operating level personnel to act with confidence.
- Policies reduce uncertainty in repetitive and day-to-day decision making to build a necessary foundation for efficient cooperation.
- Policies help resist deviation from strategies devised to guide the whole organization. Policies clarify paths to common targets. When policies are crafted with those at operating levels, acceptance is strong.
- Policies offer quick and healthy answers to routine problems. Ordinary problems are solved with dispatch. Extraordinary situations are more easily differentiated for creative problem solving.
- Policies reduce likelihood of hasty, ill-conceived, or emotional decisions in evolving operations.

Policies may be written and formal or unwritten and informal. Informal, unwritten policies are usually associated with a strategic need for competitive secrecy. Some policies of this kind, such as promotion within are widely known - or expected - by employees and implicitly sanctioned by management. Managers and employees often like the latitude granted by unwritten and informal policies. However, such policies may detract from the long-term success of a strategy.

Formal written policies have at least some of these purposes.
- They require managers to think through the policy's meaning, content, and intended use.
- They reduce misunderstanding.
- They make equitable and consistent treatment of problems more likely.
- They ensure unalterable transmission of intent.
- They specify the authorization or sanction of activities more clearly.
- They supply a convenient and authoritative reference and baseline.
- They systematically enhance indirect control on organization-wide coordination of the key purposes.

Caveat: Policies should not be so rigid that they ignore common sense, think DMV.

Policies can be externally imposed or internally derived. Regardless of the origin, formality and nature of policies, the key point to bear in mind is that they can play an important role in strategic implementation. Communicating specific policies will help overcome resistance to strategic change; empower people to act, and foster commitment to successful strategy implementation.

Most Policy will be clearly written to be included in a personnel manual for review when needed. Abuse of policy is a legitimate piece of agenda for personnel meetings. The abuse can be brought up without mentioning names; they will know who they are. The discussion on a particular policy can be on whether the policy, as written, works well or does it need modification. A democratic agreement here will enhance the team spirit and respect for adherence to the final policy.

Below are some typical subjects that may require clearly defined written policy. Each organization will have unique needs so the given examples may need modification.

ABSENTEEISM
- State the value of covering scheduled shifts and the costs to the team of absenteeism
- Put reliability in covering shift in the performance evaluation review. Laud perfect attendees.
- Provide flexible mechanisms for adjusting shift schedules. Have staff cross-trained so that a scheduled person can call another to cover. Handout updated staff phone lists often.
- Do not place such emphasis on tardiness that persons will call in sick rather than be late.

TARDINESS
Show that lateness can start the whole team with their "foot in the bucket". Occasional lateness is less of a problem than individuals who are chronically late. Chronic lateness can be cured to the benefit of the individual by noting the problem at each transgression.

DRESS CODE
Staff works best when they feel comfortable about their appearance to their peers. Obviously there must be guidelines, since a mode that looks good to peers is not always the same as a mode that looks good to your customer. Common ground can be found with input from staff. List specifically what is permissible and what is prohibited. Cleanliness must always be emphasized. Apply the standard consistently.

THEFT / DRUGS
State early and often that there is zero tolerance. Both are grounds for immediate dismissal.

> "Changing an institution's environment to increase the sense of control among its workers (is) one of the most effective possible ways to increase their sense of engagement, energy and happiness." Jonathan Haidt – The Happiness Hypothesis

OTHER POLICY
- Friends
- Phone
- Customer complaints
- Cash handling
- Safest behavior in case of robbery
- Tip allocation
- Personnel scheduling
- Time and attendance clocking procedures

"First one, then all, then chaos"

MEETINGS

Team success will depend on productive meetings. Continuous improvement for the entity's sustained competitive advantage requires regularly scheduled meetings and impromptu meetings when operations are not going smoothly. Since meetings are off-line overhead functions, planned structure of the meetings reduces the amount of valuable time of all participants to be spent with meetings. Generally, short meetings are better. Good meeting structure helps ensure focus, attention, participation, and constructive output. Well-managed meetings will be your forum to tweak and control all of the many variables of on-going restaurant operations. Participation is the opportunity to build cohesive team spirit and mutual responsibility. Cultural values and expectations develop from productive well-run meetings.

PARTICIPATION

There will be several levels of meetings. Staff-wide meetings might be scheduled monthly. Meetings for a given job function, such as wait-staff or K-staff, should be scheduled more often. Non-scheduled postmortems after difficult shifts might occur as soon as all relevant participants can attend. Time frames for start and finish are important for attendees to schedule their own valuable time. Attendance ground rules spelled out early should become part of the culture.

Absence or tardiness of key team members should have some pre-defined consequences such as reduced scheduled shift time, in order to reinforce team values.

Participation means active involvement with constructive input. Never reward poor performance or passive representation.

FACILITATE - RECORD

A Facilitator should outline the meeting agenda and the looked for gains. Focus on content and the decision-making process. Recording progress and output for recall of team meetings needs thought. Delegate a team member to capture minutes on a laptop or notebook. Minutes need not be lengthy or formal. Some capacity for display is helpful, such as a tripod for a chalkboard or chart paper. Highlight needed information and suggestions. Reserve a few minutes at the end of the meeting for a postmortem on meeting success and any required adjustment for future agendas or further information capture.

MOTIVATION FOUNDATIONS – THEORY

Since humans are complex entities and are motivated by complex needs. The foundations for motivation can only provide a way of thinking about how to mesh the organizations needs and the individual employees. Several theories for meeting mutual needs are currently in use.

Abraham Maslow's *Hierarchy of Needs* says there are 5 basic levels of needs, and that each level must be satisfied first, and in serial order.
1. Physiological needs: hunger, thirst, shelter, sex and other bodily needs.
2. Safety: security and protection from physical and emotional harm.
3. Social: belongingness, acceptance and friendship.
4. Esteem
    a. Internal: self-respect, autonomy and achievement.
    b. External: status, recognition, and attention.
5. Self-actualization: the drive to become what one is capable of becoming; including growth, achieving potential, and self-fulfillment.

The restaurant manager should not be concerned with level one, but starting with emotional harm at level two must consider all of these higher needs in interactions with each individual at all times. Satisfying the higher needs is essential for high productivity with low turnover. Status, recognition and attention will always be very important and a necessary focus of good managers.

Theory X and Theory Y from Douglas McGregor proposes two views regarding motivation. Theory X assumes that employees dislike work, are lazy, dislike responsibility, and must be coerced to perform. Theory Y assumes that employees can like work, be creative, seek responsibility, and can exercise self-direction. In some given settings, need for autocratic management might be appropriate. In the long run, Maslow's hierarchy is best met with by creating an atmosphere for theory Y of less obtrusive management. Less autocratic management allow more room for human dignity and relative status that is so essential to happy co-workers.

Two Factor Theory derives from studies by Frederick Herzberg, and measures how one's basic attitude towards work can determine the level of productivity. According to Herzberg, the factors leading to job satisfaction are not the opposite of those leading to job dissatisfaction. This implies that eliminating factors that lead to job dissatisfaction might ensure a basic level of satisfaction but may not necessarily motivate.

The set of factors reported by workers as leading to high job satisfaction were perceived as internal motivating factors. In order of importance they are:
1. Achievement
2. Recognition
3. The work itself
4. Responsibility
5. Advancement
6. Growth

Factors voiced as leading to dissatisfaction were perceived as external hygiene factors. They include in order of importance:
1. Company policy and administration
2. Supervision

3. Relationship with supervisor
4. Work conditions
5. Salary
6. Relationship with peers
7. Personal life
8. Relationship with subordinates
9. Status
10. Security

Keep in mind that voiced factors from questionnaires are always biased. Our culture does not allow us to say we are "doing it for the money", or for status. "Salary" is an extrinsic reward, and only appears eleventh in weight to such intrinsic rewards as "Achievement". Most rewards listed are intrinsic and contribute to status. Status is a need from basic human nature and is influenced by the internal set of factors for motivation as listed. Further, Herzberg was attempting to measure job satisfaction and dissatisfaction, and not necessarily productivity.

ERG Theory replaces Maslow's five hierarchical needs with the three of: Existence, Relatedness, and Growth. Also unlike Maslow's' orderly progression of basic to higher level of needs, ERG theory assumes that needs in all levels may be operating as motivators at the same time. The theory contains a frustration-regression dimension that focuses needs at any neglected level up and down. ERG theory, from Clayton Alderfer, allows for differing emphasis on needs by individuals as modified by cultural environment including, education and family background.

McClelland's Theory of Needs from a research group headed by David McClelland focuses on three needs: achievement, power, and affiliation.

1. Need for achievement: The drive to excel, to achieve in relation to a set of standards, to strive to succeed
2. Need for power: The need to make others behave in a way they would not have otherwise
3. Need for affiliation: The desire for friendly and close interpersonal relationships

With the need for achievement, McClelland found that high achievers differentiate themselves form others by their desire to do things better. They look for environments and situations where they can see a challenge and attain personal responsibility for developing solutions to problems. Achievers must have reasonable goals clearly defined, and prefer early feedback on progress. Achievement can be relative to a set of standards, especially when they are clearly defined, and where rewards both positive and negative can be measured.

Excellence in job performance may come from the desire to differentiate with the major goal of recognition by others that enhances *relative status*. Restaurant managers should have high achievement needs. Note, however, that the need to achieve does not necessarily lead to good restaurant managers, since that need applies primarily to personal performance rather than long term team productivity. The achievement need is for the individual team members only, and time and incentives are required for this ambition to be effective in the team environment.

The need for *power* is the desire to have influence and control of others. Individuals with high power needs enjoy being "The Boss". They strive for influence over others, and seek competitive and status oriented situations. Often they tend to be concerned more with influence over others than with actual high productivity. They look for control and status. Obviously, managers with high power needs can have a negative effect on employees who need their own relative status.

Affiliation can be a powerful need, and often can strongly affect the traditionally high restaurant turnover rates. The restaurant worker's internal customers are the members of the team that create the supply chain of total quality service to the external customer. That team's shift-performances and, of course, high tips rely heavily on good affiliations.

The need for both affiliation and power tend to be closely related to managerial success. McClelland's group's studies suggest that the best managers are high in their need for power and low in their need for affiliation. This view is arguable, depending on several variables in the kinds of management required. Restaurant managers deal with staff that must function face-to-face with the customer while primarily in the role of an independent agent. Empirical evidence indicates that managers of front-room restaurant staff need to operate as co-team members rather than power managers. A high degree of mutual understanding, respect, and autonomy is called for once the mission is clear and training is complete.

Cognitive Evaluation Theory discusses the influence of extrinsic rewards such as: pay, perks, and promotions as motivators on behavior that can be driven by intrinsic rewards such as achievement, responsibility, and competence. Much research has been done here, with some belief that intrinsic motivators are important and should be made part of the culture.

Goal Setting Theory says that specific and (reasonably) difficult goals, with goal feedback, can lead to higher performance. Research on goal setting is persuasive and not subject to degrees of argument as are the other theories. Key to goals is the word "Specific". Goals should be definable and measurable with clear bright lines for quality of performance. First, the goals must be "accepted", with more difficult goals providing higher output of effort. In some cases participation in goal setting can raise the motivation to achieve those goals. Further, timely and specific feedback demonstrably aids higher performance, and is an essential component of the goal-setting package. Even better is: self-generated feedback. So, it is important to build-in automatic metrics for feedback, where possible. Often self-generated feedback can be an automatic byproduct of other essential operations metrics, such as the wealth of the database from point of sale register entries, or other ongoing essential accounting functions.

Four secondary factors that influence outcomes with goal setting theory are:
- Goal commitment
- Adequate self-efficacy: the belief in personal capability to achieve the goal, or confidence
- Task characteristics
- Culture and background

Goal setting works well with most kinds of tasks. They seem to work best on simple rather than complex tasks, learned rather than new kinds of tasks, and independent rather than group tasks. Team goals are appropriate for groups. Variables will be: the kind of task and the ability and attitudes of persons.

We are familiar with *Reinforcement Theory* from our parents. It says that performance behavior is a function of rewards both positive and negative. The emphasis is on extrinsic rewards rather than intrinsic. The intrinsic feelings, attitudes, and expectations are variables that will modify the success of reinforcement. Still, we all know the value of visible concrete recognition for work well done.

Equity Theory deals with dollars. Money does, obviously, motivate. Our society decrees that it is not politically correct to say it, but money is how we keep score of relative status. When your people are happy with their work and are making good salary and wages, the job satisfaction is high and turnover low. This extrinsic reward of dollars, however, must be only part of the package with the important intrinsic rewards. For dollars to be a motivator it must be seen as directly related to performance, thus the need for flexibility and to tie to pay to specific measureable outcomes.

Most all motivation theory seems to stress the compelling importance to all individuals of *relative status*, and indirectly the badges of that status that can be purchased. Need for status is hard-wired basic human nature. While our culture discourages direct reference to status as a motivator, it may override all others.

All cultures have hundreds of words that allude to relative status, and demonstrate the pervasiveness of *relative status* in our everyday considerations and interactions. The importance of relative status to human well-being has been noted and discussed throughout the ages by Aristotle, Hegel, Hume, Fujikawa, and many others, though we have been temporarily blinded by Rousseau.

People simply need to feel good about themselves, and be perceived as good by others.

While the egalitarian society, with no class distinctions, is a cute ideal to contemplate, it will always be impossible to achieve, given actual human nature. Equality seems unworkable and destructive to human achievement. No one ever wanted equality for themselves as individuals except as a rung on the ladder to superiority. Status need is powerful. High status is always sought and usually must be earned through hard work. We benefit because work and status can be mutually supportive. Great creations are driven by striving for special recognition.

Low status, on the other hand, harshly affects human dignity. Restaurant managers, at all levels, must be ever mindful of each co-worker's dignity. When workers and team members need structure and guidance, there are always approaches that get results and still maintain dignity for all. The unfulfilled and unmotivated worker can be a "disgruntled" worker, and we all know what long-term damage can come from such a source.

The lesson to all managers is: throughout restaurant operations, maintenance of *human dignity* must govern all personal interactions. Be aware that people's beliefs and behaviors are best understood in the context of the need for relative status. Treat all with this knowledge clearly in mind for best outcomes.

TEAM DYNAMICS

While the wait-staff job function sometimes takes on the characteristics of an independent contractor, personal direct customer interaction that maximizes tips also maximizes the value to the customer that reflects on the whole organization. Therefore, at all times, every co-worker is necessarily part of a team tied by the supply chain.

SUMMARY – MOTIVATION

Motivation sustains the quality of your delivery of value. A culture of excellence is infectious as peers strive to impress. High motivation comes from attitudes about job performance excellence. Mangers do not motivate, but must supply the conditions for people to self-motivate. Creating an atmosphere for sense of control for all team members will increase their sense of engagement, happiness, and energy. That energy elevates the dining experience.

Note: we have all seen managers who felt the need to issue orders, to be seen as tough and decisive. Also we have seen managers who inspire to excellence by appealing to our higher needs to meet clear goals to our common benefit. Although there are occasions requiring clear orders, the second approach generally gets greater long run results.

RESTAURANT HANDBOOK

TOOLS & RULES

Roderick A. Clelland

FUNDAMENTALS OF RESTAURANT MANAGEMENT

PRINT SECTION FOUR

TRAINING

RESTAURANT HANDBOOK – TOOLS & RULES

TABLE OF CONTENTS – Section Four

TRAINING

    RETURN ON INVESTMENT   4- 3

WHO - FACILITATOR
      PRIMARY vs. SECONDARY TRAINERS   4- 4
      FACE-TO-FACE SKILLS   4- 4

WHO – LEARNER   4- 5

HOW - PLANNING & PREPARATION   4- 6
     CUSTOMIZE   4- 8
     ENVIRONMENT   4- 9
     BASICS   4- 9
     CLARITY   4- 10
     MOTIVATE   4- 10
     DELIVERY   4- 11
     FOLLOW-UP   4- 11
     METRICS   4- 12
     MENTORING vs. TRAINING   4- 13

HOW – BACK-OF-HOUSE   4- 14
     HOW TO TRAIN – PROCESSES   4- 14

HOW – FRONT-OF-HOUSE   4- 15

HOW - NOT   4- 15

WHAT - WHY OF EACH JOB FUNCTION   4- 16
    BIG PICTURE   4- 17
    SUPPLY CHAIN
      INTERNAL CUSTOMER   4- 17
    SPEED OF SERVICE   4- 17

WHAT – FRONT-OF-HOUSE
    SENSE OF PEOPLE SKILLS   4- 18
    SALES TRAINING   4- 19
    CONCEPTS TO COVER AS FUNDAMENTAL   4-20
    CROSS-TRAINING   4- 24
    SAFETY – HEALTH   4- 26

WHERE

WHEN - CONTINUOUS IMPROVEMENT   4- 26

TOOLS
  JOB DESCRIPTIONS   4- 27
  PERSONNEL MANUAL   4- 28
  CHECKLISTS   4- 30

JOB FUNCTIONS – FRONT
  MANAGERS   4- 30
  FRONT DESK   4- 31
  WAITSTAFF   4- 32

SUMMARY

Survival depends on competitive advantage. The best edge comes from your people. Great people need continuing education for knowledge and skill-sets that please your customers. Restaurants that educate staff most efficiently also have the highest profits.

The budget in time and dollars for staff learning cannot be avoided, but it must be employed effectively.

Most "training", unfortunately, is "Teflon training". Poor training practices produce wasted resources. This section covers how to deliver effective staff upgrades. Training material must be properly presented to be interesting, relevant, retained and to actually induce positive behaviors and attitudes. This section covers the details of powerful tools that get measurable results.

TRAINING

People who administer to your guests are your most precious asset. Each person must be nurtured. Their quality will make or break you. People-quality is your easiest path to differentiation and profit. You determine that quality by your attention to their total knowledge and skills.

Restaurant industry-wide personnel turnover can average 200% per year, and in touristy areas 400%. High turnover ensures a costly inflow of raw personnel that must serve your valuable customer. Turnover can lead to training where: buddy (b) teaches buddy(c), and buddy (m) teaches buddy (n). This process is: entropy to the nth. It leads to guaranteed chaos. Job understanding goes downhill with "buddy" training. Then you will see reduced customer counts, smaller cash flows, and dropping profits.

Your direct-labor costs are near par with costs-of-goods-sold as your greatest expense, but degree of control is much higher for labor. You control this cost, and therefore your profitability by: increasing job satisfaction, lowering turnover, and raising productivity and quality. All of this means you must have - among management's budget of rare time and dollars - an efficient system for developing quality people. The return on investment (ROI) of time and attention to your people is higher than any other cost control area.

"Training" is the label we will use for this section only because it is commonly understood and useful as a heading. The word "training", however, is a poor descriptor continual upgrade of the total knowledge and skill-sets of your entire staff, both front-of-house and back, for sustained competitive advantage.

Training is a necessary investment that competes with all of the restaurant manager's scarce attention. The approach to training starts with a healthy understanding of how people learn, because that is the only way to get a high return on this investment. The larger intent beyond tactics, methods, procedures, and mechanics, is to produce lasting knowledge that creates an attitude and team culture that promotes rewarding behavior and satisfaction.

Note: Everyone desires to grow with new skills and knowledge in a healthy and fun learning environment. Few, however, want to be "trained". The word might be better applied to pets. Further, measurement of success through feedback from many "training" programs often shows poor retention and behavior modification. People do not automatically resist change, but they do resist being changed. Like a rope, they want to be pulled rather than pushed. Much training, especially passive multi-media, makes us feel good about our actions as trainers, but yields poor returns on our training budget. Jim Sullivan calls it "Teflon training".

A better descriptor than "training" is the word "development" for excellence. Belief that a person is easily "trained" is arrogant and can have negative effects on morale. You should be a mentor, facilitator, or a coach, rather than a "trainer".

Make no mistake. Training is not just important, it is vitally critical to your success. Your restaurant concept requires essential differentiation for competitive advantage. Differentiation can be easiest with personnel who perform service cheerfully, smoothly, quickly and efficiently.

Without well-trained staff, any restaurant is doomed to failure. Poor training directly impacts both the customer and each employee. Employee frustration builds when there is a gap between what is expected and what they know how to do well.

Organizations with better training investment have the highest profit margins. Indeed, a study reported in the New York Times, shows that restaurant chains with the largest training budget generally outperform those that spend the least.

Look at restaurants that are perennial high grossers. Popular restaurants have customer counts high above average. Great performers also have higher training budgets and levels of commitment to continuous training. The cost of training is always less than the costs of ignorance. The most expensive training is no training at all.

The size of the training budget in dollars, however, does not always guarantee the quality of the training package and the results. It can be hard to measure results without metrics for planned success. Metrics should be defined in advance and viewed often. Fortunately, the tools available to measure results, in this information age, can be quick, easy, automatic, and decision-compelling.

Do not worry about the training investment for people that might soon leave your organization. That investment is a sunk-cost that must be ignored. The alternative of not training people that stay with you forever is even more costly in terms of lost future cash flows. Remember, only your people build your business. Great on-going training of skills is a powerful creator of competitive advantage, as well as a recruiting tool.

Teaching of skill-sets is only a minor portion of good training. The aim is to change the people who will administer to your customer, and free the manager of attention to routine details of operations. Equally important is establishing a culture with healthy attitudes and practices. Strong culture ensures that knowledge is eagerly shared with team members. Culture helps the team learn to adjust to inevitable change with anticipation.

Training is aimed at change, both tactical and strategic. The target is changed behavior. Changing people, even expanding their knowledge base and skills, is difficult unless people are motivated to change. A trainer motivates by starting with a clear picture of how the training will benefit the trainee both now and for life.

How well people learn depends on their personal motivation, not the strength of the trainer's commitment. Begin any training session with illustration of "what is in it for me" as it affects both immediate benefits and long run health of learners.

This section will deal with the quality of the total employee-development effort. We will cover who, what, when and how to train. The emphasis will be on training methods that yield high staff acceptance, retention, and compliance with good practices and procedures that focus on the customer.

RETURN ON INVESTMENT

The restaurant industry emphasizes the focus on the customer. Be clear that the customer is only served through staff, so that attention to staff skills must come first, before the customer can be properly served. Beyond the obvious target, a happy customer, an excellent continuing staff-education program yields these additional valuable benefits.

- Job satisfaction and morale escalate with good staff education.
- People gain confidence in their skills.
- Responsibility delegated downward frees management.
- Flexible responses are quicker and with better results.
- Teamwork is smoother.
- Service time quickens.
- Turnover goes down, with its huge costs of management time and dollars.
- Profits rise with productivity increases.
- Training for suggestive-selling increases average ticket values.
- Word-of-mouth raises customer counts and long-term revenues.
- You create an employer reputation that attracts excellent people.

Training is easiest, of course, when you have already selected the best people. Thorough training, both correctly and continually, will make personnel motivation easier. Training allows practice and repetition to teach skills for high productivity. High productivity lowers direct labor costs and allows greater focus on your primary customer.

We must get staff education right to allow all employees to expand their talents, abilities, and self-worth. We will create an environment to help our staff communicate, cooperate, and enjoy working together as members of a successful team. After all, each of us will spend a major portion of our lives in the work place.

WHO – FACILITATOR

PRIMARY vs. SECONDARY TRAINERS

We have all played the game where a story is whispered in someone's ear and the process is repeated around in a circle until it is told out loud to the original storyteller. The final hilarious story will bear no resemblance to the original. When you allow trainees to continue to train other trainees, the same deterioration of original intent will follow. Training is best done by one person who best understands the total job to be done. Bad habits, once learned, can be hard to deprogram. Often a hurdle to overcome first is unlearning poor practices. Never underestimate the value of required primary training.

Do not delegate training to anyone who is not also a primary trainer. A primary trainer is one who:
- Is experienced with the job and all of the sub-components
- Knowledgeable of the mission and common goals of the organization
- Aware of how the job function fits with the team (internal customer)
- Aware of how the job affects the delivery of the total value-package to the final customer (value chain)
- Knows the mechanics and proper steps for effective training
- Has the people skills to impart information that will be retained and practiced
- Is willing to demonstrate on-the-job examples and leadership
- Has the patience to start with basics, and persevere to total understanding
- Allows people to express emotions and concerns
- Encourages questions and feedback
- Is always aware of the overriding need of trainees to keep their dignity
- Is comfortable as a mentor

Not everyone has the skills to be a primary trainer.

FACE-TO-FACE SKILLS

The best communication is personal and direct. A trainer must have time, skills, and inclination for hands-on interaction. Face-to-face is the optimum way to communicate any concept that has complex components or material that is particularly sensitive. While there is a time and place for e-mail, telephone, or written communications, it is most effective to deal with important information in person. Body language is very important and may be 70% of total communication success. Also, direct communication allows instant feedback and interaction.

The effective coach:

- Plans the training sessions
- Demands and receives active show of support from top management
- Relates the benefits to trainees from the start
- Illustrates with real-life success
- Illustrates with mistakes and real-life poor practices
- Illustrates with humor
- Knows the difference between information and communication
- Demonstrates methods and procedures

- Asks active performance of demonstrated procedures
- Repeats demonstrations to total clarity
- Limits sessions to less than 60 minutes
- Elicits follow-up appraisals of the session and how it can improve

The Poor Trainer:

- Has never performed the work being taught
- Relies too heavily on visual aids without active interaction
- Hands out thick written material
- Covers complex material lightly without repetition

Finally, any excellent manager understands the overriding need for human dignity in all things. Conscientious and loyal staff will never allow their dignity to be demeaned. Understand this critical concept in all of your dealing with your learners. Preserving human dignity will be the strongest influence on desired behavior. You are not the boss. You are a facilitator as part of the total team.

WHO – LEARNER

Learner performance requires a basic capacity for skills. You should ensure this capacity and cognitive ability at the time of selection. Capacity for front-of-house jobs will require people-directed personalities. Young students may not yet have developed capacity, but they are eager to learn and make superb back-of-house staff as they grow from simpler job functions towards more complex skills. Lower your failure rates with teaching restaurant skills by (first) hiring people who are already hospitable by nature.

You have demands for your learners, but they also have rights to demand from you. New job performers have a right to work for an organization that is passionate about personal growth and quality learning. This job is often an entry-level position that will guide attitudes and perceptions the rest of their productive lives. They have a right for a rich learning environment. Trainees need an opportunity to perform in a supportive culture. They have a right to access and embrace new technology on the job. They will need an opportunity to build self-confidence. Self-confidence must be earned, however. You cannot just hand self-confidence to them.

Learners should have a right to make mistakes. We all learn our strongest lessons from mistakes. Mistakes, though, must never lead to any loss of dignity. Deal with mistakes with humor, and let people know that they are not the first or the worst with given mistakes. Use mistakes as a learning tool.

Learners probably should not be referred to as "trainees". Better labels might be: "Team-members", or "co-workers". Reference by their given names is even better.

Learner's time is also valuable. They have a right to be excited to learn and be satisfied with the knowledge and skills gained. Learning sessions must be productive with measurable results for the time invested.

RESTAURANT HANDBOOK – TOOLS & RULES

HOW

Effective teaching requires that you know clearly what you are trying to achieve, what the learners expect to gain, and how to link both to common goals. You will start with creating a culture that develops healthy attitudes and an eager reception to new learning. You will establish a work environment that is complimentary, supportive, happy, fun, and profitable for everyone. People will see that you care, and form a lasting bonded relationship for mutual benefit.

CULTURE

Culture deals with the guiding values and mission of the organization. Values define how you will strive to achieve the highest results for the well being of the business. Basic values are: cleanliness, good food and beverages, strong customer counts, cost control, and rewarding staff job performance that leads to the success of the operation. The overriding value that dictates all others is guest satisfaction, and guest's perception of value received. Culture leads to awareness of how best to deliver that value. Culture will solidify over time, but must guide all other training. Constant repetition of your organization's values helps to guarantee that the culture grows strong.

Change happens. Any healthy culture will expect and embrace change as opportunity.

PLANNING & PREPARATION

Plan and design all training to enhance the value of your greatest asset, human capital. The true value of any restaurant is people. Training is not just something that is required to perform, but is a key tool for quality performance. Approach every training session with the same investment in planning as for any capital budget request.

Your learners have the right to have management preplan, design and rehearse engaging learning materials and presentations. Their time is valuable and execution of skills after training determines your success. A trainer should spend at least as much time getting ready for training as in actual instruction. A presenter should know the desired results before beginning to teach.

Before any presentation or "training" session, the leader should consider these basics of planning the training structure.

- What specifically should the audience learn about the subject matter?
- What do they already know?
- Who is going to help them learn?
- What mix of tools will best help them learn?
- How will the environment for learning be accepted, with excitement or resistance?
- What behavior should change as a result of learning?
- What metrics should we establish to measure results of behavior change?

The program, in order to achieve measurable and lasting results, will require active interaction.

- The sessions should allow input from all attendees.
- Agenda will have to be informative and clearly relate to participant's future.
- The program should be entertaining with humor and fun.
- The material should be clear and simple, depending on goals.
- Material should always relate to "why" a given course of action works best.
- The materials mix should be varied, but heavy on face-to-face interaction.
- Always be mindful of the value of each attendee's time and dignity.

Learners must see a vision of what they will achieve both personally and professionally, early in the introduction. The possibility of greater income is always an incentive, but is not the most powerful motivator. Also early, you must set clear expectations for learners regarding their roles in the learning process. State what knowledge you expect them to gain and apply, and how they relate to benefits to all. They want to learn more than just the mechanics of their jobs and sharpened skills. They know that knowledge is power that leads to good economic outcomes. The training curriculum will lead to a good understanding of the value of the competitive-difference through delivered excellence.

Get learners involved rather than accepting a passive mode. Gain attention and retention from free participation. Try to determine what learners can contribute from personal experience. The whole process can be more effective with anecdotal stories of what worked in the past, as well as what does not work. What they did before is important, even if it illustrates disasters.

A blended and balanced program makes use of the new communication technologies. Technology gives us broad and exciting tools for presentation media-mix.

Your plan will yield a written syllabus that will cover all or parts of proficiency at: tasks, job efficiency, people skills, service, sales, cost control, safety and health issues, plus professional development. The plan will not stay static. Your environment is always changing as to your threats and opportunities. Feedback and metrics will drive a constantly changing syllabus. Finally, management-by-walking-around will tell you what is critical and timely to include in your evolving plan.

MIX

Trainers have great tools at hand to attack all senses with a blended and varied media mix. It is easy to be authentic, enthusiastic and excited, while still being clear, concise and respectful of the audience. However, it is healthy to retain human interaction as the major part of the training agenda. Great training materials can enhance the learning experience. Execution, however, depends heavily on direct human delivery that will reach the employee and impart memorable skills and knowledge. As much as we enjoy materials that dance and sing, the materials still need people to bring them to life through active response. Some have suggested a minimum of 65 percent delivery by people.

Many restaurant training programs feature too much teaching-by-documentation and not enough learning-by-doing-and-coaching. Text-heavy manuals and videos that repeat your manuals can lead to learning with a low shelf-life. Avoid memorization and tests on information from text-heavy manuals. You, not the learners, are responsible for results. Recognize that to be effective, our training materials ought to appeal to multiple senses and strong reactions.

Technology-based training can be embraced, but only with balance in mind. Technology should add to, but not dominate, the training session. Consider when technology-based training works best in your mix. Interactive multimedia is better than linear presentation, such as uninterrupted video, where the learner might likely nod-off. Interactive training includes reinforcement exercises throughout each session that must be completed before moving on. Interactive training works best to prepare trainees for customer related tasks or skills. For skills such as back-of-the-house procedures that require less customer interaction, linear material that outlines steps, such as video or on-line learning, can be an effective training support tool. Overheads and videos are useful, but do not start a lengthy video and leave the room.

Slide presentations are easy and fun to create. They can use the full range of video tricks with a full library of interesting sounds, as well as custom add-ins. Again, however, resist getting carried away with bells and whistles at the expense of simple, clear content. Use slides only to accompany, rather than lead interactive sessions.

Feedback is essential. Interaction can include mini-pop quizzes on covered subjects. Call on staffers by name for answers and responses to just presented material. Active responses keep the focus.

Demonstrate procedures live when possible. Games with rewards, or symposiums, change the pace. One presenter can be boring; so long sessions might employ different presenters with different styles. Learner led activities are an effective option. You have no excuse to be bland.

Tap into your food and beverage distributors for training materials. Vendors are always glad to tout their products and help sell them. The National Restaurant Association is another solid source for training information and tools.

CUSTOMIZE

You have many options for your mix, including web-based or video-conferencing technology. Developers have created training programs that are as easy to use. You can purchase off-the-shelf web-based instruction packages. All of the employees at each of your units can access the training through any computer. Some of these may aid your mix, but most restaurants have specific operating procedures not addressed by any of the off-the-shelf programs.

Your uniqueness may require in-house creation of training. Never create without soliciting input from current staff or knowledgeable experts. Current staff knows what will best fit your planned culture, concept, and designed methods. Further, such custom training demonstrates dedication to exacting policies and procedures. It might take more time to get a custom syllabus ready for delivery than off-the-shelf materials, but you can end up with a package that meets your restaurant's specific needs rather than a one-size-fits-all program. Staff input into custom development identifies critical training needs, but more importantly, will always smooth the ultimate implementation of designed change.

A balanced and blended approach gives the curriculum strength. The mix must also include entertainment value. It is very desirable to create a "fun and positive" atmosphere where learning can occur, especially when training will be tedious and involve long days and lots of role-playing with no live customers.

Throughout the mix design, do not lose sight of the need to simplify. "When it comes to training materials, it's not about quantity, but about quality and usefulness. Develop your training for the needs of your audience, not yourself". The KISS principal is valid in all presentation. The temptation to feel-good with pretty presentation can obscure learning by bypassing simple and clear content. Each slide or page should be clearly labeled, with one simple idea at a time, even for sophisticated audiences. Slide presentations, with all the bells and graphic gymnastics, for instance, are never as effective as slides that back-up an exciting presenter.

ENVIRONMENT

The environment for learning requires respectful ways to treat people. This means that the environment to preserve human dignity be maintained at all times. It does not mean, however, that people cannot be challenged or that we must automatically bestow respect. We have learned that respect has real value only when it is earned, rather than given as a feel-good form of welfare. That is why participants must be held to measured results.

Engage your staff by providing a climate where they are really involved in on-going decisions. Be authentic and follow through. It does not work if you only try to make them think their opinions are important. Encourage questioning and free suggestions. What they discover on their own is often more exciting than what you might feed them. First, they are likely to come up with better ideas than you did. Also, they will be more committed to executing the ideas they brainstormed from their perspective.

Never humiliate participants. Certainly never single out a person for correction. Rather, refer to issues generically. Remember that the learning process is often emotional with likely feelings of anger and anxiety. Create an environment where people feel free to express their emotions.

The training syllabus can be technologically advanced and proficiently taught, but if it's not fun, it won't work as well. Avoid training that seems like work.

BASICS

You can be confident that you have been perfectly clear about how you wanted something done. Yet, when staffers recreate their finished project, whether it is a procedure or a product, it often has no relation to what you thought you had asked for. It then becomes clear that what you thought you presented was not exactly what they got.

It is a common mistake for a trainer to assume that the trainee knows the basics. Just because you as a facilitator are very familiar with basic knowledge and common sense, it is no guarantee that your learner has this knowledge. Make sure that you don't over-estimate the knowledge base of the people to whom you present. This mistake is especially common with young persons starting their first job in a restaurant kitchen environment. You should always start with the lowest and simplest level of reasoning and justification for a procedure to be learned. You might explain the basics while letting the trainee know that you are starting with basics that you know everyone already understands, and request their patience. Do not, however, skip over these basics.

Find out what they actually do know. If you talk over their heads you risk losing them from the beginning. It is always useful to ask people what they need to know and what they want to learn. Answers are not always what you expect.

CLARITY

A Harvard University study on motivation and employee turnover found surprising results on the importance of clarity. The survey looked at salaries, personalities, leadership practices, work-environments, training, job performance, and related areas.

The researchers discovered that the one factor of task-clarity, as a motivational factor, was twice as important as the companies' pay scales, and three times as important as personalities. Companies that rated well in this factor had one-third the turnover than did companies that rated poorly.

Conclusions were: task clarity is the single most important element in employee motivation. Investing in both initial and continuous training on a weekly and monthly basis pays big dividends. When you build the skills and knowledge of each employee over time, you increase long-term profits by satisfying and attracting more customers.

Task clarity, then, is always one of your primary training concerns.

MOTIVATE

Think back to when you were in school. Where did you make your best grades? What were your favorite subjects? For most of us, the grades and favorites were the same. We learned because we wanted to, not because we had to. The subject was easy because we enjoyed learning. You must create the same environment.

Your training environment also directly influences motivation to learn, retain and convert knowledge to action. You must help them motivate themselves. It is clear that the most effective people are those happiest about what they have chosen to do with their time. Earning a living while also enjoying your avocation is a particular blessing, since we can spend up to a third of our life hours at work. Enjoyable work is a powerful motivator.

Motivation is about vision, standards, rewards, education, and measurement. But we cannot impose them as instruments of control. When management pushes the bureaucratic mindset through demands, persuasion, and pressure, the results are always disappointing. This top-down approach to change by managers is the dead hand of linear thinking. The demanding approach will always generate an immune system to resist it. Your organization is a living social system, and it works best through authentic engagement and dialogue.

Personal enjoyment involves a picture of individual contribution to the creation of value. Team members should see where their individual contributions are vital to the team success. Good teamwork enhances self-worth and the understanding of the desired outcomes.

Rewards motivate, so communicate rewards. Obviously people want money for what they do, but what they want more is: a sense of their own capability and recognition from others that they are capable and desirable to have on the team. People need to know the objectives of the team and have the chance to perform for their peers. Reward is the satisfaction and recognition from a job well done.

Treat your learners like customers. Such treatment pays-off with greater job satisfaction that results in less employee turnover and, therefore, less training required.

DELIVERY

Effective training is the result of effective execution. Attack all the senses. Be clear, concise, authentic, and respectful of the audience. Be enthusiastic. Energize the learners with your delivery. Let them share your passion. Show the content with relevance to behavior. Excite the learner with this education process. Keep it fresh, focused, and fun.

Be clear at the introduction that you are only a facilitator. Take the attitude that, "I cannot make you learn", but I can help with tools that will make your job easier and your skills sharper. Layout the planned agenda and the expected time line, including time reserved for feedback.

Visual aids and music can enhance any presentation. Visual aids include videos, props, slides, and flip charts. A good rule for slides and flip-charts is the KILL principal (Keep It Large and Legible). Go for few, simple, and short statements per slide or flip chart page. Make sure display is high enough for the person in the back row can see over the heads of the people in front.

Multi-media-tech makes it easy to add music to your presentation. Do not, though, allow video and audio to override your live interaction.

Delivery involves two-way communication rather than dissemination of information. You only help people with career development, if you know how to communicate. Communication is interactive. Communication avoids rote learning to focus on learning attitudes about how and why we must learn. Always promote discovery rather than lecture.

Note: you can always practice execution in front of a mirror or on video.

FOLLOW-UP

Tell your learners in advance that you will ask for feedback on what they have learned and how to improve presentation. Be sure to schedule that time as part of your presentation time-line. For a 55-minute session, allow more than 5 minutes for two-way dialogue. This follow-up allows opportunity to improve programs, but also re-enforces active interaction. This is no different than soliciting feedback from your final customers. Find out if you have met your predefined tangible goals.

Finally, celebrate your mutual successes. Recognize and reward people for executing your training standards.

METRICS

"If you can't measure it, you can't manage it". Before you started design of your training sessions, you had to address key questions. What did you want learners to gain from the subject matter, and how will you know they actually got it? How did they feel about it? What change in behavior did you expect? It is important to find objective ways to measure your success in terms of production improvements. Define the specific metrics in advance, and monitor your results.

Ultimately you will measure the success of training by the attendee's actions and execution. Do they successfully meet the performance standards? Not all success from training is easy to measure directly in objective terms, but most can be measured indirectly over time in concrete dollars.

Note that management cannot force the standards. We have learned from the decades of teaching total quality management programs (TQM), including the currently popular "six-sigma", that the actual producers of the output must have control of the metrics. When management sets standards and pushes for results, we are setting up for failure. When standards are not met, management might tend to push even harder. Experience shows that this does not work. The team will want to meet their own goals, and take pride in meeting those goals. Team peer pressure is always powerful, where management pressure can cause resistance.

Get participants to agree on the program objectives. Set milestones together. All participants should accept responsibility for meeting objectives and deadlines. You provide the atmosphere that challenges them to seek out information, solve problems and interact with all present.

The metrics selected should be specific and objective. You do not have to use sophisticated statistics. Show baselines and percentage change. Let them know the results of metrics will be posted.

While management cannot force the measurement of standards for success, they can help provide the tools. They can offer alternative metrics. They can help establish benchmark data and reasonable forecasts. Management also knows where the historical data resides, how to capture the data, store it, mine it, analyze it, and display it in a timely manner and readable format. To make results meaningful and decision compelling, the data often needs some transformation. For instance sales data represents a time series that is governed by cycles: trends, seasonal, cyclical and irregular. To be meaningful the cyclic periods can be neutralized by various smoothing methods, including moving average. (See Section Five – Control)

After measurement, it is important that you recognize and reward any progress that moves you in the direction you all want to go.

Technology helps feedback of the chosen metrics. Some major metrics are:

- Rise in sales per server, productivity
- Rise in revenues, net income
- Time spent on customer service/complaints
- Reduced costs in specific categories of direct costs. (See Section Five)

Metrics give several benefits:

- Metrics allow you to modify the syllabus to adjust to weaknesses.
- They highlight nonstandard performance of the job function for corrective action.
- They expose nonstandard product quality and show root causes.

A caveat is in order here. While metrics are necessary for tuning your training methods and material, metrics are an off-line job. Never let your pursuit of the numbers distract you from your attention to people.

Measure impact. Tie your targets to the bottom line. Teaching and reviewing targeted results makes sense because it makes dollars.

MENTORING VERSUS TRAINING

During school we all seem to have had favorite teachers. These teachers motivated us to learn. We had the feeling that they cared about us, and delivered the material in a way that inspired us to learn. You must do the same, so use them as a model to mentor your staff. Mentors invest in development and on-going guidance to produce leadership and talent. Mentors care about each learner and it shows.

Show employees how they can, within your organization, raise their pay, grow into new challenges and be rewarded for their efforts. You will gain a team that is loyal, conscientious, and effective. Turnover will virtually disappear.

Mentors always communicate while employing the three R's:

- Respect - Always be aware of the basic human need for dignity.
- Recognition - Apprise learners of progress and laud excellence. Recognition will always drive effort.
- Rewards - Rewards can be monetary, but realization of growth for future opportunity and stature is a greater motivator for learning.

Further, a mentor:

- Invests in energetic, involved, and interactive learning environments.
- Emphasizes positive sides and opportunity in every-day interaction.
- Believes in helping each employee plan for their future beyond this.
- Imparts perspective, how each job relates to the team and customer.
- Furnishes trainees with a vision of their personal achievements.
- Sets a good personal example.

Be authentic to get people excited about learning. Great mentors show that they are seriously and eagerly pursuing their own professional advancement. Mentors keep their staff open to new ideas, and are aware that they can also learn from their learners.

RESTAURANT HANDBOOK – TOOLS & RULES

Hold managers responsible for relevant program content and design. Focus on how people learn and be accountable for delivery methods that maximize involvement and retention. Support and execute some form of learning every day. Hold your staff responsible for learning something new every day and teaching it to other team members.

HOW - BACK-OF-HOUSE

Restaurant back-of-house usually requires less interaction with the final customer, and is more focused on projects, processes, procedures, and methods. Training for processes is relatively straightforward. Still, do not forget to relate each task to the overall supply chain, how if fits with internal co-worker customers, and how it follows the basic concepts of excellent production discussed later in this section.

> **HOW TO TRAIN - PROCESSES**
> **Follow three steps while training for tasks with serial components.**
>
> (1) A primary trainer should have the trainee watch the process as properly demonstrated and explained. Explanation should include the whole philosophy as well as why the steps are set up to ensure speed and ease. Show how the job function performance affects the whole team. Emphasize use of both hands. Demonstrate the need for planning so as to eliminate unnecessary wasted motion and travel. Show how the process eventually relates to providing overall customer service, and therefore everyone's paycheck.
>
> (2) Have the trainee do the process while explaining back to you all that you had said.
>
> (3) Again demonstrate the process while gently correcting and explaining the parts that the trainee missed.
>
> Repeat steps, if needed, until all processes are clearly understood and practiced.

Note: When a trainee performs incorrectly, never say, "No, not that way". Always wait until the re-demonstration for correction. You might phrase it, "I noticed you did it this way, do you see any better way to do it?" Often they will self-correct, which will have more lasting impact. After a task has been learned, ask trainees how to improve the task, because there is always-always a better way.

HOW – FRONT-OF-HOUSE

Since service-staff will deal with complex interaction with customers, their education should include interactive real-life scenarios. One approach is to have new servers wait on the staff and serve them the employee meal. The learner follows the restaurant's guest service sequence and the staff members offer their comments and critique after the meal. Staff might volunteer real-life anecdotal reactions to both common and unusual customer incidents, with outcomes both good and bad. Another approach is to have new personnel work the floor with an experienced server.

When a server is newly solo on the job, they should explain to the customer that they are new and would appreciate constructive feedback. Customers usually gladly comply.

Responsive front-of-the-house service works best when each server knows how everything works in the back of the house. Problem and service delays or snags can then be directed to the proper source for improving systems and safeguards.

HOW NOT

Do not label your learners with the name "trainee" during orientation. It is embarrassing and implies temporary and expendable. Rather, use personal names when possible.

Do not correct staff in front of others. Rather, wait for a time and place. Approach any discussion with a view of mutual goals towards best restaurant standards, and barriers to those goals. Do not start with a perceived personal attack. Present hypotheticals and allow staff to see better alternatives for themselves.

Do not imply that your knowledge in all things is superior to that of your learners. They can be very sensitive to an overbearing attitude. Treat all employees as essential parts of the team of co-workers. Allow for their experience.

Avoid short-term memorization of meaningless information that will not be applied to decision making in real-life experience. Don't require people to memorize a training manual's policies and procedures, and assume they are then trained.

Do not drop-off new personnel with a "buddy" for secondary exposure to proper training. Also do not throw warm bodies into a sink-or-swim situation because you have not planned for proper staffing for given positions.

Do not skimp training because you feel they might just leave and take those skills down the street to the competition. Do not rationalize that you cannot afford training. That would be a mistake.

Do not let enthusiasm for bells and whistles obscure meaningful content. It is okay to seek eye appeal. Entertainment uses materials that are vibrant, exciting, up-to-date and graphically stimulating. However, if the materials are lit up like a comic book, it may be hard to grasp the important principles. For example, think of your most entertaining TV commercials where you do not know what they are selling.

Do not over-rely on passive media. Video might not engage your learners. An alternative is a CD that delivers high-quality video, still photographs, audio, and graphics, plus accompanying text. Computers can train employees in skills for simple procedures. Such media are cost effective for individual as well as multi-unit operations. However, keep them short, simple and limited.

Limit off-the-shelf Web-based training. It has a place, in that it ensures that every employee receives at least minimal training prior to serving that first customer or performing a kitchen task. It is tempting because all you need at each restaurant is a simple computer with high-speed Internet access. Minimal training, however, is not in your best interest, so use it only as a part of your total mix.

Do not cram too much scope into too little time frame. Ensure the scope is realistic. Always reserve time for questioning and follow-up

Do not tell an employee to "refer to your manual" as a teaching tool. The manual is a useful tool, but good customer service is not what's being taught within. The manual cannot teach accountability or responsibility. The manual teaches that the employee doesn't have to think, or worse, not trusted to think. The manual implies that an inflexible set of rules can handle situations better than a server's intuition and instincts. "Refer to your manual" is, however, good for adhering to specific important and basic policy, especially when standards slouch.

Avoid static classroom sessions that are lecture and textbook-based. They lack context. Feedback is rote rather than performance based.

Avoid environments that allow individual egos, power plays, negativity and a lack of communication. Develop an organization that trains everyone to accept their own personal responsibilities as they relate to the team.

WHAT

WHY OF EACH JOB FUNCTION

Start with "Why". We need to give employees good reasons why their jobs are important and how they fit. Note that most of us do not like to be asked to do things without knowing why, and that includes your employees. Go beyond itemizing what to do. Remember that paychecks and demands, as carrots and sticks, are not the biggest motivators. We must give good reasons why every part of their job is important, and how it makes a difference to the customer, as well as how it impacts the income of their fellow team members. "Why" goes beyond tasks and activities. The "why" of the job gives each employee an internal compass that operates in the absence of a manager.

Ultimately the major "why" is to satisfy the customer. The customer assures everyone's job and pay. The more customers, the more opportunities for advancement and potential for pay raises. Customer counts control the learner's future, not managers.

BIG PICTURE

Allow learners to be partners in the big picture. Context is the key to new learning. Why do we learn and how does it matter?

Share the numbers. Most employees, especially your younger staff, do not know what a profit & loss statement looks like. They have little clue what it actually costs to run a restaurant, and how fragile those numbers can be. Ask about restaurant industry average profits, and you will get wild guesses beyond the reality of low single digits.

One highly productive approach to the big picture is: a large display of a simplified generic profit and loss (P&L, or income statement). You can point out that the team, not management, controls the very top line of sales revenue, with their service to the customer.

Show also that they have primary control over the bottom line. When the whole team helps keep costs low, the restaurant can then offer better prices. The lower prices means better perceived value to the customer. Everyone on the team prospers as value drives customer counts. Discuss each of the overhead costs where they have large influence. Illustrate with vivid and specific examples of waste versus good cost controls. Cost controls are in each employee's own hands. Brainstorm observed waste and cost control, and you will be surprised by the eagerly voiced examples. Show this P&L picture often while pointing to areas of excellence, and areas of concern. Facts motivate people. They will see clearly why and how they can help control costs. (See Section Five - Control)

Keeping your people ignorant will only hurt your operations. When people understand why they are doing what they are learning, they do it better.

SUPPLY CHAIN - INTERNAL CUSTOMER

We try to teach what our employees need to know to better serve our guests. Exceptional customer service is the final output from the whole supply chain. That chain includes the whole team as internal customers. Management and staff - both front and back - are customers first. When each employee understands how their output affects the health and wealth of their peers, they are strongly motivated to produce both speed and quality of service. Illustrate the internal supply chain with real examples such as, how the cooking staff and bussers rely on the dish-wash function as part of their supply chain.

Teach employees to put themselves in the shoes of their customers. This shifts the emphasis from how to work-the-job to learning how the-job-works for the internal and the end customer.

SPEED OF SERVICE

A huge factor in restaurant success is speed of service. Speed of service affects the customer greatly because the customer sees time differently. Explain to employees how speed of service so strongly affects the customer's perception of value.

RESTAURANT HANDBOOK – TOOLS & RULES

Understanding time and speed concepts gives the employee a good reason to serve customers quickly and to try to meet the customer's time expectations. Employees will know to move quickly and efficiently, and why it makes a difference. They then have a motive to prove how efficient they can be. Often spontaneous competition will arise.

Speed is especially important with limited seating capacity. Speed helps the tables turnover with efficiency. Speed and smooth, with no wasted motion, allows higher revenues, tips, and income for the whole team.

Speed also leads to the broader concepts of efficient work habits. These topics: time, speed, and efficiency are universal concepts to apply to all future projects, and are discussed in more detail below.

WHAT – FRONT-OF-HOUSE

SENSE OF PEOPLE SKILLS

Your guests come to you with different needs. It may be hard to train for, but your servers will have to sense the mood. Most guests want responsive but *unobtrusive service*. Some guests will want minimal disruption of their privacy while others will want to be entertained. Some want quiet. Some want a circus. Consider the range. You might see: a young couple on a date, an older couple with an anniversary, a birthday group, a party in a party mood, a business conference, and a family.

Each customer group can demand a different service level, but still will require attention and speed of service to complete the price/value of their dining out experience. Every guest must have a grand experience. Sometimes showbiz flair is called for. Outgoing personality type helps. Satisfying all these different demands well creates another point of differentiation for your restaurant.

Before a grand opening, I hired two starving college students for some casual labor. They soon asked to join the server staff training. Being both personable and quick learners, they became likely candidates for waitstaff.

On the job, I observed one of the pair, Al Andrzewski, in an overly familiar interaction with a dining room party. To my horror he insulted them roundly. To my surprise the party became regular patrons, and were willing to wait longer in the queue to get Al's station.

Three years later both of these waiters became principals in their own separate multi-unit operations that allowed them to become millionaires before they turned thirty.

While guests have varied expectations, there are three phases of the service that cannot be ignored.

- First is the initial welcome. The server must smile, look at, and talk to the guest.
- Next the server must meet the implied promise of all expectations throughout the experience. Guest must get the proper orders on time and on quality specification. The server will employ smile, eyes, ears, hands and feet in delivery.
- On leaving, the guest must be thanked and invited back. The guest wants to remember and be remembered.

Always develop your training programs ultimately aimed at the guests. They deserve a good time. It is a mistake to automatically assume you know what they want. A sense-of-the-mood is a skill acquired through time after good grounding in what to look for.

SALES TRAINING

Active suggestive-selling by knowledgeable staff gives measurable gains.

- The customer experience is more enjoyable and satisfying. Guests are more likely to get a total positive sense of value.
- Flag-downs are reduced. The proper order up-front allows more efficient use of server resources.
- Check averages rise. Remember, the path to prosperity is greater revenues. Revenues can only come from (1) greater customer counts, (2) higher average checks from suggestive selling, or (3) raised menu prices. Raised counts and raised average check is vastly superior to raised menu prices.
- Tips rise. Your people are happier.

Customers don't always see what is most desirable as they scan the menu. Suggestive selling, properly practiced, can help guests make more rewarding decisions. Selling anticipates guest's needs. The less the guests have to ask for their needs, the greater the overall enjoyment.

Evidence suggests that guests commonly go along with waitstaff suggestions more than two thirds of the time. This acceptance can be applied to your high-contribution menu items and the extras that add higher margins to your profit. (See Section Two – Quality – Menu Design)

Transfer your order takers into crack marketers through reinforced behavior. Selling is always easiest when the seller truly believes in the value of the described product. The same holds true for your staff, so product knowledge is a key component of successful suggestive selling. The metrics for suggestive selling are relatively objective, and easy to capture with today's computer based register systems. Examples are average customer ticket size, and suggested items as a percentage of total sales. Sales tracking can identify your most successful seller-servers and they can be recognized and rewarded with additional dollar incentives. A healthy competition can motivate all staff.

Excellent salesmanship requires (1) product knowledge and (2) belief in its value. Product knowledge has two components, (a) the ingredients and methods of preparation, and (b) the description and presentation of the finished product. Your sellers need to know both, so that the description is effective. Guests need the description plus an endorsement from the server. Proper description requires use of adjectives that fully develop the picture in the mind of the guest for a favorable evaluation. The selection of the particular adjectives to illustrate a fresh and tasty product can be suggested by anyone on the team. It may be best to get varied input at an informal muster. People can take turns describing the product. Always emphasize quality and freshness.

Description is easiest when the servers have actually had a chance to sample the product. Sampling is important for new menu items and specials. They can see, smell and taste the item while they try to describe it in their own words. The final use of adjectives in the description should be up to the server, so that the presentation does not sound contrived or canned. Try for appetizing descriptive adjectives and avoid trite and over-used adjectives.

What happens when the suggestive-seller does not personally like the product? Do they have to lie and say it is a personal favorite? The answer is no, they do not. While it is never easy to sell when you do not personally perceive value of the product, servers will still see value if they are convinced that (a) others show a craving for it, or (b) it is a popular seller on the menu. If neither is true, then it is difficult to sell, and probably should not be part of the menu.

Suggesting wine greatly increases the likelihood of wine orders that impact your average check to a significant degree. Product knowledge is important for confidence in suggestive selling of wine. Organize periodic wine-tastings for servers with the help of your wine distributor sales representative. The reps are usually glad for the opportunity to display their products to suggestive sales.

Part of salesmanship is "reading" a table, or gently probing a guest's preferences. Demonstrate the art of hand selling, or personally presenting, unfamiliar wines or menu items. Good suggestions can steer a customer to a new and fine experience. Commit to coach your staff on suggestive selling with continued re-enforcement. This is a relatively small investment for sustained high returns. Simply nodding and smiling while recommending new menu options will personalize the recommendation. The skills will become second nature. Staff will be knowledgeable, articulate, and confident. Watch them boost your sales.

CONCEPTS TO COVER AS FUNDAMENTAL

Following are some fundamental ideas that should be ingrained in the mind of your staff. These concepts are especially important to young persons at the beginning of their primary training. Start with these, because it is difficult to retrain persons who have a long experience with bad habits.

CONCEPT – *THE CUSTOMER IS ALWAYS RIGHT*

It's a cliché, but it's true. Sometimes service will go wrong (Murphy's Law). Sometimes, even when service is good, the customer has had a bad day before they came in. In these cases, do not offer excuses (they really don't care why), just apologize and try to make the situation right. If the problem is truly your fault you might go so far as to offer a gift certificate to show the customer that you believe the problem won't recur.

TRAINING – Section 4   21

CONCEPT – *THE IMPATIENCE CURVE*

We already looked at the "Impatience Curve" (see Section Two - Quality - Service). However the curve may be the single most important concept to stress to all personnel. Guests who feel ignored will always perceive poor service. The perception is irreversible and will be discussed loudly with others to your long-term detriment.

Know time passes more slowly for a waiting customer than for the server. Further, time does not pass in a linear fashion to the perception of your guest who feels ignored. Time distorts. There are no longer 60 seconds in every passing minute. As the interval past the expectation of service grows, seconds become minutes, and minutes become intolerable. Time begins to wear at an exponential rate. A customer ignored can wait 5 minutes and become crazed to argue (and sincerely believe) that they have been kept waiting 20 minutes.

As the curve for annoyance goes upward we reach a point where it goes vertical. At that point you are sunk. The problem cannot now be fixed. You can try all remedies with profuse apologies and it will do no good. The person will tell many friends of their horrible experience. So, this critical period must never-ever be approached.

As you look at the "Impatience Curve" you will note that the time values are missing, because the critical wait time is different for each step in service. For a smiling greeting at the door, this critical period may be a matter of seconds, certainly less than 30 seconds. For greeting after seating it is a matter of less than minutes. Attention should be continuous, without gaps and pauses. It is deadly to your first impression to seat guests and let them sit. Service cannot slack at the end of the meal. Pace of service is guided by each party's expectations and can be both quick and unobtrusive at the same time. Staff anxious to go home must be up to speed until you are closed and guests are gone.

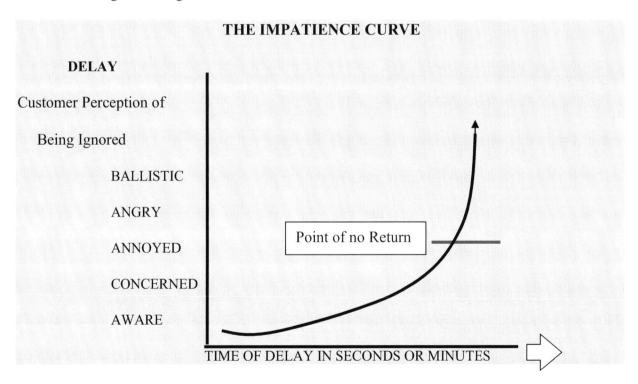

One unavoidable wait is when your waiting line for unreserved seating is large and tables appear to be turning slowly. The customer must see that you are working hard trying to accommodate. At this time your host must continually move among and talk to waiting guests to advise of developments. Candidly show guests where on the list they currently stand. If the wait to be seated is long, the host should tell the servers upon hand-off so that they in-turn can thank the party for waiting upon seating, and again thank them for their patience upon leaving. Crackers or bread and butter to the table quickly may help. "Comped" items, beverages on the house, or gift certificates will only mitigate if the vertical line has not yet been crossed.

There will be occasions where staff is overloaded. Customers might see this, but still not understand being ignored. Every staffer must keep their eyes moving for persons requiring attention. If staff is busy, it is OK to let the guest know that you are currently rushed, but you will be back as soon as you can. The words: "I'll be with you in a moment" said with a smile, or mouthed across a room, can delay the acceleration up the impatience curve.

Never forget the overriding importance of timely service to your long term reputation and profitable popularity as illustrated by this Impatience Curve.

CONCEPT – *TWO HANDS*

Some employees forget they have two hands. Consider that: whenever a trip is made, a job is done, or an order served with one hand but with the other empty, the amount of total service that can be rendered is effectively cut in half. You can afford neither 1/2 of the service nor twice as much payroll.

CONCEPT – *MACRO/MICRO MOTIONS*

Frederick W. Taylor taught us that every job component uses resources that can alternately be employed to higher productivity. Each job function can be broken into sub-units. The pieces can be analyzed for wasted motion, wasted distance, wasted time, and wasted attention. Use a workflow analysis work sheet to break down job functions. Illustrate to learners the examples of obvious wasted resources.

WORK SMARTER NOT HARDER – MICRO-MOTIONS – TWO HANDS
Job Description: Kitchen staff – Dishwash function
Sub Function: Move silverware from dishwash trays to sort bins

Observed Method: A "buddy trained" staff member had the dish-wash output silverware tray in the bottom of a stainless steel sink (knee-level). Braced with the left hand, he reached down into the tray with the right hand and moved spoons, one-at-time, laterally up to the 4-bin silverware tray on a wall-mounted shelf at chest level. Distance round-trip traveled for the hand for each piece of silverware: 6 feet. Time for each piece: 3.0 seconds.

Better Method: Place the tray at belt-level directly below the bin a chest-level. Reach into the bin with both hands and grab many utensils in each hand. Move both hands above tray and sort into proper bins. Average distance traveled per utensil is 0.2 feet (20 average utensils divided by 4 feet round trip for hands). Average time for each utensil: 0.3 seconds.

Analysis: The better method is at-least 10 times more productive than the observed method in terms of time. Also consider the reduced strain on the lumbar region.

It is easy to assume that new staff understands concepts that appear to you as universal knowledge and common sense. A common mistake of a trainer is to skip basics. This allows standards to grow wild with expensive results.

If you were trying to control your direct labor costs at 28 percent, for instance, and all of your productivity slipped only 10 percent (let alone the 1000% above) you would wipe out any chance for profit, considering the restaurant national average.

Young persons can be challenged to find a better way, because there always-always is a better way. Just try to make sure, that in re-inventing the wheel, they don't invent the flat tire.

CONCEPT – *ON/OFF-LINE JOBS*

Some persons, when faced with a list of tasks, tend to look on each as equally important. Some jobs require priority. An on-line job is any job that affects customer perception of service. On-line jobs include:
- Greeting persons at the door (This must be done immediately, and with a genuine smile. They are, after all, coming to see you and bringing their dollars. This sets the tone for all that follows.)
- Getting to the table ready to accept orders soon after seating
- Getting the order up and out
- Refills
- Getting the guest check to the guest when it is clear they are ready
- Settling the guest check when payment is offered.
- Thanking the guests as they are leaving

All on-line jobs are time critical.

All other jobs are off-line and must be put aside when on-line jobs are pending. Off-line job examples include:
- Food prep, unless you are almost out of that item (poor planning or staffing)
- Dishwashing, unless you have no clean dishes (poor supply or staffing)
- Busing tables, unless guests are waiting for seating, or your other guests view unclean tables
- Register controls (the dollar amount being controlled is small compared to the dollar value of the customer perception of service). Ringing up a check when the guest has already left, in sight of waiting customers, is a frequent and unpardonable offense.
- Paperwork
- Maintenance

All of the above may be very important but must be deferred until the customer is no longer waiting for service. This means that it can be necessary to let off-line jobs sit temporarily while you shift personnel resources and attention to any on-line job

CONCEPT – *TWO DIRECTIONS*

Every trip by waitstaff or bussers to and from dining areas should be productive. Hands should not be empty on a return trip. Waste no motion, so that service can be more complete.

CONCEPT – *AUCTIONEERING*

This is the practice of bringing an order to the table and asking who gets what, such as, "Who gets the Teriyaki?" A normal procedure for listing individual orders on any given ticket should be agreed upon by both wait staff and cooks. An example is: always start with the northern most seat and go clockwise. This does not mean that individual orders cannot be taken in any sequence; it just means that space must be made on the guest order so they can be listed in the sequence according to the accepted rule. With the rule, any server other than the order-taker can still deliver the order without auctioneering. Ladies orders can still be taken first with the correct plate delivered to each guest.

CONCEPT – *THE WORK TRIANGLE*

The work triangle describes the efficient layout of workspace in terms of a floor layout. More correctly it should include the vertical, for a three-dimensional workspace. The triangle applies primarily to work stations such as food prep or service bars, but has elements that apply to all workstations. Simply put, the triangle should be designed and set-up so that the physical inputs, for any task, that are used most often are placed closest at hand. The intent is to reduce the distance that the hands and feet have to travel to complete the value chain. (The Work Triangle is illustrated in more detail in Section Two).

Teaching the work triangle concept begins to form a way of thinking about efficient workflows that will increase service and decrease costs. The work triangle concept should become ingrained into thinking about tasks and set-up, to become part of your culture.

CROSS TRAINING

Staff is all part of a team. Teach staffers to handle other positions within that team framework. During training, show everyone on the floor everyone else's job. The supply chain becomes clear, as they understand the flow towards the guest. Cross training sets employees up for growth and long-term success as they see expanded horizons.

One powerful reason for cross training is the staff no-show. One of a manager's greatest nightmares is to have a key person miss the scheduled shift. Often the manager will have to abandon the planned agenda to roll up sleeves and jump onto the breech. Imagine customers building up at your door with no head cook on-hand.

One of the best insurance policies for no-show is to have staff cross-trained to handle several functions within the operation. Keep, and hand out, an updated phone list of all staff with X's in the columns for the various jobs for which each is qualified. Make sure your staff knows that no-show is very serious. If they don't feel like working the scheduled shift for any reason, including sickness, that should be fine. Be flexible and accommodating. Just make sure that they don't call you or surprise you. They can refer to your list and get someone who will gladly agree to cover.

Each person's self-worth rises as their utility value rises, and they gain capability to pick-up and fill-in when other team members are overloaded or otherwise unable to cover their shift. Team cohesiveness advances.

TRAINING – Section 4

SAFETY – HEALTH – HARASSMENT

Awareness of these subjects must become part of your culture. They will already be in your employee manual, but may need reinforcement in training sessions when lapses are noticed. The kitchen area deserves special attention for training regarding cuts, burns, slips and falls, fire suppression, and proper equipment use. This training is most effective with a walk-though of the areas where accidents happen. (See Section Five – Operations, for more detail)

One case of foodborne illness can destroy the whole operation. Go to the USDA website for HACCP to get their wonderful training manuals and print out reference guidelines for kitchen staff.

WHERE

We teach management skills in classroom settings, but managers practice their skills while they are dealing with the chaos and pressures of managing a shift. Trainees in the classroom have no responsibility and no surprises. Servers and managers have crushing responsibilities and must constantly react to surprises. Training, that does not use the context of real environments, can generate a glowing report about trainees who later turn out to be incompetent managers or servers.

Primary training of kitchen staff functions will use the facilities and equipment that are to be directly employed in their job. Roll up your sleeves and demonstrate.

On-the-job interactive learning provides for a richer and more easily retained learning experience. Demonstrations are clearer and more realistic when live props are close at hand.

WHEN

Mentoring should never cease. Learning must be:
- Often
- Continuous
    - Left alone, all systems degrade through entropy towards chaos.
    - Inevitable change requires flexible and quick response.
- Following shifts
- Before shifts, if staggered shifts allow
- Following 'train wrecks"

Use your program to lead regularly scheduled discussion sessions. Any manager in an organization can moderate the discussions. Waitstaff post-mortems should follow the end of any shift where a problem arose. Any person most affected can lead the session. Timing can also be spontaneous when time allows. Training can occur in brief sessions before, during, and after shifts. Timeliness ensures relevance, context, and guides quick remedies.

One opportunity for learning is the pre-shift muster. You can limit the group to a job sub-function, such as bussers or kitchen functions. Plan these sessions to cover a limited topic or area of opportunity for improvement. Also limit the time to a planned 5 or 10 minutes. Start with the big picture and common goals for service, but leave plenty of time for discussion and mutual agreement on changes in behavior or actions to implement. Encourage input from all in attendance. The session mood can be kept light, with interjection of humor. Do, however, get serious personal assurance that each member of the group sees and agrees to the value of the proposed improvements. Task clarity is essential. Provide a challenge. Such sessions will communicate the importance you hold for your co-workers, and of the value you place on the subject. Re-enforce the common values, and commitment and loyalty will follow.

Another good opportunity for teaching is during the shift. Live exposure gives an infinite variety of server-guest interaction scenarios throughout the shift. Do not, however, disrupt service to customers, or denigrate staff in front of others. A good option is to roll-up sleeves and help employees see the better methods for procedures by example. For instance, managers can prompt staff with suggestive selling. Note; always compliment servers on their successes, no matter how small.

Your coaching tactics should adapt to each situation and server, just as you adjust to the strengths and weaknesses of service throughout the shift. The laws of entropy show repeatedly that: left alone, employees tend to acquire habits that are not in the restaurant's best interest. For instance, if everyone comes five minutes late, that will become a new baseline for routinely being ten minutes late, thereby getting a shift off to a ragged start where recovery to smoothness is difficult. Another example is where bussers were taught to bus a table with efficient procedures in 30 seconds and the procedures gets sloppy to take 60 seconds. Manager might be surprised to see even the most experienced staff deviate from proven efficient modes of service. Managers need to objectively measure performance regularly and encourage good work habits. Performance metrics help keep critical tasks on path. Coach your team at every opportunity.

CONTINUOUS IMPROVEMENT

Change is constant. Restaurants typically react to change by going through growth cycles. Your job is to ensure that you are always on the upslope of the cycle. Constant reaction to change requires continuous improvement, and continuous review of your environments both internal and external.

SWOT analysis reveals your changing environments. The overall evaluation of your Strengths, Weaknesses, Opportunities and Threats is called SWOT analysis. You will have evolving strengths and weaknesses that develop in your internal environment that require constant adjustment. Internally, your strategy, structure, and systems must evolve. Your personnel will also change. All change dictates new and continuous training. You always will have to innovate and upgrade as a competitive weapon.

Externally, your environments also change, offering new opportunities and new threats. Your demographics will change, your competition will change, and your traffic flows may change. All of this change means that you are never done with learning, even after formal training sessions. All initial training must be supplemented by follow-up programs to maintain high performance standards.

Use the SWOT analysis to review your vision for the growth of your operation. Compare the changes to your specific vision. Make sure your people see the same vision with the same perspective. Usually it will become clear where you must apply new knowledge to meet the changing environments. Note that SWOT analysis is a healthy exercise that can be done quickly and easily with requests for analysis from your current personnel.

After analysis, determine what you want your staff to accomplish, and what behavior modification is required. Restructure any changed needs and put a new learning plan in writing. Circulate and discuss the new plan, and modify it with input from your staff. With consensus, put together the mix of tools and prepare a continuing agenda. Build upon each segment to get a program that matches the values agreed upon by your staff. Put the continuous teaching in place. Monitor it. Re-enforce it. Live it as an example for all to follow.

As your staff masters new knowledge and skills, measure their knowledge and execution. Then start over. Each time you build it, make it even better by adjusting to new change. There is no finish line when it comes to the skills and knowledge of both your staff and yourself. Make continuous improvement part of your job. Make expectation of change and growth part of your culture. Be a mentor. Use job situations as training opportunities daily. Your people will respond positively to the challenge. Your people must see your commitment and daily follow-up. Otherwise, training is likely to slide off with time.

If you stop growing as an organization you quickly slip into a down cycle that is often irreversible. On-going learning is mandatory commitment, and a competitive weapon.

TOOLS

Job descriptions, a personnel manual, and checklists provide a baseline blueprint for the learning syllabus. Understanding a job starts with a clear definition of functions and methods for each job. Make sure these tools are kept for easy access by all personnel.

JOB DESCRIPTIONS

> Note: many States or Counties require an education plan before hiring high-school age persons who can be such an asset to restaurant operations, especially back-of-the house functions. Written procedures and job descriptions can go far to fulfill this requirement.

The job description is an essential tool that many try to by-pass. Clear written procedures minimize the difference between people and efficient production. The differences are always produced by people. People ignore, confuse, resist, modify, misunderstand, and avoid proven standards, often turning the task into their own version of methods. Entropy means that all systems run downhill as time passes. Laziness continually tries to set a new lower baseline. If management accepts a lower baseline, entropy will continue downward from this new point. In order for the manager to keep control and to be: fair, firm, forceful, consistent, compassionate, honest, and flexible, there must be a written baseline.

Write job descriptions for all functions containing elements of the following.

- You should have a clear statement of the organization's mission or philosophy.
- Have a checklist of essential steps condensed to one page.
- Break down all of the essential steps of the job with the proper procedures.
- Relate each step to how it affects the total team effort and eventually meets the customer's eye.
- Include standards for time to complete tasks.
- Include specifications for quality.

Note that a job description is never a substitute for proper staff teaching, but they do supply several healthy values. A main value comes from the development process itself. Development of descriptions forces careful consideration of the full scope of the job and the essential details. Even better, invitation for staff input brings different perspective to the description, and gives ready acceptance and powerful credence. Staff input can improve the description, since there is always-always a better way. Another value is that it provides a guiding baseline for training. The baseline descriptions, however, should never be static; rather they evolve with the ever-changing environment. A third value is: as a tool to get a seriously derailed staff person back on track. This does not mean the deviations from the description are necessarily bad. A final use of the job description is as a tool that we hope to use very rarely: it serves to document why a failed employee should not continue as part of your organization.

Delegate the review and re-write job of descriptions periodically as a healthy exercise. Define each position as it fits into the structure of your organization. Properly constructed, the descriptions show how each function creates value as part of the whole supply chain to the final customer. Describe job positions not only in terms of requisite activities, but also in terms of results. Defining results allow people to see the jobs in perspective. Good job descriptions help each employee feel productive and a contributor to the team, the organization, and in the community.

PERSONNEL MANUAL

A written policy handbook contains standards for consistent application. The handbook will serve several functions. (1) It will keep staff informed and answer frequently asked questions that affect standard procedures, and affect morale. (2) It gives supervisors the support they need to enforce policy and, (3) minimizes legal contingencies including the rare need for employee termination. The manual need not be lengthy, but must be carefully crafted since the policies contained can be legally binding. Consult with your lawyer if you have any doubts.

Note that delivering a copy of the manual is not a substitute for proper training. Manuals are important, but again should not be a primary training tool. The age of "read this manual" is over. People are now most successful when someone takes an interest in them personally, and is on their side in terms of learning.

Following are some items that should be covered in a personnel manual.
- State your company mission or philosophy.
- Equal opportunity statement. State that race, religion, age, gender, or color will have nothing to do with hiring, promotion, pay, or benefits.
- Probationary period. Define period, 30, 60, 90 days when a new employee can be dismissed outright. Also state when any specific benefits commence.
- Proof of citizenship
- Drug policy. Drug use is grounds for immediate dismissal.
- Theft. Immediate dismissal.
- Parking lot rules
- Cell phone policy. Limit personal calls as to frequency and duration
- First Aid policy for cuts and burns and location of aid and information.
- Drills for fire in each area of the building and locations of extinguishers.
- Employee tabs and loan policy
- Covering scheduled shifts, and scheduling policy
- Dress code and cleanliness requirements
- Job descriptions may be kept in a separate manual
- Work hours. Define breaks. Provide the option of rescheduling individual hours in any week at the discretion of the floor manager. Persons can be asked to clock out if a period is slack.
- Meals policy. Say when meals can be taken and amount of subsidy.
- Time and attendance clock-in procedures. Cover signing in for others, clock-in/out too early or late, dunning for lateness.
- Pay computation rules. Set pay period and when checks arrive.
- Performance review and merit increases. Set automatic review periods and procedures.
- Housekeeping policy. Have lists of general cleaning that will be performed at the discretion of the floor manager during slower periods.
- Suggestion system. Avoid a formal system but reinforce the thought that "there is always a better way" and that management supports and rewards ideas to improve productivity.
- Complaints and grievances. Encourage staff to discuss problems first with their immediate supervisor.
- Leave of absence. Set rules for advance notice and the number of weeks that they may not exceed.
- Rehiring former employees. You will want to regain excellent staff who left under good terms for good reasons with adequate notice.
- Company parties, outings, and sports teams.
- Benefits such as group insurance.

"The manual does not have to be devoid of entertainment value. Eye appeal precedes mind appeal. Manuals can by interesting and reflective of the "fun place" you're promising they'll work in." Use color and graphics with your layout.

RESTAURANT HANDBOOK – TOOLS & RULES

CHECKLISTS

Checklists are vital tools. Lists help ensure no important job step is overlooked. Ask any pilot. Checklists are especially useful for kitchen staff where performance of elements is required in serial fashion. A good place for posting laminated checklist is on the back of doors, front of appliances, doors of walk-ins, and near complex or dangerous equipment requiring precise execution.

For front-of-house, staff checklists are important for initial set-up of stations such as bar service or waiter-stations for smooth starts. Checklists have less value for jobs with customer interactions. For instance, a list of things to do and not to do when serving customers may appear to keep things clear and simple, however, it may stifle initiative, and will not necessarily account for the employee's questions, enthusiasm, initiative, ideas and flexibility to complex customer interaction.

JOB FUNCTIONS – FRONT

MANAGERS

Floor managers must learn to stay out of the back during peak periods. All of the backroom should be perfectly trained to run on autopilot. Backroom job functions become off-line functions at peak customer periods. It is too late to be dealing with numbers or paper. Floor managers will need to move constantly to work the whole floor. They need to rove to expedite bottlenecks, aid servers who have temporarily gotten "in-the weeds", and to interact with customers. They will touch base with as many tables as possible, and not just chatting with regulars. Managers will keep their eyes, feet and hands in constant motion.

Managers should learn to show an authentic interest in customers, and do whatever is necessary to keep them pleased. "High tech will never replace high touch". Schmoozing pays.

FRONT DESK

The first impression the guest will likely get, as they enter your door, is a prompt friendly smile and warm reception from your front door staff. This impression should set the tone for all that follows. This initial impression must be great. Select host/hostess people very carefully for ability for this first impression. Note: "Front desk" might be a poor label, because this staff probably should be moving at all times.

A problem is: that this key job-function is frequently overlooked in training programs for servers, as to how they critically must smoothly integrate.

Another potential problem is: that we tend to place young servers in the front desk position just because they are not legally old enough to serve alcoholic beverages in full service.

Restaurants often hire part-time employees for some of the toughest positions, including the host/hostess position. The danger then becomes that you might have a less mature decision maker in this critical job. Must you pass up an excellent prospective employee who has great potential but needs development to handle the front desk with maturity? The answer is: retain them; the potential problems can be overcome through a proper development program.

The front desk personnel often face abuse from impatient guests, including some with a few ingested beverages. The staff must learn to never get irritated no matter how nasty an impatient customer may be on a lengthy waiting list.

They must learn to never argue with a customer. Teach them that they have the support of management. If customers are particularly abusive at any point or an employee can't handle a situation, the employee should call a manager. The primary focus is to let the customer know you are aware of their concerns. Make eye contact often, and keep them apprised verbally when possible. A good policy is to let them know where they stand, and the current best estimate of wait time for the party. The host can go further and share how they expect the tables will be breaking that might affect that wait time. Keep the wait list transparent.

This position requires a special type of person who must be carefully selected and carefully groomed. Properly taught and supported, they can be eager and quick to learn, and take pride in their success. The unceasing smile is large asset to the rest of the team. Remember, they set the first impression.

WAITSTAFF

Servers are the face of the whole team. They represent the owner and everyone in the house, from the back of the kitchen to the front dining room. Every server action is noticed by your customer, and builds the total experience and perception of value.

There are two sides to wait-staff service. (1) Technical procedures use standards for timely and efficient delivery of the product/service. (2) The personal side requires: attitudes, skills and behaviors in customer interaction.

Technical skills include these.
- Speed
- Consistency and uniformity
- Ability to plan and organize
- Understanding of efficient work- flows

The personal skills are essential
- Smile
- Friendly and personable
- Tactful
- Interested in customer
- Ability to read customers

Train staff to move fast, but stay focused on the customer. Reinforce often that we greet customers with a smile, say thank you, and ask how else they can be served. Personal skills include reading the customer to identify their desired level of service, and to pre-answer their questions.

BUSSERS

Bussers are involved both in the front and back of the house. They are a liaison that keeps both ends apprised and working smoothly together. They will always need to work closely with the host/hostess function. Anticipation of tables ready to break will allow them to be on hand instantly. In all of their work they need to keep eye contact with the hostess. Always stress the need for smooth-with-speed. They can aid servers with delivery of non-entrée items such as water glasses filled, coffee refills, or condiments.

Managers are often surprised to learn that some of the most experienced employees do not follow the proper service standards, and that includes bussers. When bussers are not closely monitored, they tend to acquire habits not in the restaurant's best interest. They usually improve their performance when they are coached, or when necessary, retrained.

Managers need to monitor performance regularly and to encourage the formation of good work habits that last until well after the training period is over. Performance tests help the managers monitor execution of critical tasks. Practice timing good bussing procedures with a stopwatch, and let them take pride in their efficiency. They usually are eager to please the server staff.

LEARNING

We train to (1) build knowledge, skill-sets and efficiency, and (2) to build sense of self-worth that comes from doing jobs well. Enjoyable work enhances self-esteem that manifests itself to the positive total customer experience. Note self-esteem cannot be granted, but must be earned with accomplishment. You create the environment.

Education research says that learning is similar to strength-training where short-run trauma produces the greatest lasting improvement. Therefore, training can employ unusual, unexpected or dramatic methods for lasting learning impressions.

> Every few months, I would walk into a kitchen and upend the dish-wash trashcan in the middle of the floor. On every instance we would find items – usually silverware – that was inadvertently discarded during the speed of operations. This drama always reduced – for a time - the cost of lost utensils. Note: this was always done at slower operations periods and without recriminations, since the evidence always spoke for itself. Also the spill was near the central-drain so that I could easily clean-up, since I was the mess creator.

SUMMARY

All restaurants need competitive advantage to prosper and even survive. The numbers show that great staff is your most powerful competitive weapon. They are the clearest, shortest and surest path to a competitive edge. Excellent staff is a clear way to differentiate. Excellence comes from a total package of superior knowledge and skill-sets of your team. People, then, are your greatest capital asset. This asset must be viewed and treated just as all of your precious capital. People must be a constantly appreciating asset. They must be nurtured.

Your job is to create a culture of excellence through continuous learning. Efficient learning requires a serious and dedicated investment of time and attention to on-going development of your staff. Return on this investment is very high. ROI is easy to measure in terms of both customer satisfaction and employee satisfaction. Increased revenues and lower direct labor costs ensure that your payback-period for this mandatory investment in people-appreciation is short and sure. Do not skimp on the budget for continued development of your staff, you cannot afford it. Evidence is clear that restaurant organizations that invest more in training have higher profit margins.

A restaurant manager is a facilitator, not a boss who issues orders. The manager is a co-worker and team member, whose major function is to put the right-people in the right-place with the right-tools in hand. When this function is performed properly, the staff is more likely to issue orders to you. You will have more net time, though, to direct your scarce time and attention properly towards your guests and not to brush-fires within your operations.

A mentor keeps working with all staff even after the learning sessions are over. They reinforce lessons through interaction and repetition. Learning must be continuous. What we want to teach is less important than how to help people learn. Mentors and facilitators accept mistakes as a powerful learning tool. At the end, what is important is what they can do, not on what they know.

Have a plan. First schedule time and attention to the details of your development program. Use the bulleted points above as a checklist to ensure that your agenda is both complete and effective. Always start learning sessions with the big picture. Give each new behavior a context relative to your mutual mission and goals. Learners need to see how each person and process works together to form the whole. The syllabus mix will include learning tools available with exiting new communications technology. Technology, however, plays a supporting role to human interaction.

Your commitment to development keeps your priceless human assets fresh and energized. You will see significantly better margins and higher market share. Your satisfied employees will help recruit their friends. Loyal employees will become loyal marketers, loyal customers, and grateful friends, even as they move on to new careers. Further, the better you teach your staff the better your own job security.

When people clearly know their jobs and have the knowledge and skills to perform, they are happiest and most productive. Management can get out of their way and let them roll.

Finally, never-ever forget the overriding need for human dignity in all learning.

RESTAURANT HANDBOOK – TOOLS & RULES

RESTAURANT HANDBOOK

TOOLS & RULES

Roderick A. Clelland

FUNDAMENTALS OF RESTAURANT MANAGEMENT

PRINT SECTION FIVE

OPERATIONS - CONTROL

RESTAURANT HANDBOOK – TOOLS & RULES

TABLE OF CONTENTS – Section Five

CONTROL – OPERATIONS

    ACCOUNTING FOR DAILY OPERATIONS   5- 2
    POINT OF SALE CONTROLS   5- 3

PRIME COSTS
  COST OF GOODS SOLD   5- 6
    PURCHASING   5- 6
      NEGOTIATING WITH SUPPLIERS   5- 6
    INVENTORY CONTROL – SUPPLY CHAIN   5- 7
      INVENTORY LEVEL MAINTENANCE   5- 8
    THEFT CONTROL   5- 9
    BAR CONTROL   5- 12
  LABOR COST CONTROL – PRODUCTIVITY   5- 13
    LABOR COST PERCENTAGE   5- 13
  COST ANALYSIS   5- 18
  BREAKEVEN   5- 18

OVERHEAD CONTROL
  FACILITIES COST   5- 19
  DEALING WITH GOVERNMENT REGULATORS   5- 21

OPERATIONS
  OPERATIONS MANAGEMENT   5- 22
    FOOD HANDLING   5- 24
      WALK-IN MANAGEMENT   5- 25
    RED MEAT   5- 25
    DAIRY   5- 26
    BEVERAGES   5- 26

FACILITY MANAGEMENT
  EQUIPMENT   5- 29
    MAINTENANCE   5- 30
    INDIVIDUAL EQUIPMENT   5- 31
    KNIVES   5- 30

HEALTH / SANITATION / CLEANLINESS
  FOOD ILLNESS   5- 33
  PEST CONTROL   5- 35
  FIRE SAFETY   5- 36
  FIRST AID – CUTS – BURNS – SLIPS   5- 35
  DISH WASH / CHINA POLICY   5- 37
  JANITORIAL   5- 37
  CHECKLISTS   5- 37

RESERVATIONS   5- 39

SUMMARY
  Glossary Section 5
  Appendix Section 5

CONTROL

Entropy and human nature continually prove the critical need for controls throughout operations. Without timely and effective control, costs always escalate and quality slips quickly. The quandary this produces is: control is essential but it is not always your highest focus. Primary attention must be given to your customers and to your staff who administer to your customers. Controls then must be designed to be thorough, but also as automatic as possible so as to free management time. We certainly do not want to spend more time and dollars on controls when the potential for dollars savings is less than the cost of control. Also control should never reduce the quality and quantity of both your service and product delivered to the eye of the customer.

Control uses the various tools of *value chain analysis* (VCA). Value analysis is the systematic activity and discovery to reduce costs and improve the performance of products and services. VCA views all activities that transform inputs to outputs, and isolates each link in that chain for improvement of value as seen by your guest. Customer value derives from three basic sources: (1) activities that both differentiate product and delivery, (2) activities that lower expense, and (3) activities that meet guest's need with speed and conspicuous efficiency.

The VCA framework has several primary activities:
- Inbound logistics include costs of obtaining inputs such as vendor relations, purchasing, receiving, storing, inspection, inventory management, and delivery of product to processes.
- Operations are all activities that convert inputs and create value. Operations include: production line efficiency, facilities management, equipment maintenance, quality assurance, and compliance with regulators.
- Outbound logistics are costs of delivering value including labor productivity.
- Marketing and sales activities advance positioning and promote differentiation.
- Services support all other activities.
- General Administration includes costs of activities of accounting, finance, legal, safety, security, information systems, and control of overhead.
- Human relations costs include recruitment, hiring, training, motivating, compensating and retaining great people.

VCA follows these steps:
- Break down the value chain to each individual link.
- Look at costs and how the activity adds to meaningful value.
- Identify activities that differentiate and add value.
- Identify activities that successfully advance the mission, and those that create drag.

VCA, then, uses examination of the materials, processes, information systems, and material flows for all of the restaurant's output. Improved productivity means better delivery of value at lowest cost for both profits and customers satisfaction. Value analysis must be a continuous part of management attention. Many *tools and rules* will guide effective control. All tools for value analysis and control require accurate and timely information from efficient data capture.

INFORMATION SYSTEMS

Information technology (IT) continues to accelerate according to Moore's Law. The high productivity from IT lowers our labor costs and allows greater focus on our customer. Control becomes more automatic. Information Systems supply:
- Timely and accurate information about sales, operations, cash flows, and suppliers.
- Relevant information for tactical decisions
- Information to manage quality issues and customer service
- Sophisticated and automatic statistical controls
- Linkages to suppliers and customers for direct supply chain control
- Efficient accounting and spreadsheets for analysis and reporting

ACCOUNTING FOR DAILY OPERATIONS

Restaurant operations call for daily decisions and strong actions that are informed by relevant data. Managers must have a basic understanding of accounting 101. (Note: if your accounting 101 is rusty – order a used book on-line.) Some studies suggest that restaurant failure is most often attributable to poor understanding of financial matters. When managers bypass grounding in basic business practices, it is prudent to study up. Restaurant accounting involves more than one kind of accounting.

Cost accounting is important for daily decisions. You must be aware of how daily operations promote long-term health. Managers need street smarts about industry standards, which give understanding on how your operation compares with the successful, and unsuccessful, of similar type. Awareness of benchmarks gives you a critical edge. Control of your profits means understanding your cost categories, and a good starting point is with industry standards. Industry benchmarks include such numbers as prime costs, average check, employee productivity, and daily seat turnover. Published standards are available from sources including the National Restaurant association. Cost accounting guides your tactical operating decisions.

Cost accounting includes awareness of *marginal contribution* of each menu item that so strongly affects survivability. (See Section Two – Menu).

Accounting for reports on financial health primarily includes the statements of: profit and loss (income statement – P&L), the balance sheet, and cash flow statements. Financial reports guide strategic decisions. Note: these are historical reports.

Accounting to government is always necessary for the many and varied taxes due to Municipal, State and Federal agencies. These include payroll, sales, and income taxes, among others. The various levels of government require accounting to bureaucrats.

Note that accounting that is available from a CPA firm primarily deals with historical data. You as a restaurant manager do not have time to wait for historical data for compelling daily decisions for strong action. Rather, you need daily feedback. Fortunately such feedback is ever more available automatically with proper set-up of information systems.

ACCOUNTING METHODS

Use the *uniform system of accounts* for restaurants to set up your P&L and balance sheet accounts. The uniform system provides a common language with classification criteria for all income, expense, asset, liability and equity transactions in typical financial statements. You will have to select the accounts that best fit your unique type of operation. Accounts will follow generally accepted accounting guidelines (GAAP) for consistent ways to integrate, view, and compare your numbers apples to apples. Set-up using spreadsheets so that you can watch percentage changes for each account. Spreadsheet software allows many built in functions for instant analysis of the numbers. There is a learning curve for full spreadsheet utility, but once mastered, you will never be able to understand how you got along without such tools for analysis to drive powerful decisions. Spreadsheets allow very timely information with short interval reporting.

This caveat always bears repetition. Accounting for the numbers is always important, but it is an off-line job. Never let it interfere with your attention to people.

POINT OF SALE CONTROLS

Sales data added to your database drives informed tactical decisions. POS systems however can be expensive both in initial purchase price but also in maintenance. Equipment maintenance costs, which are typically 10% of equipment purchase price, go up towards 20% for POS equipment. For example, two complete proprietary POS cash registers with remote printers can cost $40,000 with a yearly preventative maintenance agreement (PMA) of $8,000. Training and the complexity of the learning curve add to costs. Then we have supplies: ink cartridges/ribbons, tapes, binders, back-up systems, power surge protectors or automatic power supply - often the terminal must be on its own power circuit-, antistatic mats, and computer storage. Proprietary hardware obsolesces. Also there must be a quick manual backup for sudden downtime - as when personnel dump cola on the keyboard. So we see that the expensive tool will not pay for itself unless the information it provides is fully used for control.

There is a trend to provide all of the POS system controls with computer-based equipment with software, rather than proprietary and legacy type hardware. This reduces equipment and maintenance costs while insuring ease of upgrade. This includes excellent voice applications that allow hands free control, and remote access.

PURPOSES FOR POINT OF SALE CONTROLS

- Control cash
- Ensure that all sales are recorded to build database for analysis for profits
- Speed service by easing guest check handling
- Compute sales tax correctly
- Avoid customer errors
  - Manual check handling produces a percent of errors in the low double digits
  - Electronic data entry produces errors in the range of 4.5 to 7 %.
  - The largest source of errors is incorrect listing of items.
  - Most errors are items delivered that fail to make it to the guest check.
  - Omitted items are most often those ordered after the meal like drinks and dessert.
  - The wine order is often missed when one server takes the order and another serves.
  - 90 % of guests overcharged complain. 40% of those undercharged speak up.

RESTAURANT HANDBOOK – TOOLS & RULES

Purposes for POS continued:
- Identify voided items
- Minimize walk-outs
- Identify sales by menu Item
  - Required for menu mix engineering (See Section Two - Menu)
  - Learn what customers are buying for adjustment to raise volume
  - Eliminate menu dogs
  - Add exciting items
- Get average check (period sales divided by customer counts)
- Raise revenue by engineering raised average check
- Identify sales by server
  - Allows reward incentives
  - Informs better staff hourly scheduling
- Record discounted sales, necessary for cost control
  - Employee meals
  - Manager meals
  - Coupons (if any)
  - Promotion items
- Identify sales by time period
  - Get seat turnover (table turn, guest turnover, utilization of facilities)
  - Better match of staff levels to historical expected volume
- Tip sharing allocation computations
- Waitstaff trips to kitchen avoided
- Control labor costs
- Informed staff weekly schedules
- Get net sales per employee hour (average level of productivity)
- Remove temptation burden from staff
- Tie to purchasing in order to control inventory

Note that the primary function of the POS system should be to *speed efficient guest check delivery*. Some systems, without good design, actually slow guest check delivery.

POINT OF SALE EQUIPMENT
- Obtain quality equipment. Look for: Speedy - Simple - Sturdy - Service
- Position register so that customer and cashier can see display
- Pre check to kitchen before any meals/beverages issued
- The cash register must hold accumulative sales records
- Have pre-sets for menu items

SOFTWARE
Options include many new applications such as:
- Menu analysis
- Employee time tracking and shift scheduling.
- Inventory control
- Automated seating management

CASHIER INSTRUCTIONS

- All sales must be rung
- Cash drawer to remain closed unless sale rung
- Circle and initial over-rings on the tape with explanation at time of error
- Personal bags, purses, cosmetic bags away from register station
- Verify starting cash drawer at beginning
- Ring up each item rather than batch totals
- Inform management quickly of equipment problems
- Backup supplies handy
- Service phone number on equipment for quick response

Remember that this is an on-line task when guests are waiting for the check resolution. Registering checks is an off-line job if the customer has already left and other guests are waiting for attention. Set the check package aside for serial batch processing for when no guests are waiting.

MANAGEMENT RESPONSIBILITIES

- The manager should observe periodically how sales are transacted.
    - Customer treatment
    - SOP compliance
- Conduct spot audits on occasion, and often if problem is indicated
- Manager should keep keys – passwords - to ring out totals and produce transaction tapes. This function should be separate from the bookkeeper
- Ring totals and issue new bank at end of each shift
- Deposit no later than next day
- Issue guest checks with batch consecutive number logged
- Review daily operating report for consecutive totals
- Match guest check kitchen copies to hard copies on a regular basis
- Use spotters if numbers indicate a problem area
- Manger should not keep the daily deposit in personal possession over nights or weekends

Note that POS can reside on generic small computers with software that can provide much power and flexibility. Off-shelf remote components are enabled with wireless technology such as Bluetooth. Remote components can be flat screens in food production areas, remote slip printers, remote cash drawers, and voice applications. These systems allow for quicker service to customers while your labor costs lower as staff avoids walking to deliver paper.

RESTAURANT HANDBOOK – TOOLS & RULES

PRIME COSTS

Prime costs are your costs of production of goods and services. The two components are your two largest cost categories: (1) direct cost of goods sold (COGS), and (2) direct labor costs. Since these direct cost categories are largest, they are the most fruitful targets for control to ensure profit maximization. Prime costs generally range in the low 60's as a percentage of total sales. If this number approaches 65%, you must act to lower to avoid danger. When prime costs are out of control, survivability is doubtful. Fortunately, we have many tools and rules at hand for cost-volume-profit analysis.

COST OF GOOD SOLD

COGS must be managed at a target percentage of sales. You will hear of a 1/3 rule, but that cannot work for many venues. This percentage is necessarily high for steakhouse operations - approaching 50% - and low for items that are pasta based, or rice heavy menus. Pizza and some ethnic food menus can have a COGS target in the high teens.

COGS control involves the whole value chain, from procurement of inputs to the final delivery of product to the guest.

PURCHASING

PROCUREMENT GUIDELINES

Dependable relationships with your suppliers are essential to long-term health and growth. Supplier benefits can include: financial support, timely and reliable service, consistent quality materials and complete supplies. Your supplier representative informs you of products and quality. Occasionally the rep might even have to bring a quick emergency delivery, possibly in a personal vehicle. Supplier relationships involve:
- Quality products
- Breadth and depth of choice (One truck, one check)
- Pricing and discounts
- Delivery accommodation or flexibility
- Reputation of abilities and services

NEGOTIATING WITH SUPPLIERS

Single restaurant units do not have great leverage with suppliers. You have even less at start-up, since you have no history of sales volumes and reliable behavior. Further, the industry record with failure limits the amount of credit that can prudently be extended. Still reputable suppliers will work with you to help you succeed.

Approach suppliers with the same business plan material that worked for your finance sources.

You will not need to limit your options with a sole-source, but also do not jump between competing suppliers based on temporary price advantages. Suppliers need to rely on reasonably stable volumes of items that may be unique to your menu and operation. Both you and the supplier are best served as you move closer to just-in-time inventory levels.

ELECTRONIC PURCHASING

Electronic data interchange (EDI) is remote computer-to-computer exchange now available from most large restaurant suppliers. The supplier often provides the free client software to allow standard procedures for product and price search with an electronic catalogue. Software allows direct ordering and purchase orders, invoices, and payment methods. Direct ordering bypasses phone calls, mailed documents, and some sales-rep face time. Most suppliers can integrate with your inventory procedures to supply several advantages.

- Product availability is evident
- Ordering time is speeded.
- Electronic ordering lowers the supplier's clerical processing costs and reduces errors. Savings can be passed on to buyers.
- Transactions go to a database for better analysis opportunity.
- Clerical document processing costs reduce for the buyer.

The Internet as a tool will continue to evolve as your purchasing becomes increasingly automatic to free your attention to people rather than things.

INVENTORY CONTROL – SUPPLY CHAIN MANAGEMENT

- Match inventory of key items to sales on a daily basis (20% of stock is 80% of total value)
- Deliveries should be checked against the invoice with counts and weights
- Organize storage for natural flow when taking inventory. Label shelving.
- Keep good records of spoilage and "Bad meal Report"
- Personnel should leave by front doors.
- Some storage of high value items should have limited access.
- Check trashcans and dumpsters on a spot basis

TAKING INVENTORY

- Use software or pre-printed form that matches the physical organization of how items are stored
- Major items can be inventoried more often and others estimated
- More frequent inventories give these benefits:
  - Theft and waste are better controlled
  - Storage area stay better organized
  - Items are more easily found
  - Hidden waste and spoilage are eliminated
- Purchasing is easier and more automatic
- You become quicker and more efficient with frequency

Make sure you relate COGS to sales on a regular basis for timely control.

Note: RFID, radio frequency identification tags, are becoming rapidly ubiquitous, as well as barcode. Couple these tools with handheld wireless input, including voice, to gain endless options for quick and accurate inventory measurement.

INVENTORY LEVEL MAINTENANCE

Ideally inventory control calls for "just-in-time" delivery upon "Stock-out". Efficient restaurant inventory is slightly different than general business, because stock-outs that affect the customer's perception of your menu can be intolerable. Remember a menu is your half of a contract that implies "we have it, and it is good".

Therefore we want to: (1) Keep the minimum on hand, while (2) Avoiding stock-outs, and (3) keeping deliveries restricted in number and to best time of day.

There are several reasons to keep the *minimum on hand*:
- Dollars tied up in the pipeline cannot be employed elsewhere.
- Square footage in the building should go to customer space not storage.
- Shelving can be reduced.
- Handling and rotation are reduced.
- Inventory counting is reduced and more accurate.
- Product is fresher and out-of-date - spoilage is eliminated. Line cooks will not reach past day-olds.
- Pilferage is controlled.
- Better awareness of raw inventory improves production yields. Portioning will be more exact.
- Purchasing specs will be tighter.
- Comparative pricing with vendors can be more competitive.
- Food costs will go down.

Avoiding Stock-outs is a special case for restaurants. Most inventory management allows for some stock-out because the item is not critical, or has a substitute, or can be gotten quickly from a close source. Obviously restaurant safety margins must be at higher levels. Guests should be able to rely on your menu, with the exception of daily special items that are limited quantities by implication. Note than many inventory items can be purchased in emergency from the 24-hour grocery store, but this is always a costly use of people assets. However, stock-outs can be even more costly in the long run.

Automatic Order Points must be established for each item so that as stocks reach a minimum level the order kicks in.

Par Stock is the level to which the item will be raised using the economic order quantity.

Economic Order Quantities should be based on efficient shipping & handling amounts, as well as; total purchase dollar amounts, possible discounts, and shelf life. This must raise stock to par or slightly above.

Just-in-Time Supply means that if you have a regular and reliable source of some items, the par can be lowered.

Mini-Max is control using Automatic order points with Pars.

Rotate all stock upon delivery. *Label* shelving space so the eye scans in an orderly fashion. *Locate* most often accessed supplies closest to area of need or use.

THEFT CONTROL

A Justice Department study found that about 1/3 of employees steal in one form or another. Some insurers believe that employee theft accounts for 1/3 of all business failures. You get no tax breaks or deductions for losses from pilferage. In fact you can be made to pay sales taxes on goods that were stolen, such as bar sales not rung. Younger single males are the largest group of offenders, partly since they apparently have less to risk in; wages, status, and seniority. A profile of internal thieves includes persons transient in their jobs and employed less than one year. Persons between the age of 16 and 22 commit over 2/3 of all theft. This unfortunately describes many employed in our business. Estimates are that theft eats up 4 % of every food sale, an amount well below the commerce departments' belief of 15% for general retail sales.

We do not mean to scare you here, just make you aware that theft is pervasive and a part of doing business. If you are aware, you can take many specific steps to avoid becoming a victim. Theft deterrence requires a systematic policy from first concept. You do not have to contribute to the hundreds of billions lost in theft annually.

The one best theft deterrent is to have a low-turnover staff with high morale who work together as a team and develop a family type peer structure. Persons in this family type atmosphere are motivated to be honest.

Vigilance and special attention to the risk with young-single-males calls in the question of profiling. To not discriminate reminds us of the classic cartoon: Looking for lost car keys down the block from where they were dropped, because "the light is better down here".

MANAGEMENT AND THEFT

The manager is the one person able to both (1) control employee theft and (2) steal the most. Management agents have the most opportunity and ways to be dishonest, with the least probability of early detection. Managers often work longer hours at lower pay than most of their staff. In fact, few may want the "promotion" away from high tips as a server.

I listened to one restaurant ex-manager brag about how prodigious and rewarding his theft efforts were over a long period of time, and how stupid the ownership interests were in not seeing the flagrancy.

The manager sets the example for all. If the manager; skims, creates an atmosphere where corners are cut, or follows lax control policy, then personnel will quickly catch on to the general culture created and join right in. The manager must:
- Keep on the move
- Compare inventories to sales daily. Look for percentage changes
- Limit the number of persons handling cash
- Make cash deposits daily
- Check personnel out of the door and require vacating the area directly

BOOKKEEPING AND THEFT

The bookkeeper has much temptation because of the amounts of cash handled and the isolated nature of the job function. Embezzlement, as we see often in the news, can be endemic. Do the following:
- Compartmentalize input to the bookkeeper. Staff can balance their own drawers to the managers' tapes.
- Review the historic and stable relationships of credit cards to cash.
- Balance deposits to daily sales.
- Use statistical controls to monitor standards and relationships.

VIGILANCE FOR THEFT

Most of dishonest employees will be of two types (1) Opportunists and (2) disgruntled.

Limit opportunity for theft. Most persons are honest, but opportunists lurk. You can easily envision the scenario where a basically honest person, for instance, is behind on rent. This person may take advantage of a glaring opportunity to steal with the intent of a one-time only occurrence. After that, of course, events slide down hill, and we have helped create a dishonest person. Therefore proper controls are for the benefit of the business, but also vital for the sanctity of each person's long term self-worth. The victims are both the theftee and the thief. The theftee has only lost something that can be replaced. The thief has started down the path to lost dignity that might never be replaced.

We try hard to avoid creating *disgruntled personnel*. Still, some people can feel that the business treats them unfairly, and further, owes them something in addition to their current wage or salary. Often they will take a wage they have not earned. The feeling of being exploited is apparently a prime cause beyond the cause of opportunity. Some employees just feel that they are smarter than management, and like the thrill of challenge. Also keep in mind that disgruntled ex-personnel initiate most business burglaries and robberies with adolescent friends. Proactive anti-theft steps include:
- Briefly mention theft as a firing offense in most meetings.
- Separate job responsibilities where dollars are involved for check and balance
- Look out for cliques that allow collusion in the face of job separation.
- Establish an easy path for whistleblowers.

A good friend and employee asked for a wage increase. I thought I argued against it using fair and reasonable logic. Later I discovered that the person's total apartment place-settings were the restaurant's unique china, silver and glassware.

SOCIAL CONTROL OF THEFT

Peer pressure appears to be the strongest factor in honesty and dishonesty. Policy should begin at hiring.
- Set good examples of integrity.
- Bring up subject of theft at hiring interview, and at staff meetings
- Show that national average profit is only about 3.5%, and that theft can erase profit and destroy all the jobs including teammates.
- List the benefits they already receive including uniforms and meals.

- Note that a dishonest employee is just as likely to steal from a co-worker's purse or wallet. If such instances occur, be diligent in investigation, since there is prima-fascia evidence that a person with that flawed mindset exists in your organization.
- Stress: honesty, integrity, and loyalty at the top of job descriptions, handbooks, and appraisals.
- During hiring personnel evaluations, question for cues as to the person's general level of job satisfaction.
- Treat staff as responsible. Praise performance as you correct deficiencies.
- Allow staff to make good wages. Refer to a starting wage rather than minimum wage to show opportunity for growth.
- Do not allow drug culture to infect staff. Make zero-tolerance clear.
- With clear proof of theft, make the termination highly visible.

PHYSICAL CONTROLS ON THEFT

There will be some who accept theft control as a challenge. However, there are pervasive systems of control available that can render theft problem nil. When systems are well put-together, there will still be persons who try to beat the system, but ultimately they will suffer detection, which will be a deterrent to others. Prudent steps are:

- Check with last employer or references before hiring.
- Keep product storage areas and safes locked.
- Change locks on a regular basis and limit access to keys.
- Put kitchen keys on a large ring (to loop over neck).
- Carefully monitor cash and product inventories.
- Give special attention to: meat, beer and wine (quickest source for underage), and all high cost items.
- Separate accounting to avoid collusion. Example: broiler staff can balance daily steak inventories.
- Check dumpster contents on occasion.
- Minimize clutter and foliage at rear of restaurant.
- Issue numbered guest checks.
- Examine voided checks carefully.
- Required accurate logging and order slips for customer adjustments.
- Conduct surprise audits and inventory on occasion.
- Avoid delivery at busy periods.
- Assign delivery reception as a function separate from ordering.
- Avoid if possible union contracts that make it hard to fire thieves and collusive delivery drivers.
- Be aware that plastic bags containing high cost items can be put inside clothing, personal packages and bags.
- Spotters are called for, if indirect evidence point to a given source of loss.
- Extreme measures are: surveillance cameras, security hardware and lie detectors.

Note: this is just a partial list. Collusion and contrivance can take creative forms. This list presents a bleak outlook, yet most people are honest. The best defense is always screening at hiring, treating staff with dignity as co-workers, and never putting temptation under anyone's nose.

INDIRECT RELATIONSHIP CONTROLS

Aside from daily reports on sales and inventories you will find that many apparently unrelated items have stable long-term relationships. Since the item counts can be captured as an automatic byproduct of other input, they can be quickly and easily analyzed for relationship change. An example would be the number of Strip Loin Steaks sold as a percentage of total menu items. You can establish, for instance, the 95% confidence level in simple correlations. You need not bother with this relationship unless your computer throws out a red flag that the confidence limits have been out-ridden. You can look for variance on the means with help of spreadsheet functions. these statistical controls will give you timely warning and direct your attention when problems have first begun, but will not bother you otherwise.

BAR CONTROL

There are many jokes in the industry about the number of honest bartenders. A few of the 101 areas for attention are:

- High pouring costs (PC). Pouring costs are: beginning inventory plus purchases, less ending inventory divided by sales. Average levels are the mid to high twenties. Some chain operations try to tightly control PC to the high teens. PC above thirty calls for action.
- The short pour, keeping track, and not ringing sales. This allows cash to pockets with pouring costs still at target levels.
- Liberal use of freebies to the customer to raise bartender tips. (I believe some allowance here is OK, for several reasons that cannot be covered here)

Hire inexperienced bartenders and train. You can select for personality rather than the easily trained limited knowledge of pouring. You don't want to inherit someone else's experienced pilferer. Learning to pour drinks is relatively easy. Unlearning to steal is probably impossible.

Other bar policy is:
- Keep on-line or weekly inventory depending on volume.
- Establish alcohol delivery and handling guidelines
- Teach free pourers the proper count for the volume of the pour. Have them demo many counts into a large glass and measure contents with a shot glass. A liter bottle filled with water should empty with the consistent number of counts.
- Require a log sheet for freebies.

THEFT POLICY

Theft will require immediate firing and possible prosecution. With poor employee performance in all other areas, you have many opportunities to help retrain staff, however, with theft, cut your losses now.

"You owe it to yourself and all of your employees to keep temptation from under their noses." R.A. Clelland - Administrator of many large hospitals with thousands of employees.

LABOR COST CONTROL

The second leg of prime costs, after cost-of-goods-sold, is labor costs. Labor cost is also a major cost and therefore a prime target for control that greatly affects profits.

Your business, like all others, owes its existence to the ability to provide value to the customer. Taking care of the needs of people is your only primary responsibility, and all other functions are overhead. Low direct labor costs allow resources to flow to added customer value. Note that efficient labor utilization does not mean quality-compromising staff cuts, or low pay. The goal rather is productivity, which is a measure of how well staff is utilized.

PRODUCTIVITY

Productivity is the value of outputs of goods and services divided by the values of input resources. Productivity = Output/Input. Calculations are only approximations since many variables influence the numbers. Still, with clear definitions for inputs and outputs, the productivity measurement can be very useful against baselines, and to see trends.

Labor productivity is an index of the output per person or hour worked. An example for waitstaff efficiency would be: Dollar Sales (output) / Hours Worked (input). Use this number to spot trends and areas for attention. Look out for unusual or short-term variables that might affect this pure number such as special activities, prime quality hours, assigned stations, and days of week.

The operations-managers play a key role in determining productivity. Their job is to increase the value of output relative to the cost of input. They strive to generate more output, or output of better quality, using the same amount of input. Productivity also increases if they can maintain the same level of output while reducing the use of resources, including people inputs. Judicious staff scheduling and use is key to high productivity.

Note: we can never afford to be understaffed since service is so essential to our customer's needs and perceptions. Neither can we afford to be overstaffed since it is so costly after all labor costs, including benefits and the government's big share. A normal labor cost that escalates 10% through laxity can by itself wipe out the industry average net profit. Often labor reports are designed for upper management and do not guide the person who must produce the daily staff schedule that so affects your people. If we can get meaningful numbers automatically from our control database we can ensure that labor costs are where we planned. There are several tools for labor costs control.

LABOR COST PERCENTAGE

Labor cost targets as a percentage of total revenue differ according to type of menu and service. Industry averages range from mid-20's to low-30's. Still you must find your own target and try to find ways to hold to it. Labor cost percentage is simply: period payroll divided by period sales. The period can be monthly, weekly or daily. Further it can be broken to time of day and by job department or job function.

The drawback of labor cost percentage is that it ignores peak productivity values, also being weekly or monthly; it is historical (old) data.

LABOR HOUR TO MEAL RELATIONSHIPS

Productivity is driven by guests and not cost. We therefore require a forecasting tool that is tracked in a timely fashion and is useful to the staff scheduler. Daily staff-hour to meal relationships gives insight to better staffing decisions.

LABOR- BY- FUNCTION BUDGETING

Discuss your labor target against actual standing often. Set specific weekly labor targets for each job function (waitstaff, bussers, prep, etc.). Measure labor hours by function daily and relate to the weekly goal that you have budgeted. Let people know how they stand. Mention the targeted clock-out times for each job.

Foster competition to meet the goals by involving teams with the numbers. Often staff will take pride in their productivity numbers if you give them timely and accurate information. Have staff in each job function deliver a list of ways to collectively lower costs. Offer rewards both for good suggestions and meeting productivity targets

Note that smartclocks allow easy capture of labor hours by job function with automatic comparison to budgeted hours.

SCHEDULING

Large labor cost savings can be achieved with staggered shifts. Schedule your staff just-in-time to coincide with planned peak business hours. Track your volume levels by time of day. It should also be made clear to staff, at time of hiring, that policy is: if conditions dictate, staff will be asked to clock-out early. Notice the next time you are dining out, how often you see staff "hanging-out" and socializing when they sometimes outnumber the customers. How expensive is that?

CROSS TRAINING

Staff scheduling can be further tailored to peak customer loads by pulling staff from "off-line" jobs to cover on-line (customer attending) jobs temporarily, until the staff schedule catches up. This requires staff to be cross-trained so that they are instantly up-to-speed. A side benefit of cross training is lowered personnel turnover, as people become more involved and comfortable with total operations. You, the manager should be in a position to roll-up your sleeves and jump in to help any staff that is temporarily "in-the weeds"

Cross training will usually be separated into front-of-house functions and kitchen staff. However, since everyone is part of a team of internal-customers, some knowledge and appreciation of all jobs is healthy. The K-staff can be rotated through all kitchen functions regularly. The dish-wash function will command a wage differential, or in the case of tip sharing a tip-differential. The pay differential allows rotation through K-staff jobs without preference for one job function over the other.

ABSENTEEISM

Have as many persons cross-trained as possible. Provide each employee with an up-to-date phone list of all other staff, with columns showing job functions for which they are qualified. When persons do not feel like working, one or two phone calls will find a co-worker only too glad to cover. The person will not have to interrupt you the manager and lie (call in sick), or worse fail to show. This policy helps avoid giant headaches and should be part of your culture clearly stated at time of hiring and reinforced as policy by dealing directly with staff that cannot follow policy.

TARDY

Tardiness demands more attention than most mangers ascribe to it for several reasons.
- It affects your direct labor costs. Payroll costs are expensive and greatly affect your bottom line. Therefore, you only schedule staff to be present when operations absolutely need them to be productive in adding value to the supply chain towards pleasing your customer. People must be on hand and being productively up-to-speed at the time scheduled.
- It affects morale. When promptness standards are relaxed, everyone on your team notices. Lateness becomes a slackness standard that affects attitudes. Further, standards erode as lateness becomes accepted. Lateness becomes a new baseline and the lateness-interval grows as standards are abused by those inclined to be perennially late to the job.
- It affects your customer, and therefore your overall organization profits and long-term health. Your staffers are all members of a team. Team members have starting checklists of preparation tasks in order to be ready to serve their customers promptly and efficiently, for both internal customers of fellow co-workers and the final paying customer. When a late staffer tries to set-up while also trying to serve, the service can suffer. The employee starts the job with their "foot in a bucket". The team is less efficient and it affects their income. Team resentment can escalate as overall service is negatively affected.

Combat tardiness. First, discuss the importance of prompt time and attendance, in the context of the above. Speak up during team meetings, when standards are visibly tending towards chaos. Second, capture time and attendance with a computer-based system (smartclock) that will track and document exact times of arrivals and departures.

Remember that the primary way to control labor costs is to hire the best people to begin with. Develop their skills, and properly motivate them to raise productivity and job satisfaction, and lower costly turnover.

PAYROLL PROCESSING

Labor, as noted, is a large chunk of costs and therefore highly fertile ground for productivity improvement and cost reduction. Another piece of cost overhead is the distracting and time-consuming function of payroll processing. All clerical tasks detract from people tasks. We therefore need to reduce both payroll and payroll processing where possible. There have been two main kinds of aids to payroll processing, (1) off the shelf payroll accounting software which helps those that process payroll totally in-house, and (2) payroll paycheck outsource services.

Both kinds of aid can greatly reduce payroll processing, but both only do the back half of the total payroll-processing job. The back half is: tax accounting, historical reports and paycheck printing. You will also need the front half: data capture and reconciliation of time-and-attendance with the proper accumulation of work code and rates. Smartclock software can do the front half.

SMARTCLOCK

Smartclocks use inexpensive off-the shelf hardware and software to prove accurate time-and-attendance tracking. They also provide many built in labor cost controls. Their input will bridge directly to payroll accounting to lower clerical costs and errors. Smartclock systems can be easy and inexpensive. Input can be: clicking on an icon, barcode badge, magnetic swipe badge, keyboard employee number, voice, RFID proximity badge, or fingerprint pad. The features of smartclocks allow much flexibility and reporting tools for control of budgeted job function times and dollars.

Payroll makers can be divested of all the work required to get the data ready for the back half of the software or service. The smartclock software automatically does the work leading to the rest of the job done by your service, or imports directly to your payroll service through a software bridge via the internet.

The smartclock software eliminates most all of the steps of spreadsheet preparation, and the calculations with the inevitable arithmetic and transcription errors. You will have tools to reduce your total payroll dollar amounts. Smartclock software should provide these other advantages.

- Give on-line labor analyses without keying
- Work with any input device; barcode laser, magnetic swipe, keypad, voice, proximity badge, etc.
- Fit on any computer platform, portability
- Bridge to the major services
- Be intuitive with a small learning curve
- Be upgradeable

Benefits of good smartclock software are:
- Save time
    - Better scheduling
    - Reduce paper trail
    - Shorten clerical tasks
- Save dollars
    - Tighten gross payroll
    - Eliminate errors (4 to 7 percent with manual transcriptions and keying)
    - Better focus on operations
    - Better use of staff
    - Less physical record storage
    - Increased work product
    - Target labor costs
    - Reduce overtime with red flags for those approaching OT.
    - Reduce tardiness
- Quicker more informed decisions
    - Target staffing needs
    - Timely, decision compelling reports
    - On-line labor status (who is here)
- Control
    - Simple reliable management reports
    - Customized Reports
    - Better personnel history retention

- In-house instant information v. historical pipeline
- Better accounting
- Ability for projections
- Make life less complicated
- Meet demand reports (Government and Insurance)

A major tool with the smartclock is: the ability to budget hours by job-function and have real time feedback on progress to the budgeted goal.

For the regularly-tardy persons, set the program to dun the late clocker with a voice message, or computer screen multi-media graphic reminding the person of the infringement and the consequences. The smartclock should be able to set a reasonable tardiness limit in minutes, and round towards the next nearest 10 or 15 minutes. Pay will therefore be only for actual time on job, and negative reinforcement is an option.

I had a valuable and productive co-worker who was 15 minutes late automatically for every scheduled shift. No amount of jawboning could change this habit pattern over years. Finally the smartclock was set to play a silly tune about "late again". This annoying reminder was sufficient to finally ensure that she was never late again, as a new habit pattern. Incidentally: she recently sold her own popular restaurant for $3.2 million.

COST ANALYSIS

Cost accounting relates to the determination of product, process, or service costs. Cost-volume-profit analysis is a valuable and necessary tool for tactical decisions. It requires an understanding of the nature of fixed and variable costs as they apply to your operations. *Variable costs* are the direct costs of inputs, raw material and labor that are associated with producing a given product (a cost object such as a menu item, or service). They vary because total costs are tied to volume, as volume rises those costs go up.

Fixed costs do not vary with volume. Total costs stay the same, but when applied to a particular production item they become a smaller portion of total item costs as volume goes up. The distinction between direct and indirect costs is not always clear. Some management, for instance, is general management and therefore fixed, and some management is directed towards the production of products and services. A way to view costs is: an indirect cost is one that would continue to be incurred if the product or service was discontinued (examples are rent and insurance). Direct costs stop when the product or service is stopped.

BREAKEVEN

Know your breakeven before you start, and re-measure it at all times to control your profits. Be sure to include your own salary and perks in the fixed costs. Also, it is helpful to break down your main menu items for breakeven contribution. Breakeven is the point where revenues equal all costs. Spreadsheet software has functions for breakeven analysis. The formulae are given with examples of how to use them.

RESTAURANT HANDBOOK – TOOLS & RULES

OVERHEAD CONTROL

We discussed the direct costs of producing goods and services. They are cost-of-goods-sold and direct labor costs. All other costs are overhead. Any time we can reduce overhead we can direct more resources to people (customers and personnel) and thereby strengthen and grow the organization. Overhead costs are all those that are not directly associated with units of production. Overhead costs are called fixed costs, but several categories allow room for reduction. We want to spread these fixed costs across the greatest volume of sales possible in order to keep total costs per unit down. Sales volume is always a function of our primary focus of delivering value to people. Value includes price, which we can lower when we control overhead.

Look at your monthly income statement. Most every-one of your expense categories have opportunity for cost control. Some are more fixed than others. Rent and insurance, for instance, are not usually variable in the short run. Take each expense category one-by-one, and brainstorm the opportunities for cost reductions that will not compromise perceived value.

Where your staff has any direct control over an expense category enlist their valuable input. First, they will have good ideas on how to control costs, but the exercise will also raise awareness and make change much easier. Tie some rewards to good suggestions, and where performance towards cost savings is measurable, also give rewards and recognition. People can take competitive pride is achieving common goals.

A view of costs – One perennial favorite restaurant in Lake George NY, has long seasonal waiting lines due to great food and service combined with wonderful decor in a large log building above the lake. During off-peak hours and seasons, the skilled owner will chat with guests and often "comp" dinners or drinks. The server will quietly tell a guest that, "Dinner is on George". What is the net effect of the comp on costs and long-term cash flows?

First, notice that the out-of-pocket costs of a comp are only the incremental direct food costs. An example would be primarily the cost of one additional steak (say $10). Remember that all of the other costs - including kitchen and wait staff - are fixed, because staff and facilities still must be adequately scheduled for off-hour guests-on-hand, given the posted hours of operation.

Now what happens? The guest feels good and gives a huge tip to the servers considering the "free" dollars not spent, and might hang-out to order an extra round, which largely covers the other direct costs. The enhanced tips keep the staff happy without adding to direct payroll costs.

Further, the guest will likely return often with friends and family, while giving that best-of-all promotion of word-of-mouth. Do the math on costs and cash flows.

FACILITIES COST

The real estate you occupy is usually your largest fixed cost. Costs are in the form of rent or mortgage expenses. Even if you own this real estate free and clear, this cost must still be accounted for because it is an opportunity cost. The cost is the value of your space if it was rented on the market to someone else, or sold and rented back. You have little control over real estate costs, since the market governs them.

Facilities do have ongoing *maintenance costs*. Planning for these costs and procedures will help avoid unexpected high costs with little time for flexibility.

UTILITIES - ENERGY COSTS

Electric utilities usually charge commercial rates based on peak utilization. For example, if you have three air conditioning units running at the same time, the power load will be high. The utility will capture peak load, even if it is only for a few moments when large electric motors start up when there is already a heavy load. The rate for the whole month will be will be based on those few moments. Try to schedule big-amperage equipment to run in staggered shifts. For example, compressor units for walk-in refrigerators and freezers draw heavy amperage. You can place a 24 programmable clock in the circuit to alternate use periods.

Use programmable thermostats for air conditioning. However, pay attention to air-conditioning for manual override. If outside ambient temperatures are due to rise dramatically, start lowering temperature gradually in advance. Always remember that densely packed human bodies put off large numbers of BTUs in heat. An expected packed-house must call for anticipated temperature control so as not to be overwhelmed.

Architects use tables to consider air conditioning equipment size, but do not routinely figure in the possibility of a crowded space in the heat of summer. Consider over-engineering on air conditioning. Bigger equipment operating at a moderate pace is better than smaller units at screaming capacity.

Pay attention to hood exhaust fan usage, and return air. Try to avoid exhausting conditioned-air. Have variable exhaust controls for fans to fit the current cooking need. Turn fans off or down when not generating smoke from grills.

Pay attention to hot water usage, and put dishwasher temperatures at the lowest range for effective and efficient use. Note minimum temperatures dictated by the health code.

Natural gas, if available, powers cooking equipment and air heating at a much lower cost than electricity. Turn down burners when not in full use.

Water and sewer rates are often governed by the size of the incoming water supply pipes. Use ¾ inch rather than one inch, if it will serve your needs adequately.

RESTAURANT HANDBOOK – TOOLS & RULES

THERMOSTAT POLICY

Extensive studies show, despite Jimmy Carter, that ideal temperatures in a restaurant from the customers' point of view are: from 68 degrees Fahrenheit in winter when people are more heavily dressed, to 72 degrees in summer. The best degree of comfort is not too far from this range and depends on outside ambient temperature and humidity. Computer programmable thermostats can save energy during non-business hours, but quickly changing conditions may call for manual override.

Try to limit the access to thermostats to key personnel, and certainly locate away from the reach of guests. The hot and cool settings should remain not more than six degrees apart. When moving the settings, move both at the same time, but never more than about 4 degrees at a time. Do not slam the settings to the stops. Think of the settings as being bound together with a six-degree spacer and with stops glued in place at 66 and 74 degrees. Start with temperatures on the low side in anticipation of heavy business peaks.

LIGHTING POLICY

Lighting depends on your menu, customer, and time of day. Dining area lights should be on multiple rheostats for selective dimming. Start evening shifts with lights full up. As twilight nears, begin to turn lights down in multi-stages. 1/2 hour after darkness, lighting can be fairly low. Late in the evening, depending on whether the guests are: intimate couples, elderly, or family groups, lights can be low to enhance candlelight ambience. Some dining areas can come down more quickly, but hall lights should come down last and least.

DEALING WITH GOVERNMENT REGULATORS

From the time you start planning your operation, you will come face to face with an endless supply of bureaucrats. There will be planning boards, environmental engineers, building inspectors, health inspectors, fire inspectors and any number of license inspectors from many jurisdictions. Their collective charge is to protect the interests of the public at large. Always - always treat these people with utmost respect. They have the power to destroy you if they feel slighted.

Many years of dealing with inspectors reinforces the awareness of importance to pay strict attention to their requests. Take time to talk with them face-to-face when possible to know their exact wishes. Try to start the initial relationship on a friendly note with a compliant attitude. Unfortunately, many bureaucrats are more protective of their power and egos than the public. They are armed with thick books of rules and regulations that can be interpreted at their whim, and bear no relation to actually protecting the public. When slighted, a contest of powers is likely. They have the full weight of government assets to force your compliance. You have paid the taxes for their salary, but to go against their assets with yours is most always a losing effort. "You can't fight city hall".

Bureaucrats take their power seriously. Many have never operated in the world of providing goods and services at a profit, so they have a separate reality of how the world works. Cost-benefit is a concept that they do not consider. They can try to achieve zero risk by absolute compliance towards their rigid standards. Take them very seriously.

Many inspectors appear to feel that they are not doing their job if they do not find something to write up, and will hunt until it is found, no matter how minor. Your regular fire inspector, for instance, will look for certain items predictably. If inspectors find minor things to write-up, some are satisfied. When regular inspectors go on vacation, the new inspectors will look at different sets of items. Note: An inspector can never have as much serious concern for health and safety than you. Inspectors will not go out of business and lose all of their reputation and assets if you fail to protect your people and the public.

The above discussion shows the difference with academia and business environments. Such frank discussion of the real world will offend many. Nevertheless, it is a true-and-accurate discussion of activities and situations that you will face constantly. Be prepared.

I once had a regular health inspector that wrote me up several times for not having a thermometer on the front of the racks in my beer cooler. The bartenders would move it back so as not to bang it when grabbing multiple bottles with both hands in the heat of battle. I finally lost patience and told the inspector that, "The thermometer in front is not controlling anything that affects the public health. Besides, if the beer cooler was not cool, my customers would tell us in a heartbeat." This display of disrespect was a huge mistake with much long-term cost as pay back. Never make such a mistake.

OPERATIONS

Restaurants supply both goods and services. Operations management deals with the efficient production of those goods and services using people, capital, information, and materials to meet the goals of supplying quality and value for competitive advantage. Operations are the day-to-day systems that drive the total supply chain, with the ultimate end of the chain focused on the customer. Operations management always includes primary attention to people, both the external customer and the internal-customer-co-workers who administer to the paying customer. This section, however, will not focus on people management (See Sections 3&4), but the efficient management of things. When these things: systems, procedures, and methods are smooth and efficient, the restaurant manager can apply greater attention to where it belongs with making people happy. Efficient operations comprise a competitive weapon for the restaurant manager.

Beyond human resources, operations include:
- Product handling, processing and preparation
- Equipment management and maintenance
- Health, sanitation, cleanliness, and safety
- Accounting and control systems
- Management Information systems for compelling timely decisions
- Supplier relations
- Inventory – value chain control
- Scheduling and capacity management

OPERATIONS MANAGEMENT

Overall restaurant strategy guides both the direction and control of processes that transform inputs into finished goods and services. Processes are activities that employ one or more inputs to modify and add value to them to provide output for a customer. Inputs and outputs vary along the whole restaurant value chain. Inputs are food/beverage product ingredients, production, support, and wait staff. The final output is cheerful and efficient delivery of high quality product/service to the customer.

Note that everyone in the organization has customers, both external-end-customers, and internal customers in adjacent job functions who rely on their inputs. Each link of the value supply chain has inputs and uses various processes to provide outputs such as services or information to their co-workers. Communication and understanding keep the flow along links smooth and efficient. The ultimate focus on customers drives all operations management throughout the organization, especially with the unique restaurant mix of product and service.

Remember that: there is "Always a better way". Operations are systems, and all systems are legitimate targets of *continuous improvement*.

OPERATIONS MANAGEMENT AS A SYSTEM

Operations management describes a complex system that processes inputs to create outputs, while modifying those processes through constant feedback. Restaurant operations use a mix of these Inputs.
- Managers
- Staff
- Equipment
- Facilities
- Cash
- Supplies
- Raw materials
- Information
- Services
- Energy
- Land

These capital inputs are transformed into higher value through operations and processes into the goods and services mix. Customers both internal and external provide feedback on performance to adjust processes and inputs. Daily attention strives for *continuous improvement* for *sustained competitive advantage*.

OPERATIONS MANAGEMENT AS A SET OF DECISIONS

Operations management (OM) forces decisions of different types that define both the scope and content of restaurant operations. Some decisions are strategic in nature; others are tactical. Strategic plans look farther into the future than tactical plans. Thus strategic decisions are less structured and have long-term consequences, whereas tactical decisions are more structured, routine, and repetitive and have short-term consequences. Strategic choices also tend to focus on the entire organization, cutting across functional lines; tactical decisions tend to focus on departments, teams, and tasks.

Many operations decisions are types of decisions that must be made with others, or in teams. Some of types of operations decisions fall into categories.

(1) *Strategic Choices* call on the operations managers to help determine the company's competitive priorities such as: the concept, the menu, the kind of equipment, the methods of improving existing processes, the ways to help staff facilitate change, ways to structure the organization, fostering teamwork, the degree of specialization, or description and methods of jobs created by processes. Strategic decisions may include capacity, location, and layout design. These types of decisions will require long-term commitments. Operations managers help determine the system's capacity, the location of new facilities, the organization of personnel, and facility configuration.

(2) *Quality* issues underlie each processes or work activity. Operations managers help establish quality objectives and seek ways to improve the quality of the organization's products and services. A formal path for objective measurement and feedback of both internal specifications and customer reactions is important to sustained quality produced by the various processes.

(3) *Operating Decisions* influence the infrastructure after design and completion of the fully equipped operating facility. Operations managers design and coordinate the various parts of the internal and external supply chain, forecast demand, manage inventory, and control output and schedule staffing levels. They also make decisions about quantities to be purchased or produced.

Operations Management is a function requiring the following skill sets:
- General management business and restaurant knowledge
- Generally accepted accounting principles (GAAP)
- Organizational behavior insight
- Human understanding & communications skills
- Facilities management
- Accounting for profitability and government
- Liaison to government agencies
- Quantitative methods
- Economics, micro and macro
- Information systems basics
- Business ethics and law
- Understanding of efficient food value-chain processes

FOOD HANDLING

Food product inventories: raw-materials, food in process, and product ready for consumption, represent fragile capital assets that require careful attention. Quality value-chain-management relies on efficient inventory management procedures as outlined later in this section. Those items in inventory that that represent the largest value and cost are generally the perishable items such as meat, dairy, and produce. This part of your inventory on hand, obviously, needs the most attention.

RESTAURANT HANDBOOK – TOOLS & RULES

REFRIGERATION HOLDING TEMPERATURES

Produce generally keeps well at 36 to 46 degrees Fahrenheit. Some particular fruits and vegetables do best at warmer temperatures.

On the other hand, meats and dairy have the best long-term quality shelf life when maintained near to, but not below, freezing. The 33 to 37 degree Fahrenheit range is ideal. Roasts, steaks, and chops can be held for two to four days at 38 to 40 degrees F. This dictates separate temperature controlled zones or equipment for produce and for meat/dairy.

FROZEN FOODS

Note that seafood seems to accept freezing without damage to quality. Meat products, however, and especially red meats, sustain damage from freezing. Red meats seem to gain damage to texture due to the expansion of ice crystals. Upon thaw, red meats experience "purge". This bleeding-out carries away part of your juiciness, flavor, and tenderness. An excellent steak can never come from frozen meat.

Frozen products should go onto the freezer as soon possible upon delivery. Freeze temperatures are zero degrees F or below rather than just below 32 degrees.
- Freeze time maximum for beef, *if you must*, is about six months.
- Hold frozen poultry only five to six months.
- Hold frozen lamb and veal for less, three to five months.
- Hold frozen pork for only two to three months.

Note that restaurant operators have *no business* holding any frozen meats beyond very short periods. Limit capacity by limiting freezer space and equipment.

Label all frozen product by type and date and try to store each kind of product in a labeled area. Never refreeze thawed meat. "Purge" in cryovac packages of red meats is always evidence of prior freezing that requires careful handling if not outright rejection.

Re-cooling of meats exposed to warmer temperatures should happen as soon as possible. Re-cooled products can only be held for a few days since the spoilage process on the surfaces has already started a hard-to-reverse course.

WALK-IN MANAGEMENT

Product in the walk-in-cooler comprises your most expensive and perishable inventory. Temperature control is imperative. Have thermometers highly visible. Use hanging plastic curtains to inhibit flow of colder air to warmer at doors and sections. Use stainless steel shelving widths that are not deep in order to avoid losing product behind and in corners.

Keep the surfaces and shelves scrupulously clean. Schedule the takedown of whole shelves periodically to clean wall, floors, and wire racks. Liberal use of diluted chlorine is a safe practice.

RED MEAT

You may buy Meats in pre-cut portion controlled sizes, such as a 10 oz. New York strip steak. More often meats come in 9 to 15 lb packages called primal-cuts that are vacuum-packed in cryovac. Examples of primal-cuts are: strip loins, whole top butts, ribs and tenders that yield filet mignon. Packaged primal cuts have a several week shelf life at temperatures from 33 to 40 degrees F.

BUYING CHARACTERISTICS OF HIGH-QUALITY BEEF
- Fat should be creamy white rather than yellowish or gray
- Marbling should be even and fine-grained, rather than heavy
- Avoid zero marbling
- Meat should be bright red and not deep red
- Avoid meat with two-tone coloration

DRY-AGING

Carcass beef can age from 4 to 6 weeks at temperatures near 34 degrees. Dry aging refers to unpackaged primal cuts that are exposed to several weeks of low temperature aging. Dry aging allows a dry thin-coated surface that protects the valuable juices while increasing flavor and tenderness. The dry aging of beef should be approximately 2 weeks to 28 days for beef, and about one week for lamb and veal.

USDA GRADES

Prime steak comes from steers that are 10 to 14 months old. Generally, this means Angus or Hereford cattle that have been "finished" in a lot with corn feed. Genetic science has improved the product along with advances in care, feeding and processing. The U. S. Department of agriculture oversees and grades prime and choice meats. The familiar purple stamps appear on the fat caps of primal cuts. All meats that are shipped interstate must have these stamps.

The quality of the meat shows up in any section of the animal's carcass and will dictate flavor and texture and juiciness. You are looking for an even fine-grain marbling consistent throughout the meat. Course grained marbling often comes from older heavier steers. Thick and uneven streaks of fat within the meat will usually mean tougher, less-juicy and less-tasty steaks.

CHOPPED AND PROCESSED MEATS

Chopped meats such as hamburger have a shorter shelf life and require temperatures closer to freezing. The reason for this is that spoilage always begins on a surface. Chopped meats have greater surface to volume ratios. To visualize this: imagine a cube cut in half. Each half has ½ of the original volume, but two new surfaces are created. This phenomenon continues as each half is further divided down to the infinite sizes.

DAIRY

Most dairy products start an irreversible path to spoilage if exposed to temperatures above 60 degrees F. for extended periods. Cooling down after refrigeration takes time, and is too late. Therefore, try to keep dairy products from heat. Refrigerate deliveries directly. Any dairy dispensing equipment will require thorough cleaning between shifts.

BAKED PRODUCTS

Consider the opportunity to bake your offerings in a glass-faced convection oven that is visible to customer areas. Let them salivate from the look and pervasive smell of fresh baked goodies.

RESTAURANT HANDBOOK – TOOLS & RULES

BEVERAGES

WINE

Wine inventory for restaurants rules are similar to rules for all other inventory. You want to turn that inventory rather than put aside wine for the future. Still, some wines can be delicate, and good *wine storage* will consider the following.
- Store at a constant temperature. Temperature fluctuations expand and contract the liquid as well as the cork.
- Store in cool temperatures. Wine cellars seek 55 to 60 degrees.
- Avoid high temperature spikes. Short exposure to temperature over 104 degrees will alter a good wine within two weeks. Above 86 degrees the shelf life is near 30 days. While high temperatures can damage the wine, the remedy is to open and serve those bottles soon. Since your goal is not to hold the wines, temperatures above 60 degrees are not critical as long as the inventory is turning over in a matter of weeks.
- Store in low light. Light penetrates even dark green glass. Never buy wines that have been displayed in shop window.
- Avoid vibration. Tannin maturity is affected.
- Store in moderate humidity. Dry air affects corks that might admit fatal oxygen.
- Store bottles on their sides if they will be held more than a few weeks. Sparkling wines can be stored upright.

Wine aging affects quality. From a restaurant business point of view, you should not be involved with the aging process, but do consider age at purchase. There is currently much debate on aging. In modern times aging is less critical to wine quality. Two reasons for this are modern methods and equipment that process grapes with more control, plus controlled temperature shipping.

Wines that *age best* are fortified wines such as port and sherry. Wines that generally *age well* are based on Cabernet Sauvignon and its blends such as Barolo and Riesling. Italian Nebbiolo based reds also age well. A rough guide is: Bordeaux type wines with high shouldered bottles age better than those in slope shouldered Burgundy style bottles.

Wines to *age with caution* are:
- Pinot Noir is more delicate and is usually best at less than ten years old. Some say less than five for the newer fruitier California vintages.
- Chardonnay probably should be less than five years old. It is more apt to be rich and buttery when new.
- Shiraz/Syrah wines can age well, but 10 years might be the limit for most.
- Sparkling wines are usually best when young.
- Merlot can age well, but is usually just as good new.
- Zinfandel is probably best at less than five years.

Wines that most agree are *best when new* include:
- Sauvignon Blanc is a fresh wine to serve now.
- Pinot Grigio does not age well.
- Any wine that costs less than $15 on release is probably best now.
- Blush and Rose' are drink-now wines.
- Self-proclaimed oenophiles are fanatic about Beaujolais Nouveau.

Most people do not realize that the subtle flavors in wine come from the aroma in the nose, whereas tannins and astringency are tasted in the liquid.

COFFEE

A superior cup of coffee can help make a great meal more memorable. Your customer is happy, and you have a low-labor high-margin item with high turnover. The aroma as the cup nears the nose is the most powerful part of the taste. Taste determines your customer's view of quality. To ensure consistent high *quality coffee*, consider the following standards to be set for your delivered cup.

- Select quality and fresh beans. There are many species of coffee but the two most widely cultivated have the common names of "Arabica" and "Robusta". Arabica beans are more fine, light and delicate with aromatic flavor. Arabica beans are also more expensive. Robusta, on the other hand, is heavier and earthier in flavor, and also less expensive. Many commercial coffees are blends of both, so it pays to know the mix. When in doubt, go with higher portions of Arabica. Work with your supplier. Know source of the beans and how it reacts with preparation.
- Store coffee in a cool dry place.
- Measure properly. The final product cannot be too thin or heavy for local tastes. Testing and adjusting may be required to tune and control waste. About Three gallons of water to one pound of coffee is normal. Use good water. Coffee is over 98% water, so if the water does not taste good the coffees will not either. The water can be filtered but should never be softened water. A separate cold water supply is desirable.
- Grind just before brewing if possible. Ground beans begin to lose flavor.
- Match grind to the filter and the equipment. Spread the grind evenly in the filter.
- Adjust for proper brewing time and temperature, which controls sweetness and bitterness. Brewing temperatures are 200 to 205 degrees F. Best holding temperature is near 195 degrees F.
- Clean equipment regularly using a checklist. Lime deposits and residual oils must be cleared or bitterness can result.
- Remove grounds as soon as possible. This must be taught to staff. Drip through stale-grounds adds bitterness.
- Never re-pour through old grounds.
- Avoid excessive holding times. Urns can hold for an hour, and hot plates probably about 1/2 hour. Holding for longer periods can be done in vacuum type air-pots, since no continuing external source of heat is applied. Preheat air-pots with hot water.
- Never re-heat

Coffee *equipment selection* is guided by these considerations.

- The quantity of coffee served at peak periods will dictate type and size of equipment. Urns can produce more output than bottle brewers. Some claim brewing by the pot ensures quality. The average cup is 6 ounces, and the average serving is two cups. Yield is about 20 cups per gallon.
- Urns should have variable controls for pot fill, timing and temperatures. Grinders can pre-measure.
- Where will you place the equipment and the water supply? Location must be quick at hand for servers.

Coffee service may be best when you check-off these items.

- ✓ The access to coffee should require few steps for waitstaff.
- ✓ Disburse, if necessary, hot plates for holding both regular and decaff. Staff should always carry both, if hand is free. When filling a request for coffee, look at tables that are nearby for top-off.
- ✓ During peak periods, delegate the brewing of an uninterrupted supply to an off-line staffer possibly from your kitchen. The waitstaff should not take time from customer's attention to brew or wait for coffee. Brewing is an off-line job.

Coffee merchandising can raise average ticket and tips.

- Consider stagecraft. Location of pretty equipment in view of the customer can be part of the appeal, such as antique grinders. The aroma can sell. Display of fresh beans and whir of the grinder can be part of the showbiz.
- Waitstaff can instead of saying; "coffee?" can use descriptive words about your coffee, or say "Espresso? And "how about some Gran Marnier or anisette with your coffee."
- Flavored coffees and decaff can be held safely in air-pots.
- American *blends* are generally thinner and slightly acidic. Other blends are; 'Viennese" which is richer and full bodied for after dinner, "French" which is smooth and sweet for cafe au lait, and "Italian" black and oily for espresso.

FACILITY MANAGEMENT

EQUIPMENT - MAINTENANCE

Keeping your equipment in good operating order is an ongoing expense of normal operations. We tend not to think of it until key equipment fails. Failure, because of Murphy's Law, seems to occur during rush periods that affect customer service. To avoid expensive surprises, we must plan for costs, and set policy and procedures for regular maintenance.

Service contracts and preventative maintenance agreements (PMAs) for new equipment traditionally run near 10 percent per year, and for legacy-type cash registers 20 percent. You must add the cost of capital to any amount of PMA cash flowing out at the beginning of the period covered, which further raises costs. PMAs can be profitable for the equipment supplier and expensive to your operations.

If you have to call for service, without a PMA however, keep in mind that the service company might bill you for each hour from the time they leave their shop until they return. The service technician may have to make a visit for analysis and then another to return for proper parts.

Whether you opt for PMAs or not, it is reasonable to assume that actual yearly maintenance costs will run between 5 to 10 percent of the purchase price of the equipment over the long run. It is prudent to plan for funding this ongoing expense that will affect cash flows.

A larger cost of equipment maintenance can be the cost of downtime and interruption of customer service. How quickly will the service technician respond? If existing staff has the skills to read the manual, tools at hand, and the time to do repairs on the spot, then downtime can be reduced.

You will find that parts on some heavily used equipment such as dishwashers, ice machines, oven door springs and cooler fans will fail with some frequency. It is not always rocket science to repair. If parts are not large or expensive, buy a *backup part* at the time of replacement and twist-tie the backup part in a clear plastic bag in a handy location for ready access.

Refrigeration fans and other small motors can seize after long hours of continuous use. Often a simple oiling of the motor shaft bearings will extend motor operational life by several months or more, until replacement can be convenient.

MAINTENANCE POLICY AND PROCEDURE

- ✓ Keep *user and repair manuals* for each piece of equipment in a specific handy location. Manuals should have a list of replacement part and their numbers. Put manuals in a clear sealing bag, and file where they will always be quickly reachable.
- ✓ Keep common size screwdrivers and an adjustable wrench in a handy rack for all to use
- ✓ Keep a lockable toolbox with handy common mechanical tools on hand
- ✓ Keep light-oil lubricating can with tools in a sealed bag
- ✓ Keep a Grainger supply catalogue on hand, or search on-line. The catalogues have replacement parts for most all types of restaurant equipment. If a supplier is local, the part is always in stock and can be picked up directly. Alternatively, you can often get quick delivery in hours, or overnight if not.
- ✓ Use Radio Shack for replacement of some common electrical switching component failures.
- ✓ Put a label for emergency equipment failure procedures and phone numbers on each piece of equipment, if possible.
- ✓ Store a master list of emergency maintenance procedures with the manuals. Log the maintenance history of each piece of equipment in this master list to avoid wasted diagnostic time. The master list should have a schedule for regular inspection of high maintenance equipment and parts to anticipate and avoid failure.
- ✓ Have temporary back-up plans for emergency equipment failure.

ELECTRICAL BACKUP - After experiencing periodic electrical power outages, I engineered a feedback for an electrical generator to the broiler exhaust fans for each of my restaurant operations. Previously when power went out, the dozens of steaks on the broiler had caused the building to fill quickly with smoke forcing shutdown and evacuation. The resultant loss of revenue was in major-dollars for each episode.

With the generator, all employees were ready for the drill upon power failure. The generator was started quickly to keep the exhaust fan turning, and the emergency lights were strategically aimed. All cooking equipment operated on gas, and the candles on the dining tables provided for no interruption of the dining experience.

Business always continued with smooth continuity. Indeed, the customers seemed to always enjoy the candle light experience. The dollars savings over time were immense.

RESTAURANT HANDBOOK – TOOLS & RULES

INDIVIDUAL EQUIPMENT

KNIVES

A knife is the ultimate food processor. It is good to have one integral kitchen tool with no moving parts and small depreciation. When properly maintained, knives will last a lifetime.

When *purchasing knives*, decide first what you are going to do with that knife, and then consider these points.

- Let the menu needs dictate what style knives will be most functional versus pre-purchase of a large inventory. Knives can be expensive if not regularly used.
- Do not necessarily go by price or brand names. (A Solingen knife is merely made in that town.)
- With size, think of larger versus smaller. Let the larger mass and longer blade do the work. A 4-inch paring knife is better than a 2 or 3 incher unless you have small hands.
- Select high carbon stainless with a hardness rating of around 65 (International Rockwell scale). To keep an edge, the steel in the knife should be hard but not harder than your sharpening steel with a rating of around 70. Avoid pure stainless that can have ratings of 75. The carbon steel knives of the past are easy to sharpen but also can rust.
- Look for knives with a tang (the continuous part of the metal) that runs the full length of the handle. Three rust resistant rivets are necessary for wood handles.
- Handles made of molded plastic are less aesthetic but easier to grip and clean. Some health departments disparage wood handles.
- The blade should be fairly thick at the back edge with a uniform taper to the tip. The cutting edge should be uniformly thin from the bolster to the tip. The bolster, the non-cutting metal between the edge and the handle, provides strength, balance, and slip protection. The thinner the blade, the thinner the slices.
- Consider general kitchen knives that will be handy to all kitchen staff, but also sets of cutlery to be kept separate for meat cutters and chefs. Unsupervised kitchen personnel have been known to use knives as can openers, for instance.

A basic set of cutlery depending on function and tastes could be:
- 10-inch chef's knife for all purpose dicing and chopping
- 4-inch paring for fruits and vegetables
- 10-inch scimitar for cutting fish without scoring
- 7-inch boning knife
- 12-inch butcher knife for cutting steaks with a Bowie point for stripping ligament silver.
- 14-inch thin blade serrated meat slicer for roasts.

Knife maintenance guidelines include the following tips:

- Always keep knives clean. Clean only by hand, never in the dishwasher. Use a brush. Pay attention to the bolster area where the blade meets the handle.

- Keep knives sharp by steeling. Less force is required for the work. A look at the edge with a microscope will show an edge that is not smooth but has small teeth. A sharpening-steel realigns these teeth. Use a steel 3 to 6 swipes before each job and periodically after so many cuts. Keep sharpening steels handy to the cutting area. After each steeling you will readily notice the change in cutting resistance The sharpening steel should have guards at the handle. Some prefer to put the steel point down on a surface and stroke downward. Start at the bolster and slide the length of the

OPERATIONS – CONTROL – Section 5

knife blade to end at the full length of the sharpening steel. Alternate sides, as you hold the same angle for each side. The angle should range from 15 degrees for razor sharp to 35 degrees for a cleaver. Most knives should be sharpened around 20 degrees. To see the approximate angle, fold a piece of paper at the 90-degree corner to get 45 degrees then refold to visualize 22.5 degrees.

- Now and then, a knife will need a new edge. There are sharpening services, but honing with a stone or ceramic stone can repair an edge. You may see people putting oil on a stone but water keeps the abrasive from filling with steel residue. Use a constant angle using the same as the steeling angles. Try to avoid cutting against hard surfaces. Avoid electric sharpeners that remove too much material.

- Knives can be *stored* on handy magnetic racks above the work area. Slotted racks can be unsanitary. Do not store knives in drawers with other knives or implements where edges can be nicked, or knuckles nicked. Special carving knives should be wrapped and kept un-handy to the full kitchen staff.

Knife safety requires that staff learn good habits. Eventually staff will be cut. (See First Aid Cuts)

- ✓ Teach cutting in a direction always away from hands and other body parts.
- ✓ When laying a knife down, place the blade edge away from the work area to avoid cut knuckles.
- ✓ Use the proper knife for the proper job. Avoid excessive pressure or force.
- ✓ Clean by hand, but do not drop knives in soapy water.

CARVING

- Use knives of high quality steel and keep them sharp.
- Select the proper type/size of knife for the given job, just as with any other tool.
- Keep the angle constant after the initial incision.
- Use long sweeping strokes rather than a saw-like motion.
- Cut across the grain whenever possible.
- Chain mail gloves are essential for high volume cutting

THERMOMETERS

Most health departments require thermometers on the management's person and in all cooling and cooking areas. Bi-metallic types respond quickly and are good for most food areas. A bi-metallic with a pocket clip should be handy at all times. Thermometers with different sensitivity ranges are required for the different functions; coolers, freezers, griddle tops, internal roasting temperatures, dishwasher rinse. Some applications need thermometers that can be re-calibrated. To calibrate: check for 32 degrees by swirling in ice water. Bi-metals can be checked against mercury thermometers, but avoid mercury filled thermometers in food areas. Other types are digital, remote, and recording thermometers for tracking 24-hour temperatures.

HEALTH / SANITATION / CLEANLINESS

FOOD ILLNESS

FOODBORNE DISEASE CAUSES - REPORTED BY FREQUENCY
- Poor refrigeration
- Holding foods at maximum bacterial incubating temperatures. USDA HAACP guidelines say above 41 and below 140 degrees Fahrenheit is dangerous.
- Food preparation too far in advance
- Infected personnel and poor personal hygiene
- Incomplete cooking
- Failure to re-heat to proper temperature, 165 degrees Fahrenheit
- Adding raw or contaminated ingredients to food without further cooking
- Poor cleaning of kitchen and failure to disinfect equipment and surfaces
- Cross contamination from raw foods of animal origin
- Creating conditions for pathogens to grow and inhibiting competing organisms.
- Foods from unsafe suppliers
- Serving food left from previous meals
- Use of metal utensils for handling of acid foods
- Over use of additives or toxic chemicals

Possibility of foodborne illness is serious enough that you must have pervasive policy and practice to reduce risk near zero. Failure here is fatal. Most health departments provide classes that your staff can attend to gain knowledge of healthy practices.

A National Restaurant Association study said that a single foodborne illness outbreak can cost a food operation as much as $75,000 in legal fees, medical claims, lost employee wages, cleaning and sanitation, discarded food, and lost income. As serious as that figure sounds, however, it doesn't even begin to tell the whole picture. One U.S. government report (1999) claimed that the estimated annual costs of medical care and lost productivity due to foodborne Salmonella infections were $700 million to $2.8 billion, depending on the method used to calculate lost earnings.

The Center for Disease Control of the USDA gives us these numbers.

- Estimated number of foodborne illness cases annually   76 million
- Number of hospitalizations   300,000
- Number of deaths   5,000
- Medical costs and productivity losses $5.6-9.4 billion
- Number of known foodborne illnesses   >250

SIMPLE PRECAUTIONS

Simple and small controllable measures like time/temperature control and proper hand washing are still the culprit in many foodborne illness incidents

OPERATIONS – CONTROL – Section 5

Food handling factors often associated with the occurrence of investigated foodborne incidents are: incorrect storage of food, reuse of food, lack of employee hand-washing; lack of thermometers; and the presence of any food protection violations. CDC studies indicate that factors commonly associated with foodborne illness are: improper holding temperature, poor personal hygiene, inadequate cooking, contaminated equipment and food from unsafe sources. Simple guidelines include:

- Establish temperature-monitoring times for food to be held. Allow for lead times and temperatures to avoid entering the zone for microbial growth, 41 to 140 degrees.

Hot foods

- Holding equipment must hold at 140 degrees or higher.
- Do not use holding equipment for reheating.
- Stir foods to keep heat distributed evenly.
- Keep food covered to retain heat and prevent contamination.
- Measure internal temperatures at least every two hours.
- Never mix freshly prepared food with old held product.
- Prepare in smaller batches for faster turnover.
- Throw out foods after four hours if not held above 140 degrees.

Cold foods

- Use cold holding equipment at below 41 degrees.
- Do not hold food directly on ice except for fruits and vegetables.
- Ice bins should be self-draining.

Server guidelines

- Servers and line staff must wash hands if crossing over to bus tables.
- Handle glassware by stems, middle, or bottom. Hold dishes from the bottom or edge.
- Avoid stacking glassware and dishes when serving.
- Hold flatware and utensils by handles, not food contact surfaces.
- Use gloves or utensils to contact food rather than bare hands.
- Use plastic or metal tongs or scoops to get ice, never glassware or bare hands.
- Good personal hygiene includes keeping hair pulled back and covered. Avoid touching face or hair when serving food.
- Cloths used for food spills should be used for nothing else.

Kitchen Staff

- Use only utensils with long handles. Hold serving utensils so that handles extend above the rim of a container or are placed on a clean sanitized surface. Keep spoons or scoops used to serve food such as ice cream or mashed potatoes in containers with running water.

- Only use clean and sanitized utensils for service, and only use for one food at a time. Clean and sanitize utensils after each task. Clean and sanitize all utensils at least once every four hours while in continuous use.
- Avoid bare hand contact with cooked or ready to eat foods; use gloves or utensils instead. Change gloves often if cross-contamination is possible.
- Practice good personal hygiene, properly washing hands after using the restroom, coming in contact with food, or handling dirty equipment or utensils.

The above guidelines all seems simple, but must become automatic practice as part of your culture. Your dire interests include staff awareness of holding temperatures and personal hygiene. Stay in strict compliance of sanitary guidelines. Post procedures conspicuously, and reinforce practice by highlighting both compliance and malpractice by staff.

Hazard Analysis and Critical Control Points (HACCP) provides Standard Operating Procedures that can be adopted or modified by any restaurateur. These provide clear documentation for many practices that should be followed in every well-run operation. Go to the USDA Website for HACCP. They have wonderful training manuals on safe food handling. Print out a reference to keep handy in the kitchen.

PEST CONTROL

The best control of pests is cleanliness. Check all external doors for tight seals. Contract with an exterminating service for monthly visits.

FIRE SAFETY

Keep all fire suppression equipment serviced and handy. Staff must be familiar with equipment locations and procedures for use. Discuss at orientation with a walk-around, and review with staff periodically. Keep cooking and exhaust hoods free of grease. Contract with professional hood cleaning services for regular steam cleaning from intake to outlet

FIRST AID – CUTS – BURNS – SLIPS

A high production kitchen produces accidents over time even in the face of aware safety practices. Keep a fully stocked first aid kit mounted in a handy location. Post procedures for cut policy.

Cut policy will include:
- Put pressure on wound to stop blood loss
- Quickly wash wound with soap and water, and reapply pressure.
- Dry with sterile wipe
- Butterfly bandages work for smaller cuts
- Apply sterile bandage over butterfly
- Cover with gloves for minor cuts.
- Do not continue service with larger cuts

OPERATIONS – CONTROL – Section 5

Note: for adolescent male K-staff regarding cuts:
- Do not hold wound under running water. It promotes maximum bleed.
- Do not continually blot wound on your dirty apron for most visible blood.
- Do not wrap wound in wet terry towel for continued blood loss.
- Do not adopt wounded warrior pose.
- Do not wander up front to seek sympathy from female co-workers.

For *puncture* type wounds:
- Promote bleeding by manipulation near wound.
- Wash with soap and water.
- Dry with sterile wipe and bandage.
- For minor wound apply Bacitracin type disinfectant.

First step in *burn treatment* is to reduce the latent heat of the burn to reduce skin damage by immersing in cold water. Do not apply grease to a fresh burn where the superficial part of the skin is missing. Grease is occlusive, non-sterile, and promotes bacterial proliferation on the surface of the wound. It may lead to infection. Vaseline is not to be used as initial first aid for burns, but it can be used as a later dressing for minor burns.

For *slips* consider non-slip tiles in kitchen areas with high traffic, but use smooth tiles under equipment. Use washable mats in high traffic areas that might build up slippery footing.

DISHWASH / CHINA POLICY

Maintain dishwasher equipment to use proper chemicals and amounts. Keep temperatures at the proper range for health specifications.

Dishware needs pre-rinse, wash, rinse, and air dry. Use gloves to stock handling by edges. Do not towel dry, it is unsanitary, is extra handling, and adds to breakage. For scraping, use the spray-rise head and scrapers of rubber or plastic, not metal. Do not scrape a plate with another plate.

Stainless tableware is highly resistant to stain & corrosion, but corrosive food chemicals need to be removed.
- Remove all food remnants immediately after use
- Presoak in plastic or stainless pan using non-abrasive presoak solution
- Wash in Hot water using non-corrosive cleaning agent
- Rinse in water of at least 180 degrees F. A wetting agent may be used if using water of high mineral content
- Dry Immediately

Caution: With low temperature dishwashers, avoid over concentration of bleach, which can cause staining and corrosion. Follow Manufacturer's instructions.

CHINA

Choose vitreous china kiln-fired through entire thickness versus kiln-fired glaze over clay pottery. A typical permanent ware plate should cycle over 6000 times before chipping or breaking. The cost per use is therefore small and high quality should be selected. Care, however, depends on practices for bussing, scraping, racking, washing, storage, setting, and serving. Good Bus practices include:
- Bus dishware first to lay flat. Stack dishes vertically.
- Cups and glassware go on top and in corner.
- Avoid overloaded bus tray.

JANITORIAL

Have closing checklists for cleaning for all staff functions. Keep lobby brooms handy near wait-stations Do not clean however if it intrudes upon customer experience. Also, school-age staff should not be kept late.

Pay attention first to all cleaning that affects food and sanitary conditions. Then you can contract for routine cleaning of customer areas for later at night or early in mornings. Again, agree on a checklist of mandatory duties.

CHECKLISTS

Throughout restaurant operations we promote the use of checklists to ensure that best procedures are followed, and to avoid unpleasant surprises. Reasons for restaurant operations checklists are many.
- Stimulate thought on how to best get each function done with attention to:
  - Expediency
  - Order
  - Avoiding omissions
  - Quality of value added
- Training:
  - New staff
  - Cross training
- Define each job for differentials
  - Pay
  - Duties and responsibilities
  - Authority scope
- Control of performance
  - Establish a baseline for execution
  - Personnel review
  - Documentation of performance

Each job function within operations is an alternative application of resources directed to producing value. Who, when, and how is important to getting the job done quickest, with the fewest mistakes, with quality, and at the lowest cost in terms of time, talent and dollars.

OPERATIONS – CONTROL – Section 5

DEVELOPMENT OF CHECKLISTS

Have each person, who might perform a given job, write their own list of tasks in the order of importance. Some tasks must necessarily precede other in a serial fashion and some can be done in parallel. Compare lists with your own, and revise. Discuss the draft with team members. Apply times for each function to be completed. Periodically review, reorder, and update.

Input from teammates ensures a complete coverage of vital tasks, and aids acceptance and implementation of standard procedures as defined.

RESERVATIONS

Restaurant reservations must balance the need of both patrons and the need to fully utilize capacity. Patrons can plan their lunch and dinner engagements several weeks or days ahead, and make reservations in advance. Operations benefit from reservation efficiency that guides work force scheduling. Work force scheduling is crucial to measures of performance such as customer waiting time, waiting line length, utilization, cost, and quality as related to the availability of server.

Reservation policy provides management the ability to prepare in respect to:
- Number of people expected at any given service period
- Timing and indication of a rush-hour
- Opportunity to recognize, divert and spread the rush-hour
- Allocation/distribution of table, staff and food preparation
- Smooth workflow during operations

In short, advance reservations provide an opportunity to avoid surprises both to customers and the restaurant management, and a tool for effective table management.

All restaurants that take reservations experience *no shows*, sometimes as much as a third. Some people try reservations at more than one place and don't cancel. Overbooking to a limited degree may be permissible depending on your experience. If your guests must wait, you must take very good care of them. Never ignore those waiting. You might provide some comped beverage or appetizer

Request credit card and phone numbers for very large parties or for special occasions. You might keep a computer listing of no-shows so that you can ask to call to verify an hour before. Have a written procedure.
- Take names
- Phone numbers
- Call back same day to verify for large parties.

Try to be protective of reservation makers and seat them as close to time as possible

Reservations are traditionally maintained in book form. Diners need to call the restaurant during operational hours to make a reservation. Lately, restaurants are moving in the direction of on-line reservations. The growth of the Internet offers the patrons the flexibility to make reservations from a place and time convenient to them.

Many electronic reservation systems are now available off-the-shelf. The decision to select an electronic information system depends on utility and ease of use. Advantages might be the tapping of potential resources to increase revenue through effective floor management, eliminate overbooking, reduce errors while taking reservations, and capture of customer data for future target marketing.

Considerations in decision for selecting electronic reservation system (ERS):
- Fit to menu type and mode of operations
- Reliability – the ERS should be reliable in terms of volume handling with proven track record.
- Personalized interface – the ERS console should aesthetically blend with restaurant interior
- Availability – The ERS should be accessible at all times for clear reading
- Ease of use – The ERS should display the restaurant layout. It should have touch screen input device. Should be user friendly and easy to install.
- Costs - Consider total cost to purchase, support costs for supplies, annual fees, and any fee per reservation through vendor website.

Note, always have manual backup to electronic systems.

SUMMARY

Entropy and human nature continually prove the critical need for controls throughout operations. Without timely and effective control, costs always escalate and quality slips quickly. Therefore, control is absolutely necessary. Yet, all control detracts from our primary focus on the needs of people. The costs of control in the form of diverted dollars, time, and attention must never surpass the potential savings from control. Neglected people are always costly. Careful design of controls will assure maximum of feedback for decisions balanced with a minimum of assets diverted away from people.

Fully use today's information technology to capture meaningful data as an automatic by-product of normal business functions. Set up the controls to import that data into template spreadsheets for timely decision compelling information for both revenue increase and control of costs.

Costs fall into two primary categories. (1) Prime costs are the direct costs of producing and delivering your product and service. The two major components of prime cost are cost-of-goods sold, and direct labor costs. Both of these costs are large and provide much room for control that so greatly affects your fragile bottom line. (2) All indirect costs are overhead. Any time we can reduce overhead, we can redirect resources to producing value to the customer. To control overhead, set up a uniform system of accounts, and brainstorm each expense category with staff to lower costs.

Control uses the various tools of *value chain analysis* (VCA). Value analysis is the systematic activity and discovery to reduce costs and improve the performance of products and services. Use the tool & rules provided for smooth and efficient flow of value.

Remember: Do not lower any cost, if it will lower customer perception of value.

RESTAURANT HANDBOOK

TOOLS & RULES

Roderick A. Clelland

FUNDAMENTALS OF RESTAURANT MANAGEMENT

PRINT SECTION SIX

RESTAURANT- VALUE
VALUATION FOR BUY/SELL

RESTAURANT HANDBOOK – TOOLS & RULES

TABLE OF CONTENTS – Section Six

VALUATION FOR BUY/SELL

    REASONS TO KNOW THE VALUE   6- 1
FAIR MARKET VALUE   6- 1
SELL   6- 2
BUY   6- 4
INCOME CAPITALIZATION
   CASH FLOWS DISCOUNTED   6- 5
   CAPITALIZATION RATE OR MULTIPLE   6- 6
COST OR REPLACEMENT
   ASSET VALUATION   6- 9
     LAND   6- 9
       HIGHEST AND BEST USE   6- 10
      BUILDING   6- 11
      OTHER ASSETS   6- 11
AREA SALES COMPARISON   6- 13
NEGOTIATE
   THE DEAL   6- 14
   PLAN   6- 15
   ATTITUDE   6- 16
   STRATEGY   6- 17
     STRATEGIES FOR SELLERS   6- 20
     TECHNIQUES & TACTICS   6- 21
LEASE   6- 23
FINANCE   6- 25
SUMMARY

CHECKLISTS – TEMPLATES - FORMS
   VALUATION BY CAPITALIZATION CHECKLIST
   BUYING CHECKLIST
   OPERATION
   FINANCIAL INFORMATION
   BUILDING AND LAND
   COMPETITOR ANALYSIS
   LEASE
   PURCHASE AGREEMENT

VALUATION FOR BUY/SELL

How much is it worth? Information on restaurant valuation is scarce. The problem appears to be that the diversity of restaurant concepts does not allow easy comparison, as compared to generic commercial real estate such as office space. Objective valuation is important, however, to determine a reasonable fair market value as a basis for transactional values. Accurate value is necessary for many reasons. Do not leave big dollars on the table.

REASONS TO KNOW THE VALUE OF A RESTAURANT OPERATION:
- Sell
- Buy
- Lease
- Estate purposes, wills, transfer to heirs
- Finance & refinance
- Pro-Forma basis for business plan
- Shareholders agreements
- Arbitration & mediation
- Stock incentives
- Partnership dissolution
- Divorce
- Insurance settlements
- Property tax assessment verification
- Justification for IRS deductions

Deal from strength. Whether you are dealing from the buyer or seller's perspective, you must have done your homework. You will need a solid objective basis as a starting point for negotiations.

FAIR MARKET VALUE

The primary value you seek, for most reasons, is called the fair market value (FMV). The FMV, the marketable value of any property, is ultimately determined solely by the market. That is: the amount willingly paid. This open market, in turn, is influenced by many less tangible factors, including human emotions. It is almost impossible to measure a buyer's motivations. Ultimately, the business is worth whatever a buyer and seller thinks it is worth, based on criteria selected, including the subjective. You can create a "fair" estimate using several different objective tools to value the business, and then choose the mix that reflects a reasonable basic value. It is always practicable to determine a fair market value as a benchmark. How you use that knowledge in negotiations is up to you. The objective numbers will document a final transactional value.

There are generally three separate ways to arrive at objective valuation. Each of the three is only an approximation of the FMV and should be used to establish a range of values. The three are described briefly below, with more detail to follow later in this section.

Cost or Replacement - This valuation method deals only with the assets. The value derives from adding the dollar value of all assets less depreciation. Assets to include are: real estate (if owned), equipment, furnishings, fixtures, inventories and supplies. Asset values will be adjusted for physical condition relative to new assets.

For real estate, especially if newly built, it is relatively easy to get the prevailing front-foot values of the land on your street, and the construction costs or leasing prices for space per square foot in the locality. Building values derived must then be adjusted for depreciation, condition, functionality, age and obsolescence. This *cost or replacement* approach does not account for the value of the operation (its ability to produce income through goodwill and reputation), and generally understates the value of the total package.

Area sales comparison - This valuation approach works well for residential real estate, but is less powerful for commercial real estate. Comparing restaurants often is an apples/oranges problem. Still it is useful for the value of the real estate itself. A number of factors influence the value range. These include: location, financing costs that shift with interest rates and tax policy, demographics, type of operation, parking, access/egress, age of building, management abilities, labor costs, seating, owned versus leased equipment, kitchen, goodwill, etc. Most local papers publish, by law, the Real Estate transactions with dollar amounts that are easily accessed through research.

Income Capitalization This method of valuation often has the highest validity. There are two major components, (1) the value of the business operations based on discounted future cash flows, and (2) the value of the assets including real estate. More detail will follow.

Note that whatever sale price is established, the *terms of the deal* are almost equally as important, and will greatly influence any negotiated price.

SELL

Selling a restaurant calls for a truly comprehensive valuation. This valuation will involve an understanding of the business, the client base, personnel, market niche, competitors and demographic trends. Triangulate FMV by using more than one of the standard methodologies to estimate the value of the business. The process will uncover the strengths and weaknesses, and the threats and opportunities that will alter the final numbers. The end product will be a solid basis for negotiation.

As a seller, you are primarily responsible for establishing the initial asking price. You will have the advantage of access to the complete inside-information about the operation's cash flow, financial structure, assets, employees, and business trends. Your perspective allows you to use real numbers to provide solid tangible evidence of your organization's worth.

You may have to seek a comfort level with the degree of full disclosure about your operations details. The most well documented approach, using the valuations tools provided below, will give the seller the highest leverage.

Favorable conditions for a maximum price are:

- When you are selling in an up-trending market with solid profitability.
- When you have several buyers at the table
- When the sale is not forced

Preparation for sale requires a planned exit strategy. The sale process until closing can be lengthy, so preparation must begin with orderly steps.

First, you should build the case for a realistic valuation of the business worth. One approach is a professional appraisal of value. An outside source will give extra weight and credibility to valuation. The outside appraiser will use the same tools that we will provide below. A comprehensive appraisal will give you your market position, financial situation, and your strengths and weaknesses. Also active marketing with a professional firm might bring several potential buyers for active bidding. Outside sources include accounting firms, regional business brokers, and investment banking firms. You will look for a firm that has direct recent experience with restaurant appraisals and sales.

Next, make sure your accounting of financial information is up to date and accurate. The best indicator of the value of operations, beyond the assets, is the proven statement of operations and the balance sheet. Three years of income statements allow trend and smoothing analysis for showing expected maintainable cash flows. Strong verification of the revenue portion of your income statements will come from actual sales tax filings. The more orderly your financial statements: the greater the weight to the buyers. Good books allow easy due diligence and high confidence for your bidders.

Adjust cash flows on the profit and loss statement to make them more meaningful of true profitability. You will have a variety of non-operational expenses. Examples would be: business paid automobile lease, personal life insurance, bonuses, non-performing employees, and corporate overhead. You will also usually have some unusual or non-cyclical expenses and revenue sources. Non-recurring expenses such as: moving expenses or unusual legal-fees should be adjusted to find regular cash flow projections. Solid documentation of non-recurring expenses always helps.

Understand your personal and corporate tax options to maximize the structure and financing of any sale. This may require the advice of professionals. Have all your corporate legal documents current and close at hand. Ultimately you might require a team, including: accounting, legal, and business broker services.

Know your reason for selling. Buyers will always ask, so you should be prepared to reply. Also, the buyer might ask for help in management succession. You should have a way to help the changeover with smooth continuity. What are you prepared to supply in terms of time and talent, and at what consideration?

Do not neglect to qualify each potential buyer. Due diligence means the seller should understand the buyer's business background, motivation for purchasing the business and financial qualifications.

RESTAURANT HANDBOOK – TOOLS & RULES

Note: It is important not to neglect daily operations, while working on the sale. The latest profit-and-loss trends will carry the most weight when calculating an objective valuation of the business.

BUY

A buyer's position is similar to that of the seller, except that you will use objective review of the numbers to try to keep the value as low as possible. You will work to establish a value that can be held with strength in the face of pressure by the seller to raise the asking price. The seller holds more inside information on the true cash flows and details of the operation. You as prospective buyer must therefore use due diligence to try to best establish those numbers. If you have properly done your homework with the numbers, any disagreement will require that the seller provide documentable details of better numbers. The burden of proof will shift to the seller to provide additional credible information to assess true value. Note: it is always fair to ask to see the books.

As a buyer, you must already have some concept of your planned market target. This target is partly defined by the demographics of the geographic location under consideration. The planned market target shapes your intended menu, which in turn influences your planned furniture, fixtures, equipment and mode of service. You will have a template of needs that defines value to you as a buyer.

Any existing restaurant will only partly meet your needs. Unless you are accepting a "turnkey" type of agreement, the valuation of assets will need some adjustment to fit your required template of needs. As a buyer, you should still determine value by triangulation with the three methods for valuation, however it will pay to value each of the asset categories separately according to your needs profile. Naturally, you are looking for the lowest total price that you can obtain. Using the *valuation checklists* provided will ensure you cover all considerations, and will give weight to your negotiating position.

Buying a restaurant might be seen as cash flow exercise. You will want to delay and minimize actual cash outflows until you are up and operating with a positive cash inflow.

INCOME CAPITALIZATION

Income capitalization gives a truer picture of value. It will follow these steps:

- Determine expected future cash flows.
- Select a capitalization rate to determine value of income stream.
- Determine value of assets after depreciation.
- Add value of assets to value of income stream.

CASH FLOWS DISCOUNTED

Income capitalization valuation is a discounted cash flow technique. It requires good data and seeks a *net present value* (NPV). Final decisions should never come from a purely mechanical technique, however. After all, cash flow estimates are merely estimates, and flows rarely proceed as anticipated. It is important to look behind the numbers to see how the operation will actually work, and what might go wrong. Still this technique is a valuable tool to establish reasonable and objective start points.

Step one is to determine expected future cash flows. The best basis for future flows is past and current net profits, if available. Value of the business operations is easiest with a history of earnings - unless you are working on a pro forma for a proposed new restaurant. The earnings figure to use should be yearly net profits. Again, three years history is helpful for averaging and trend analysis. This figure can be derived from sales and net profit percentage, but must be adjusted for items such as: depreciation, interest plus principal on debt, and owner salaries (see checklist). Think of the business as a stream of cash. You valuate the business by finding a value for that stream of cash.

Consider also the economic life of the planned operation, since it will influence the duration and pattern of those cash flows. A lease might define that life unless there are easy optional renewal clauses.

> Note: Some use total *sales revenue* with a multiplier, which is a cruder approximation of a restaurant's value than use of net profits, but might also be a starting point. The capitalization rate for revenues will be much lower than the cap-rate for net profit.

With the estimated earnings in hand, you can project the future cash flows and then determine how much that income-stream is worth to you, given the relative surety of those cash flows. Note: never assume that future earnings will be stable. Many variables can act to change the threats and opportunities of your future business environment. Change will include competition and changes in the local demographics. It is healthy to develop low, middle, and high expectation scenarios for cash flows. A more precise term for this valuation basis is "maintainable" cash flow. Maintainable flows are the net income that a restaurant can expect to earn on a consistent basis before depreciation, income taxes and debt service. When historical earnings are not available you will base a restaurant's maintainable cash flow using results of comparable type restaurant operations.

CAPITALIZATION RATE OR MULTIPLE

Now take step two and discount the projected cash flows. This is necessary because the value of future dollars is less than cash in hand, and cash always has the opportunity cost of alternative applications. The cap rate considers these realities to convert the maintainable earnings into business value. The cap rate is determined by either selecting a (1) multiple or (2) calculating a rate.

RESTAURANT HANDBOOK – TOOLS & RULES

(1) Find an earnings multiple by researching purchase prices of comparable restaurants and estimating the maintainable earnings. The multiple will be in the form of a number such as 5 times earnings. This is not always easily available information, but guidelines exist. A lower cap rate (20% = 5 times earnings, to 25% = 4 times earnings) sets a higher restaurant value and a higher cap rate (25%, to 40% = 2.5 times earnings) creates a lower restaurant value.

Selecting a multiple is not precise because of the variables with each deal. A seller will select a high multiple and a buyer will argue for a lower value. Bankers have an abundance of available data on specific industry multiples that can be used to estimate a business's value. They adjust these over time as they observe trends in the selling price of businesses. Multiples are simply a summary version of these trends. They are industry-specific and generally used for smaller businesses.

Multiples for restaurants are generally lower than less risky categories of business. For instance, some public companies may have price/earnings multiples of more than 20, based on expected stable future earnings growth, while restaurants will be worth only four to five times earnings. There are several reasons for the differentials in multiples.

- Restaurant diversity means you are often comparing apples to oranges.
- Privately held organizations are not liquid, as are the public held. You cannot easily transfer your capital to another investment opportunity.
- Restaurants often seek to minimize taxes, while public companies maximize profits. This disparity alters the net profits that are the basis for calculations.
- Public companies have capital structures of debt/equity that are similar. Restaurants do not.
- The risk profile for restaurants is much higher.
- Restaurants operate in a narrow market niche.
- The restaurant operations management group is dependent on a small sample.

Note: you also cannot use the multiples of publicly held chain restaurant operations as a guide. Chains are included in a broad based industry, a different animal. You can see how the valuation of a single private restaurant is complex and often cannot be determined through the direct application of an industry price/earnings ratio.

While multiples provide a guideline for the price of a restaurant, accurate valuation requires consideration of unique attributes of an individual business, a geographic location or the current economic environment. In addition, simply using multiples to value a business means that no benefit can be made in terms of truly understanding how to increase the value of the business by addressing changing opportunities.

(2) Calculating a capitalization (cap) rate might be an easier approach than a "multiple" to the same results. This rate is determined by looking at the cost of capital and adding a "hurdle rate" based on risk factors. To illustrate: if you invested cash in treasury bills you would suffer little risk and return near 5% compounded return on your investment. (Note: T-bill yields often settle about 1.5 points above inflation. The historical average of inflation is near 3.5%. Both are un-naturally low during "quantitative easing" periods.)

Now consider that there is an *opportunity cost* for all money since it can be employed in alternative pursuits with reasonable returns given risks. To invest the same amount in a restaurant you will need a substantial hurdle rate above the T-bill rate to allow for the much higher risk. This discounted value is the present value (PV) of those future cash flows. Note that the selected discount rate effectively establishes a multiple.

As with the multiple-approach, you first determine the potential future stream of cash earnings, its quality and duration. You then discount by selecting the best capitalization rate to determine an amount to pay for the projected income stream. The cap rate reflects the return on invested capital while also considering risks. Remember that the restaurant industry has a high rate of failure and that reward is usually commensurate with risk. The restaurant cap rate has traditionally resided near 20% and above, or around five times earnings or less. For example, an investor requires a 20 % annual return (ROI) in order to recoup the principal in 5 years (Payback Period). The rate, however, is moved by opportunity costs of alternative investments. When inflation is low the cap rate comes down. Conversely, as the rate goes up the value of the business component comes down. Rates are based on mortgage rates that are further based on U.S. government 30-year (long) bonds. In the "Carter years" of double-digit inflation, the cap rate went way up.

The restaurant risk requires that the hurdle rate be added on top of the base rates. For example add these components of alternative uses of cash.
- 5% for no risk government bonds (long-term historic rather than current yields)
- Plus 3% for moderate risk
- Plus 6% for higher risk in stock equities
- Plus 6% more for even higher risk of restaurant business

This adds up to 20%, which is the proper neighborhood before adjustments.

> Warren Buffett appears to use the similar discounted cash-flow analysis he encountered in his professor's "Graham & Dodd" textbook on fundamental financial analysis to become mega-wealthy. Steps are; look at current cash-flows, projected cash-flows, and risks related to cash-flows, to establish a net-present-value (NPV) using a hurdle rate for risk above the basis of "no risk" long-term treasury bills. He shows that he abhors risk, and seeks to minimize risk. Note that Excel™ has an NPV function for your easy use.

A quick illustration is to divide the current yearly earnings by the long-term Treasury bill rate. For example, if the operation earns $50,000/year and T-bills are returning 5 percent interest, the business worth is equivalent to $1,000,000 (50,000 / .05). That amount invested in T-Bills would return the same $50,000 income with small risk and no management effort. You must add a hurdle rate to account for risk and effort. A hurdle rate of 15 percent added to the 5 percent T-bill rate lowers value to $250,000 ($50,000/ (.05 + .15)). This approach assumes that the operation will have the same maintainable earnings year after year, and ignores all non-monetary considerations.

Income capitalization is a healthy methodology for establishing value for your restaurant. The value is based on earnings of a well-managed operation. The tangible assets such as equipment, furniture and fixtures, and licenses are necessary to generate maintainable earnings, and are all part of the business value. If you also own the real estate, land and buildings, that is a separate value to be added to income capitalization value.

These valuation techniques: cash flow analysis, earnings multiple, and asset valuation only value the financial side of the business. Non-financial considerations will always come into play. The use of these objective methods will help you avoid letting your dreams influence the valuation too much, and keep you grounded near reality.

FMV – FAIR MARKET VALUE

Once the maintainable earnings and capitalization rate are established, to calculate the *Fair Market Value,* simply divide the maintainable earnings by the cap rate or multiply the maintainable earnings by the earnings multiple.

Simplified examples:

Given: The adjusted net profit for the year is $60,000.

A. The cap rate for the buyer is 20 %, or 5 times earnings

$60,000 / .20 = $350,000 = Value of business component

B. The cap rate for the buyer is 25 %, or 4 times earnings

$60,000 / .25 = $240,000 = Value of business component

Note that multiples are useful for providing an immediate ballpark of a business's value. They are simplified shortcuts. Multiples do not substitute for a comprehensive valuation analysis based on more in-depth valuation methodologies. The understanding of the complex data underlying the multiples requires systematic use of all of the valuation tools.

COST OR REPLACEMENT

ASSET VALUATION

You start by looking at the value of all the business's assets. A balance sheet, if available will show what the business owns. What equipment? What inventory? Any operator would have to buy similar productive assets to start a restaurant. Therefore, the business is worth at least the *replacement cost*. Be wary if a current balance sheet does not exist. It is a difficult and lengthy process to create accurate numbers if accounting is not up to date. The *value of the assets* includes tangible and intangible assets (see checklist). The major component is *Land and Buildings*. Getting this value is less complex if you have already looked at area sales. To fine-tune the value of assets, start with the largest value, the real estate (when owned).

LAND

The market determines real estate values, and values are only modified by the knowledge and motivations of the buyer and seller.

The easier way to value the real estate is to treat the land underneath as unimproved. Improvements are the buildings and structures built upon the land. Unimproved land can be valued quickly and accurately by comparison to similar property in the area.

Front footage is an important measurement for commercial property. The front footage is the linear distance of the property facing a commercially zoned high traffic street or highway. Dollars per front foot for prevailing similar property are easy to get from published real-estate transactions in your area.

The shape and size of the property influences the value of dollars per square foot. A "shotgunned" property is one with small frontage but with narrow width and a long depth. Note that traffic counts are powerful influences on front-footage values. Also remember that a property only 100 feet off the main high-traffic-count thoroughfare may be 100 feet "too far".

Always read the zoning regulations through carefully while underlining those possible restrictions to your future plans and abilities for flexible response to changing opportunities and threats to your concept. Find out about grandfather clauses for any existing improvement configuration.

Location variables modify land values. Consider this list:
- Visibility (view amenity)
- Access (driveways, cut-throughs, turn lanes, traffic lights, etc)
- Proximity to neighborhoods
- Parking (on site, parking requirements/sq. foot of building,
- Landscaping
- Setback
- Distance and direction of major streets (number lanes, dividers, medians, posted speeds
- Traffic counts
- Traffic patterns (Going home or to work)
- Side of street
- Growth or decline of commercial area (age cycle)
- Zoning enactments
- Free standing, outparcel, or strip
- Restaurant Row?

HIGHEST AND BEST USE

It is axiomatic with commercial real estate that it be employed to its highest and best use. That is: the front footage of the property and the square footage of any structure should house the kind of operation that will return the highest dollar amounts for that property. The operation must provide a cash flow to support not just what the property last traded for, but also the current fair market value.

Over time the value of commercial property will change. It will appreciate or depreciate with the evolution and demographics of the area. The area can outgrow the longtime use of a property that ultimately leaves it below its highest and best use. As an example, when a city grows fast into a rural area, the use of the land and buildings quickly becomes obsolete to the potential best employment.

A longtime popular restaurant and bar had a patio that overlooked Sausalito with the marina and San Francisco Bay spread below. The large daily cash-flow from the operation did not sustain the current fair market value of the property as residential property values rose over time. The property footprint was more valuable as a $4 million lot for a house.

As a buyer, you would look for underemployed property. Look beyond the owner's stated reason for sale to see true motives. Is the property being "flipped" for short run profit? Has the owner operated at that location for many years? Has the current concept been outgrown, with room for a trendier concept? Are there new opportunities? Are the demographics changing to a higher per capita income area? Is the commercial area in a general decline or re-growth cycle?

Research the last time the property was sold and at what price. A title search might give you a better insight into the seller's true needs.

BUILDING

We must repeat that: "you must try not to limit your seating capacity", since much of your overhead can be the same for few seats as for many. This has to be a primary consideration with any restaurant building, so consider total square footage and how that space will be designed including kitchen and public space. (See Section Two - Design)

Consider that any existing building, with its location, commands a dollar per square foot market value. The planned operation's cash flow must support that value. An existing restaurant building may actually detract from value, especially with a history of previous failure or with poor functional design. If the building is ugly, your best path may be to bulldoze. (See Section One – Location)

The value of land and building can be approached from another direction: by the rent it commands and the real estate capitalization rate. The real estate cap rate is different from and lower than the operations cap rate because it is secured by a tangible asset. For restaurant real estate, however, the capitalization rate will again be higher than general rates.

Example of land and buildings valuation using rent:

- Rent is $3,500 / month, or $42,000 / year
- General commercial mortgage rates for a current period are 9 %. Restaurant rates may be 12.5 %, which represents a premium for higher risk.

    $42,000 / .125 = $336,000 =$ Value of land and buildings

A majority of restaurant operations are in leased property rather than owned. *Leasehold improvements* are assets that can be physically removed. They include such items as signage, partitions, counters, wall coverings, floor coverings, and woodwork trim. They will usually belong to the current owner, though a landlord might require their removal as terms of ending a lease. Leasehold improvements are valued using the market approach based on substitution.

OTHER ASSETS
Segregate all other assets and use the best valuation techniques for each category

FFE – Furniture, Fixtures, and Equipment FFE is tangible property to be valued with the cost approach. Make a list. Use the headings of: Item Number, Description, Manufacturer, Replacement Value, Depreciation Allowance, and Depreciated Value. FFE items can all suffer from various amounts of wear and obsolescence. They suffer physical deterioration, age, functional obsolescence and economic obsolescence. Equipment may need to be replaced with models that are more energy efficient, convenient to use, or less costly to maintain. Gas powered equipment, for instance, can be very much less costly to operate than electric.

Segregate out all *Leased FFE Items*. They have no value here.
Expendable Values are items such as *Pots, Pans, and Tableware*. They have minor value. Use the cost approach.

Accounts Receivable must be discounted heavily. They have little value.

Notes Receivable – avoid these as any part of a deal unless there is solid agreement on their value.

Pro rate any *Prepaid Expenses* such as *Insurance, Advertising, and Taxes*.
Note: always check to see if any current *License* such as liquor license or catering is assumable. If new licenses are readily available from the controlling government agency, the old have no value. Liquor licenses often must come only from the current licensee and may have large value.

Grandfather clauses might have value. If zoning allows grandfathered configurations, then reconstruction will not be required in order to meet new codes.

The *Leasehold Interest* has value. The length of any existing real property lease, and the contracted lease payments for that period, may be favorable in the current market.

Are there current *Assumable Loans?* Check existing loans rates against current rates for re-financing. If current rates (including any fees) are the same or lower, the existing loan has no value. However, if the seller is currently burdened with unfavorable rate loans, the buyer can have leverage in negotiation to eliminate that debt.

The seller might deserve consideration for *finding financing* for the buyer. The seller also might consider *carry back financing* by accepting notes from the buyer. Current financial positions of the parties and the ability to assume debt at favorable rates will influence the terms of the deal.

Administrative Systems may have value. Systems might include point of sale (POS) systems, and any other accounting and control hardware and software. Note that such systems obsolesce quickly, so look at the age and functionality. Do the systems automatically build a database for future meta-analysis and data mining as an automatic byproduct of normal operations and control?

Look at any *unused space*. Survey all of the square footage to employ it at the *highest and best use*. Is there space or land area that can be turned into an additional revenue generation source? Value this unused space using the income stream approach, after considerations of any costs of remodeling that space. The net present value (NPV) is the discounted expected cash flows of the unused space less conversion or renovation costs.

Existing personnel may have positive or negative value. Highly trained key staff may help smooth changeover, but the value is somewhat intangible. Any staff retention will depend on the view of value to the buyer, and can depend on negotiations with that key person rather than the seller. Note that much of existing personnel will turnover either voluntarily or otherwise. Often a fresh start with properly trained people is desirable. (See Section Five – Training)

A *union shop* will have a large negative value to a buyer. The buyer has incentive to close and restructure in order to avoid any existing union contract.

A *customer list* may have some small value as a mailing or contact list.

Recipes only have value if the product is unique to the location.

Look for *favorable operating expense* values such as a natural gas hookup.

Antiques will have unique value beyond normal operating FFE.

Consider a *non-compete clause*, but do not fear honest competition.

Seller assistance on startup can have value that must be negotiated.

Tax credits will only have value if the operation is a corporation.

Goodwill is the excess of earning capacity over and above the fair or average return that ordinarily would be earned on the company's tangible assets, name and reputation. This value is very subjective and will always be higher in the mind of the seller.

POTENTIAL LIABILITIES

Accounts Payable - Usually the seller should wipe these clean before any deal. They can be assumed if buying a corporation. If the current business is in bad shape the creditors usually will accept a negotiated partial payment.

Check to see who will be responsible for any *Contingent Liabilities* such as coupons, or pensions.

Verify that the land does not risk any liability for past *environmental hazards*.

AREA SALES COMPARISON

Ultimately, the strongest indicator of value is the market. Worth is only what people believe, rather than dictated norms. Only people who actually vote for value with their dollars determine prevailing area transactional values.

A major challenge for use of area sales comparison for restaurants is finding similar property that is actually comparable. Area sales comparison will give a reasonable guideline for the value of the real estate. The value of assets and the value of income stream will modify any numbers derived from area sales comparison.

First, define the area. Standard Metropolitan Statistical Areas (SMSA's) define major markets in cities by demographic characteristics. These numbers are available from several sources including marketing publications and from the U.S. Census. You must further breakdown your area of interest to a smaller geographic area, including neighborhood. The neighborhood, and access to it, will place constraints on your concept and your menu plans. Several kinds of maps will define your area of interest. Maps can include street maps, aerial views available on the Internet, and the county plats in the public records. The local chamber of commerce can often be helpful.

Walk through the immediate local area, and drive through the surrounding streets. Note neighborhood traffic flows, relative affluence, and proximity of other restaurants. Look at area trends. Evolving neighborhoods offer opportunities for new concepts.

Area sales are available in the public record. Offerings are available in the real estate multiple listing Service (MLS). You are looking for recent transactions in your area of interest that might compare. Price paid per square foot is a base number. Uniqueness of the real estate depends on a very long list of variables partly covered in the checklists appended to this section and further detailed in Section One. Use several recent area transactions for a base value and modify number by variables on the checklist.

Use Google Earth™ to look at the drawing area density and demographics.

NEGOTIATE

Every restaurant owner has, at times, thoughts on selling the business. Further, there are many who would like what that owner might have. That means that any restaurant can be bought or sold if the price is right. That price at which a deal can arise will depend on the negotiations of the parties with their best skills and knowledge.

THE DEAL
The deal will depend upon an acceptable price to both parties

Deal from strength. To buy, sell, or lease restaurant facilities, someone will have to negotiate a deal. Note that negotiating from strength does not come naturally for most of us that did not come from a bargaining culture. Since the final deal will involve substantial dollars, we must treat preparation for negotiation with the level of seriousness shown any capital budget decision.

RESTAURANT HANDBOOK – TOOLS & RULES

It is important, for a successful deal, to understand the anatomy of successful negotiation. Success will depend on planning, strategy, attitude, techniques and tactics.

Since a deal only happens when both parties feel they will receive net benefits, the approach to negotiation has to be non-adversarial. It sounds trite, but "win-win" is the only proper attitude in negotiations. A popular term is "principled negotiation". Principled negotiation, partially developed out of the Harvard Negotiation Project, is a way to produce maximum outcomes. It strives for the just and mutually beneficial resolution of conflicts while acknowledging the value and importance of ongoing relationships. Principled negotiation tries to avoid the "hard" approach, which stresses winning, and also seeks to avoid the "soft" techniques that lead to regrettable deals.

Principled negotiations, as outlined by Fisher and colleagues, rests on four main principles: separate the person from the problem, focus on interests not positions, invent options for mutual gain, and insist on using objective criteria.

PLAN FOR NEGOTIATIONS

Due diligence requires us to properly prepare for inevitable negotiations. The return on investment of time in planning is high. Some advocate spending three times as much time in planning than in expected meetings. Planning will seek to provide a solid basis covering the following issues. You cannot avoid your homework here.

Start with objective criteria. Strength and confidence builds on the solid basis of carefully derived values from all of the valuation techniques described above. Take time to do the numbers.

Know what you want. Before negotiations start, take time and write down the concrete numbers. Your goals provide a strategic structure for the negotiations. Be as clear as possible on what you are asking for and terms for settlement. Know how far you will go and what you can accept. You cannot wait for the other party to state the positions. By then it is too late.

List all alternatives. The greater the options, the greater the negotiating power. Alternatives allow you to be flexible and gain major concessions while giving up the less important. Make a wish list. Start with high goals that will allow room for giving up items that you can live without.

Know you bottom line. There is a danger with getting caught up in the negotiations frenzy that you will forget your objective criteria in an effort to "win". Plan when to cut-and-run. Save yourself from emotionally driven decisions. You will know when it is time to stop before you agree to the unacceptable.

Between your highest wish and bottom line, establish one or more fallback plans. Know also your plan B, in case of failure of negotiations. Do not be afraid to walk away.

Try to *know what the other side truly wants*. Seek to understand what the persons you are negotiating with want in terms of end results. Their stated objectives might not cover their total objectives, including emotional needs. Put yourself in their shoes to get insight into their goals and therefore their negotiating agenda. Otherwise, they can take you by surprise.

You must know their needs in order to counter effectively. What benefits are they seeking and how does it shape their strategy. Try to quantify their probable needs in specific terms such as dollars, percentages, or time.

Seek to *know who the other side is*. First, qualify the other party. Can a prospective buyer handle the probable financial requirements? Does the party have authority to make the deal after all negotiation and agreement?

Make sure the other party is seriously *negotiating in good faith*, rather than just to gain information. You do not wish to lose valuable time and inside information to a party not intending to reach a deal. Bad faith negotiators can have several devious motives. They might want to delay your market plan or get information for a potential lawsuit. Be a skeptic until you have a picture of the persons and their motives.

Get to know as much as possible about those you will face. Call people with whom they have dealt. Ask about the principals and the company they might represent. Anticipate the negotiating style, strategies, techniques, and ploys. Ask about the negotiator's personality and successes.

Learn what the other team is gaining personally. Are they principals seeking development, professionals gaining a fee, or a broker with a deal percentage? Are they rewarded for closing deals or saving money? What is in it for them? Is the deal a "must-have" for them, or just a nice-to-have deal? What are the stakes win-or-lose?

Find out if the other party has a track record. If so, see how the deals evolved. Most of the answers are found with basic research. Google the trade publications if the deal involves a larger organization. Check with, suppliers, competitors, locals, etc. One source of information is simply to ask others that might know them or have done business with them.

You might even ask them directly. "Who" are you and what are you looking for in this deal? What is your title? Are you the principal, and do you have final authority? Where can I learn of your other projects? Can I have permission to do a credit check? You may not get perfect answers but you may have gained credibility by asking. You might ask such questions in a pre-negotiation lunch where the deal itself is not covered. Since much is at stake, do not be afraid to get personal. You will be surprised how much information is out there. The time to get informed and form a working structure is before negotiations start.

Finally, planning will include time to *rehearse and practice what you will say*. Have a knowledgeable person you respect cover the expected scenarios. Learn how you will react to the suggestions and demands of the other party. Learn to stay calm and on course for a good deal.

NEGOTIATION ATTITUDE

A healthy attitude is easiest when you have done your homework. Your objectively derived numbers allow you to deal from strength. But there must be a balance of strength. Recognize that the deal will only work when both parties see value. Never believe the other person has all the power, or that more authority means more power.

You do not need to be either hard or soft in negotiations. When you stick to your planned goals, you can be reasonably authentic without giving away valuable points in advance. Believe that a win-win can be achieved and work methodically to get it.

Armed with objective facts, you need not accept anyone's announcements or opinions as fact. When the other side quotes facts to be assumed as given truths, consider the source. Question who gathered the "facts" from where, and the methods, motives judgments, assumptions, and biases in the gathering. Look closely at any such facts. Ignore quotes that cite averages. Nothing about you or your operations is average. Also, do not automatically accept as truth any findings presented with statistics. Statistics are a great tool for both parties with the correct context. We know, however, that statistics can always be used to spin a perspective.

Take time. Never negotiate in haste. Allow adequate time to listen to the other side. Hear what the other side has to say, what they want, and what might be given up. Be a good communicator not just a good talker. Be attentive and observe behavior and body language. You will gain much by asking questions that elicit open-ended answers. Together the parties can explore options to help smooth negotiations towards mutual benefit.

Strive to discuss rather than argue when covering the tough issues. Listening will help you attune to a working agreement that is truly win-win. Go in ready but relaxed. Stay cool. Ignore theatrics and emotional reactions. Be prepared for intense reactions to various proposals. When the other party steps over the line, be authentic and speak up. If you see an impasse is looming, be ready to create a tactful time-out. Be mature and in self-control with your reactions. It all pays off.

NEGOTIATION STRATEGY

Negotiation is a process that is both art and science. It is never a rigid process, but is governed by rules that can be interpreted differently or even violated by either party. Each unique case proves that every principle has an exception. While there are no absolute rules in negotiation, there are proven guidelines towards high probability of success. The guidelines are strong starting points for negotiation, and are generally in the best interests of all parties involved.

First, start with a *good atmosphere*. Your opposites are more likely to make more concessions if they're convinced each party wants a deal fair to both sides. Display friendship and goodwill, trust and integrity. Both sides of the table will seek win-win opportunities. This is a necessary mindset. Opportunities will arise to allow both sides to meet needs. Know what items are a must, and which might be conceded. Know when to be *flexible*. When you flex, it is acceptable to assume the other party will also be flexible to find workable compromises.

Further, with any *concession* made, try to get something in return. If you give up any part of your bottom line with nothing in exchange, your credibility drops. Clearly point out the reduced value to your position with your concession, and the grounds for reciprocal value from their side. Otherwise, you will set up for future inequitable demands.

Start with *high goals*. You will get only what you ask for. The higher the start, the more you will get at closing. Ask for more than you expect. Remember, though, if you state a clear price, you will never get more than that price, and probably less. Rather, let the market dictate the price. The surest path to a market price is with multiple buyers, and that all are aware of that state.

Be reasonably *candid up front* to save time and effort. It is very important to have both parties reveal as much as possible of what they seek. Openness demands and creates mutual respect. Never negotiate with the intention of getting everything you can while the other party walks away with little. Your reputation as an ethical and fair dealer is on the line. Long-term relationships are more valuable than cheap victory.

Assess the current environment. Did someone come to you, or did you seek the negotiation. If *you are sought out*, you can start with higher targets. Present your demands and minimum concessions, but do not imply that any item is non-negotiable. You cannot appear as demanding and unyielding without possibly killing the deal.

Early in negotiations concentrate on emphasizing the *benefits* that both parties will realize from your preferred alternative. Both sides are seeking perceived value, so match benefits to their wants. To gain your value, you have to provide value. When you see what they want, look to your inventory of value to match their needs.

Try for the *home-court advantage*. A preliminary decision has to be where to meet. You will be more comfortable and confident in your own place of business, and behind your own desk. If not at your own office, arrange to meet on neutral ground, if possible. A luncheon meeting at a restaurant is one possibility. Eliminate distractions during the meeting so the discussion can flow uninterrupted.

Try to maintain *confidentiality*. When word leaks that you're selling, employees, customers and competitors may react to your detriment

Stick to your plan. You have already outlined clear goals. Keep from flinching on your critical goals, and you can always find compromises that allow both sides to come together without losing real value. When you offer a solid proposal, and can back it up with objective numbers, stand by it. Let the other side fuss and fume, and then refocus on value. Force the other side to show that value is not there. Don't wimp. Make the other party work to get what they want. They will appreciate the deal more at closing. However, always leave room for negotiating. Unreasonable demands kill deals.

When you make an offer *be patient*. Wait for a response. "By waiting, you avoid the possibility of rejecting your own offer and making further concessions in a revised offer. If you don't wait, it encourages the other side to hold off its response in hopes of getting a better offer, and you lose the opportunity to learn from the other side's response."

RESTAURANT HANDBOOK – TOOLS & RULES

Patience and perseverance are virtues in negotiating. Lack of patience weakens your position and can even kill the deal. Lack of patience, likewise, will harm the other party. Conceal your *critical deadlines*. Deadlines can be used against you to force a yield to meet a timetable.

Prepare for stalled talks. Inevitably discussion will reach disagreement. Both parties must try to keep focused on value, rather than personalities. Repeat important points of agreement using the right language and paying attention to what the other side is really saying. Look for creative ways to overcome the disagreement. Maintain respect to allow free interchange to continue.

Always *ask for new disclosures* at each round. Every successive volley in the bid-ask process must open up new information to support the latest proposed adjustment in the deal. Objective information can help you approach a value where both parties feel comfortable.

Communicate with confidence. Listen for feelings and ideas from the other side. What do they see as important? Attune to non-verbal communication - the tone and body language - which many believe is the larger part of total communication. Be concise in response.

Save *aggressive* negotiation for when it will count. When you start out with a more passive and receptive attitude, the other side might be more willing to be candid. You can then be very strong when the need arises. A negotiator that is too aggressive from the beginning will be resented and resisted.

Never accept the first offer. The other side expects you to reject the first offer. If you accept they will feel that they started with a proposal that was too weak. When you eventually say yes, they will be satisfied that they have pushed you to your limit.

Also, don't make the *first concession* if you can avoid it. You may have advantage when the other side concedes first. If you must go first, try to make it a minor point. Save concessions until they can count towards reciprocal concession of value. Concessions will be necessary, even if it is to allow the other party a feeling of gain in the negotiations. Decide, however, in advance what key concessions you absolutely will not make - those that severely erode your value position.

Piecemeal concessions are a mistake. Wait until you have heard all of their demands before you consider any concession. If you start giving early, it will set the tone, and your opposites will be encouraged to ask for more, and you will become a serial conceder. Listen to all their issues first, and take good notes. You will then have an overview of the playing field. Only then should you consider what concessions to make and what to request in return.

As you near agreement, *ask for the business* just as in any other contract talks. Good negotiators ask for everything they want. Be explicit about what you do and do not want.

Do not use their form contract. The forms will contain boilerplate that will drive all negotiation to their side. Rather, start with a *fresh draft* based on the progress of negotiations.

Do not commit before a deal is nailed down. If one party commits, all options come off of the table. It becomes impossible for parties to go elsewhere. *Early commitment* can destroy movement to mutual value, or even provoke a lawsuit. If the other side starts acting as if you've got a deal, call a halt and return to reality.

Often the two sides cannot narrow the bid-ask spread sufficiently to close a deal. Do not hang on and try to make something happen where clearly there is no deal to be done. This is throwing good resources after bad. Always reserve a *walk away option*. If you cannot achieve satisfaction let go. View your vested interest as a sunk cost, and turn to plan B. Other deals are just over the horizon.

Good faith negotiation allows sides to come to agreement and both feel they have gained value. It's a win-win event. Now get it on paper quickly so that it can be signed before the other party's resolve or memory on agreement falters. A *written contract* helps resolve any dispute. Written agreements stand up when the original negotiators are no longer around. They document the intent and quality of the negotiations. Review by legal counsel before signing is appropriate and advisable, but resist the *deal-killer legal veto*, without working to resolve problems first.

As a young negotiator for my fourth restaurant property, I was naively overconfident in my powers as a dealer. I was purchasing the unimproved property from a firm of wealthy lawyers, and the discussions went smoothly. The negotiations produced a verbal contract and handshake with an agreement that fit my valuation guidelines. The contract was left for drafting by the legal firm. I was then informed that the partners had reviewed the deal and that the terms had changed. We renegotiated, and again came to verbal agreement. Just before signing, I was informed that the deal had changed yet again. (The flamboyant lawyer that did the negotiating was later indicted for multi-million dollar fraud and disbarred) The lessons are: (1) the deal is not over until signing on the written draft, and (2) do not leave the contract draft to their lawyers.

STRATEGIES FOR SELLERS

A *third party intermediary* such as a business broker will cost you fees. Those fees, however, can be reasonable if the intermediary can produce a better deal and the owner/seller does not have the time and inclination to do all of the work required. Operations sold by owners often can be undervalued. The reason may be that owners tend treat buyers as customers that need to be pleased. Often sellers are too busy to properly valuate the operation. Intermediaries are more practiced in knowing what information to release to buyers and when. Intermediaries as negotiators give the advantage of an emotional buffer. On any sticking point they can defer to an absent decision maker. The owner avoids the pressure and can focus on the operation of the business. Also, a third party can bring multiple buyers to the table that can result in competitive bidding and a sweeter deal. Dealing with *multiple buyers* is the best way to get the best deal. As a seller, you have no way to validate the value a single buyer has placed on your company. A buyer, knowing that there are other players in the mix, might be induced to start with a higher initial offer of their own accord. If one offer is accepted but the due diligence turns up bad information, you can have options to push back from the table and consider alternatives.

RESTAURANT HANDBOOK – TOOLS & RULES

NEGOTIATION - TECHNIQUES & TACTICS

The following list includes some suggestions for dos-and don'ts that have worked for others. Not all will apply to your own negotiation needs, but be aware of their availability both to you and your opposite. Use them when tactically favorable and recognize when they are used on you.

DO:

- Start with highball and low-ball amounts that will leave room for concessions. Your opposites will be doing the same.
- Get agreement on some initial point, even a hypothetical. Initial agreement allows a basis for further progress.
- Ask questions, but avoid questions with yes/no answers. When your counterpart begins explaining, they cannot intimidate, but must discuss.
- Be ready to say "no" to unacceptable positions. Instead, be ready with plausible and constructive alternatives.
- Plan your concessions. Concessions are a normal part of negotiation, so you must be ready to concede wisely.
- Keep track of your concessions. If you are moving beyond your planned bottom line with concessions, stop and backtrack. Renegotiate.
- Constantly employ joint problem solving techniques. They are powerful tools of successful resolution.
- Take notes as you go. Write down the statements made by the other side for future refreshment. Ultimately the notes will help in drafting the final deal.
- Refocus on the important issues when discussion deviates. Bring the discussion back to basics: dollars, time periods, and percentages.
- Put money on the table. Cash up-front is a powerful inducer. Cash incentive can be in the form of down payment or offer to hold paper.
- Slow the pace when there is pressure for concession. Pause, take notes and consider answers. Offer to think it over, and move to another topic.
- Cite the all-powerful marketplace. Point out the competition and what else is available as an alternative course of action.
- Point out the negative consequences of not reaching an agreement. The impact might be lost time, lost dollars, and lost opportunity.
- Look for emotional undercurrents. Emotions often override rational decision processes.
- Look for, and be aware of possible hidden agenda. Negotiators are not always authentic in their statements and dealings.
- On impasse, return to prior agreements. Start again to see where problems arose, and how to head them off.
- On impasse, call for a break. Emotions can escalate and preclude progress. A time-out allows for cooling of and reevaluation.
- On impasse for one issue, leave that issue behind, and go forward with other agreement. Agree to return to the tough issue later.
- Always look for more than one option. Be creative when difficulties arise. There is usually a way over, under, around, or through a particular hurdle.

- Remember that the deal is not over until you shake hands and sign on the dotted line. Until that point each item is fair game for renegotiation.
- Get the final agreement in writing as soon as possible. Do not sign the document until it has been thoroughly reviewed. Reserve the right for review.

DO NOT:

- Accept the first offer that comes in. No matter how good the offer appears, it is only a starting point. Your reaction sets the tone for negotiations to follow.
- Accept a heavenly reward promise: "If you give in now, I will be good to you later".
- Fall for the good cop/bad cop routine. The tag team approach is an old tried and true producer.
- Agree quickly to the 50-50 split. That may be the other side's original target. Upon this suggestion, counter with "I can't afford it". Try 70-30 if it fits.
- Fall for the limited authority ruse: that the real decision maker has only authorized up to a limit. Usually that limit can be breached.
- Negotiate for the other side. After you have made an offer, shut up and wait for a response. Avoid further concessions until you see the reception.
- Accept the "It is out of my hands" response. All items should be adjustable at some point in the negotiations.
- Fall for meaningless concessions from the other side. Each concession has weight and measurable value. Treat each with the weight deserved.
- Accept the words, "trust me", without full measure of due diligence confirmation.
- Throw good money after bad, as in poker. If you have invested much time in negotiation, be ready to accept that as a sunk-cost and walk away.
- Get yourself into the fait-accompli predicament. Do not commit to a path where the other party knows you have run out of options to a jacked up price.
- Fall for an irresistible low ball-bid that is only a precursor to a series of unacceptable concessions.
-

After several bids on a plumbing contract for a new restaurant building, I received a very low bid from a contractor who dropped by at ground-breaking. I accepted the bid as a verbal contract. Upon completion and billing, I found the bill was many thousands higher than the quote. The extra amount was claimed to be extra work beyond the verbal agreement. His employees told me that he used this ploy routinely.

I refused to pay the added amount, and was taken to court. Acting as my own lawyer I showed the original plans, as filed with the county, to prove the work was in fact not extra work, but clearly in the original specifications. I lost. I then hired attorneys to appeal and he capitulated.

The two obvious lessons are: (1) Get it in writing, and (2) don't think you are an attorney.

LEASE

Every restaurant operation occupies space that has value. In the case of owned real estate, any mortgage and its terms dictate cash flows for occupancy-costs, but the prevailing market-rates dictate the actual value in the form of the *opportunity costs* of that space. For leased space, the annual rent becomes the largest component of your overhead. Rent is a major influence on your breakeven level of sales, and therefore your profitability.

Viewing a potential lease site requires due diligence. First make sure that you can adapt a menu concept to the local demographics. Don't' compromise here just because the space is available. Think about the area five and ten years from now. Following are some preliminary checklist items.

- Square feet available (Do not limit your capacity)
- Term of lease in years (5 years minimum)
- Renewal options
- Cost per square foot
- Security deposit required
- Common area expenses in addition to base rent
- Parking
- Insurance, who pays, how much
- Taxes, who pays, how much
- Utilities - who pays, how much (Natural gas available?)
- Costs of renovation, who pays, how much (Negotiate here)
- Get list of all possible restrictions (zoning, building, sign)
- Contract rights of both parties
- Personal guarantees from you as tenant

Use realistic numbers for your sales and rent in your pro-forma income statements to avoid emotionally driven pursuit of a given location. Note that rent is a relatively stable cost for the life of the contract, since it cannot be easily lowered by efficient practices as can much of your other overhead. Therefore, the time to control occupancy costs is in the planning and negotiation of the lease before you sign the contract. You can be tough and thorough in negotiations for a lease and still have both parties benefit.

A sad fact is: that most lessees view their landlords as adversaries. It is much better for the relationship to be that of long-term symbiosis dedicated to mutual success. Approach a potential landlord as a partner. Deal in good faith to treat the landlord as an investor in your business. A supportive landlord will offer assistance to help a worthy tenant succeed. Assistance might be in the form of build-out assistance or other financial allowances. When both parties show good faith, it shows the landlord wants long-term success rather than just the monthly rent.

As the lease site moves toward a contract, it is important to seek a good working relationship for both parties. Your job, then, is to show that you are a worthy tenant with potential for strong revenues. A prospective lessee, however, should avoid being overly optimistic in initial sales projections, and the monthly rent budget. Research the comparative rents in the surrounding area before negotiation. Use these metrics to keep lease costs low. Approach the negotiations with alternative sites in consideration, either as a back-up plan or as leverage.

The National Restaurant Association says that typical occupancy costs average 5% of total sales at full-service restaurants and 7% at limited-service operations.

Before negotiations, operators should have knowledge of two key terms of many restaurant leases: (1) percentage rent, and (2) tenant improvement dollars (TI).

(1) Paying *percentage rent* often is unavoidable. Institutional landlords generally require lessees to pay percentage rent, a figure based on sales volume, in addition to base rent. You should avoid it if you have any choice. It is often better to rely on a fixed monthly fee, because your success can have a higher potential net profit. If you cannot avoid a percentage rent, negotiate a high point for sales before the percentage rent kicks-in.

Triple-net leases are common with retail properties. These require the lessee to pay all tax, insurance and maintenance expenses in addition to the rent.

(2) Lease agreements, especially those relating to mall or in-line properties, often include provisions for *tenant improvements*. This is money the landlord will provide for work done on the interior of a space.

Sometimes the two are connected. If a landlord puts TI dollars in, there is the expectation to want a share of your success and to take a bigger percentage of your good fortune with a percentage rent.

Base and percentage rent are only starting points for fixing the true costs of a lease. Landlords can build in a long list of additional and potentially costly provisions. Lease agreement contracts will usually contain standard amounts of *boilerplate clauses*. You should read each clause carefully. Note that you do not have to accept each clause as written. Each is subject to modification or elimination through negotiations. The basic structure of a lease can include any number of specific clauses, with several designed to protect the lessee. It may be a good idea to have legal representation close, to keep an eye on details. Below are some clauses that might require special attention.

- Include an *allowance for contingencies*. For instance the deal can be dependent on securing the necessary financing, zoning, and licensing. Allow for termination if contingencies cannot be reasonably attained. Allow for termination in case of natural disasters.
- Determine common area *maintenance charges* for such items as lighting and parking lot. Negotiate a percentage cap so you don't end up with large surprise charges.
- Keep the *use clause* as broad as possible. You need to allow for possible changes in your concept.
- Include a *go-dark clause*. This is when a major co-tenant, anchor, or several tenants go out of business to leave vacant space. Allow for financial relief or termination.
- *Escalation clauses* provide for rent increases over a period of time, and work to the advantage of the lessor. Restaurateurs not only should make themselves aware of how the landlord calculates planned increases but also how the figures historically have risen in the area.

- *Exclusivity clauses* depend on the landlord and the intended use of the property. These supposedly protect against competitors. For most restaurant operators, they should welcome other food operation to their proximity for symbiotic attraction. The net effect is usually complimentary rather than competition. An exception might be a franchise for a particular similar food type such as pizza.
- *Security deposits* and *personal guarantees* potentially are points of contention. While in many cases operators can avoid security deposits based on the investments they make in equipment and property improvements, landlords who oversee choice real estate often have the power to exact such concessions for their properties in a tight market.

When you get down to detailed contract negotiations, a review by legal counsel might be prudent.

FINANCE

Finance possibilities can be from several sources that allow you to be creative in your quest for adequate capital. Finance is always easiest when you have a credible and complete business plan. (See Section One) Following are some potential sources.

The Real estate (when not leasing) can always be leveraged with a *mortgage*. Keep in mind that the percent of equity requirement will be higher for a restaurant if the space is not readily convertible to general-purpose use.

Construction loans are secured by the real estate. Funds are usually released as milestones in the construction process are reached.

Seller financing is very common as part of a deal structure. Seller financing can give the buyer confidence that the seller believes the business can thrive at that location. Often the terms of seller financing can be more favorable than traditional financing sources, especially if it raises the sale price. The rate should never be much above the current bank rates for such loans.

The seller should determine the ability of the buyer to perform. Ask for written permission to see their credit record, especially when the buyer is an individual. Credit records can be queried via the Internet. The buyer should cover the query fee. Also ask for financial and business references.

Seller financing can provide benefits for both parties. Make sure both parties are comfortable with the other's ability to deliver what is promised.

Incorporation and sale of stock is another financing option. If your business plan is good, it can be relatively easy to persuade several *investors* to own shares in your business. Potential investors are business associates, friends, and family. Ask for recommendations for parties that might be interested. Owners as shareholders can be induced with special perks such as 50 percent discounts on meals. One caveat is: Do not allow one single investor, or small group, to own over 50 percent of outstanding shares, unless you can stand the risk of losing all control.

SUMMARY

There are many important reasons to know the value of a restaurant operation. The main reasons are: to buy or sell. The buyer and seller each have different perspectives, but both must start with objective valuation methods in order to deal from strength with any negotiations.

Information on restaurant valuation is scarce. The problem appears to be that the diversity of restaurant concepts does not allow easy comparison, as compared to generic commercial real estate such as office space. Objective valuation is important, however, to determine a reasonable fair market value as a basis for transactional values. Three conventional valuation techniques: cost or replacement, income capitalization, and area sales comparisons, help triangulate a value that will stand on documented numbers.

The use of forms and checklists will guarantee that you do not overlook valuable considerations in arriving at a fair market valuation. The calculated objective valuation figure, however, is only a starting point. Human motives will always modify such numbers. Negotiations can be detailed and lengthy.

Each deal will be unique. It is important, however, to follow proven guidelines for successful negotiation. First you must budget much time preparing for negotiations before sitting down to the table. The most successful negotiations result in a win-win deal for both parties. Win-win is especially important in lease negotiations, since a long-term relationship should be symbiotic for the lessor and the lessee.

Lease contracts generally have standard boilerplate for the various clauses. Do not feel bound by boilerplate. Each clause should be subject to scrutiny, negation, and modification.

The long-term commitment to high dollar cash-flows mandates that time and due diligence be applied to planning for valuation and negotiations of any restaurant package.

VALUATION BY CAPITALIZATION CHECKLIST

Tangible Assets: Land .... _____
                     Buildings.. _____
                     Inventory .... _____ (List separately)
                     Equipment, furniture, fixtures .... _____ (List separately)
                     Leasehold improvements and interest rights _____ (List separately)
                     Licenses (type) .... _____
                     Other .... _____
Intangibles: Business trade name .... _____
                     Goodwill .... _____
                     Non-compete covenant (years, miles radius) _____
Estimated Total Market Value of all assets........................... _____

Operations: Income:
                  Gross Sales.................................... _____
                  Cost of goods sold .... _____
                        Gross Profit .... _____
                  Expenses: Rent
                                   Utilities
                                   Telephone
                                   Advertising
                                   Insurance
                                   Employee salaries
                                   Contract Labor
                                   Auto Expense
                                   Accounting/Legal
                                   Maintenance
                                   Repairs
                                   Depreciation
                                   Taxes
                                   Equipment Rental/Lease
                                   Office supplies
                                   Interest Expense
                         Total Expenses.. _____
                Net operating profit before Income Taxes   _____
                Add: Seller's salary plus benefits
                          Loan Payments
                              Total Adjusted Net   _____
                              Operations capitalization rate   _____
Estimated Value of operations   _____

Total Value (combine estimated total Value of Assets and Estimated Value of Operations
Also consider: Down Payment
                     Interest rate, terms   ==========
                     Broker fees
(See also buyer's checklist and uniform chart of accounts in appendix)

RESTAURANT HANDBOOK – TOOLS & RULES

BUYING CHECKLIST

OPERATION

Name of Business _____ Principal _____
Phone _____ Address: _____
_____
County/City with jurisdiction on codes _____
Business Type: Proprietorship __ Partnership __ Corporation __

For Sale: Building ___ Land ___ Equipment ___ Leasehold Improvements ___
Inventory _____ Other _____

Type Operation _____ Breakfast __ Lunch __ Dinner __
Liquor __ Beer __ Wine __ Licenses _____
Type of service _____

Number of seats _____ % Capacity: ___ Breakfast ____ Lunch ____ Dinner ____
Interior: Excellent ____ Good ____ Poor ____ Comments _____
Exterior: Excellent ____ Good ____ Poor ____ Comments _____

Menu:
  Breakfast # of Items ____ Price range _____ Average price _____ # Covers ____
  Lunch   # of Items ____ Price range _____ Average price _____ # Covers ____
  Dinner   # of Items ____ Price range _____ Average price _____ # Covers ____

<u>Site</u>
Good visibility _____ # Parking spaces ____ Access: Great __ Good __ Fair __ Poor __
Nearby:
  Residential _____ Yes ___ No ___
  Shopping Center _____ Yes ___ No ___
  Schools _____ Yes ___ No ___
  Recreation/Parks/Museums _____ Yes ___ No ___
  Central Business District _____ Yes ___ No ___
  Industrial Centers _____ Yes ___ No ___
  Mass Transportation _____ Yes ___ No ___
  Freeway (include projected) _____ Yes ___ No ___

Traffic: Pedestrian count ____ Auto count _____ Auto speed ____ Destination _____
Fire Station _____ Police protection _____

<u>Customer Base</u>
Metro area population _____ Projected _____ Unemployment rate _____ RAI _____
RGI _____ Immediate Area: Offices ____ Work Sites ____ Malls _____
Residential _____ Other _____
Avg. Household size _____ Avg. Household income _____ Age composition % _____
Ethnic Groups %: Hispanic ___ Oriental ___ Black ___ Caucasian ___ Other _____

FINANCIAL INFORMATION

Last 5 Years Financial Statements Available (yes/no) _____ Any Financial Statements ___
Prepared by: CPA _____   Accountant _____   Other _____

Sales Information _____

Verification of Financial Statements:
  Audited Financial Statement _____
  Compilation or Review   _____
  Books and Records   _____
  Income Tax Returns   _____
  Sales Tax Returns   _____

Will a Pro Forma Financial be Prepared? _____

Will a Cash Flow Analysis be Prepared? _____

Estimate Annual Sales   _____

Sales Trends   _____

Profit Trends   _____

RESTAURANT HANDBOOK – TOOLS & RULES

BUILDING AND LAND

Appraisal by M.I.A _____ or Estimates, 3 sources (1)_____ (2)_____ (3)_____

Available for use other than restaurant _____
Adequate for future renovation_____
Age of building _____General repair: Excellent ____ Good ____ Fair ____ Poor_____
Comments:_____Soil
sample_____ Drainage problems? _____ Other land problems_____
_____
Potential ordinance problems _____
Restaurant ever forced closed? ____

Square Footage: feet   %
    Total   _____   ___
    Dining Room   _____   ___
    Bar   _____   ___
    Kitchen   _____   ___
    Restrooms   _____   ___
    Storage/utility   _____   ___
    Office   _____   ___

Restaurant Equipment

Append complete list with age.
Available? _____
General condition of equipment: New-like _____ Good _____ Fair _____ Poor _____
Additional Equipment necessary _____
_____
_____
_____
_____

Any unusable equipment? _____
Leased equipment w/terms? _____
_____

Labor:
Union? yes/no:____ Availability of personnel _____

Parking for staff _____ Bus Service _____

Approximate Rates: Manager _____ Chef _____ Cooks _____ Servers _____ Bussers
_____

COMPETITOR ANALYSIS   (list for each)

Name _____ Location _____
Distance and characteristics
_____

Accessibility _____ Visibility _____ Comments _____

Interior: Nice _____ Good _____ Poor _____ Comments _____

Exterior: Nice _____ Good _____ Poor _____ Comments _____

Hours Open _____ # Seats _____
% Capacity: < 50 %   50%   75%   Full   Wait list   Weekends   Weekdays
  Breakfast   _____   _____   _____   _____   _____   _____   _____
  Lunch   _____   _____   _____   _____   _____   _____   _____
  Dinner   _____   _____   _____   _____   _____   _____   _____

Name _____ Location _____
Distance and characteristics
_____

Accessibility _____ Visibility _____ Comments _____

Interior: Nice _____ Good _____ Poor _____ Comments _____

Exterior: Nice _____ Good _____ Poor _____ Comments _____

Hours Open _____ # Seats _____
% Capacity: < 50 %   50%   75%   Full   Wait list   Weekends   Weekdays
  Breakfast   _____   _____   _____   _____   _____   _____   _____
  Lunch   _____   _____   _____   _____   _____   _____   _____
  Dinner   _____   _____   _____   _____   _____   _____   _____

Name _____ Location _____
Distance and characteristics
_____

Accessibility _____ Visibility _____ Comments _____

Interior: Nice _____ Good _____ Poor _____ Comments _____

Exterior: Nice _____ Good _____ Poor _____ Comments _____

Hours Open _____ # Seats _____
% Capacity: < 50 %   50%   75%   Full   Wait list   Weekends   Weekdays
  Breakfast   _____   _____   _____   _____   _____   _____   _____
  Lunch   _____   _____   _____   _____   _____   _____   _____
  Dinner   _____   _____   _____   _____   _____   _____   _____

RESTAURANT HANDBOOK – TOOLS & RULES

LEASE

Lessor: Name _____ Phone _____
Address
_____
_____

Original Lease Date _____ Expiration Date _____ Renewal Provisions
_____
_____

Can lease be assigned and conditions?
_____
_____

Option to Purchase? _____ Deposits _____

Rate: Minimum Payment _____ Percent _____ Escalation Clauses _____
_____

Who pays Taxes? _____ Who pays Repairs? _____
Internal? _____ External? _____

Any provision for major Renovations?
_____

Insurance paid by: _____ Coverage _____
_____
Fire _____ Liability _____

PURCHASE AGREEMENT

Buying Stock _____ (If buying stock see attorney first)
Buying Assets _____

Total Purchase Price Allocation:
   Building .... $ _____
   Equipment: .... _____
   Leasehold improvements .... _____
   Value of Lease .... _____
   Covenant not to compete .... _____
   Recipe values .... _____
   Goodwill .... _____
   Customer List .... _____
   Management Value .... _____
   Franchise Value .... _____

Sub-Total .... $ _____

Other:
   Liquor License .... $ _____
   Prepaid Expense Allocation .... _____
   Personal Property Tax .... _____

Total .... $ _____

Subject to transfer of Liquor License (yes/no) _____
Subject to transfer of Lease Agreement _____
Subject to Verification of Financial Information _____

Terms:
   Down Payment _____   Assumable Loans _____
   Interest _____   Assumable Leases _____
   Payment Amount _____

Special Items:
   Operating Inventory: Buying (yes/no) _____ Method of Valuation _____

Liability Assumptions
_____

RESTAURANT HANDBOOK – TOOLS & RULES

Made in the USA
Columbia, SC
08 May 2018